Acclaim for James Wood

"Breathtaking . . . [Wood's] writing is alive, crackling, and sparkling with electric energy."

—*The Washington Post Book World*

"Thoroughly rewarding . . . no one has written better about most of what he writes about."

—*The Boston Globe*

"Perhaps the strongest, and the strangest, literary critic we have."

—*The New York Review of Books*

"Brilliant . . . famously rigorous . . . [Wood's criticism is] profound, searching, and bogglingly learned."

—Daniel Mendelsohn, *The New York Times Book Review*

"[Wood's] literary criticism has been the most fruitfully polemical of recent years. . . . [Wood is] unforgiving of complacency, unsparing of triviality, and unrelenting in his assault on the half-formed or the overwrought."

—Wyatt Mason, *Harper's* magazine

"Impressive . . . ingenious . . . lively, learned, and enthusiastic . . . Wood is one of our strongest literary critics, a diligently close reader who tethers his critical rigor to an admirably expansive vision of the place of fiction in our imaginative and moral lives."

—Chris Lehmann, *Newsday*

"James Wood uses his humor and perspicacity to glance over the history of literary comedy."

—*Esquire*

"Literary eviscerator James Wood defends tragicomedy in fiction."

—Elissa Schappell, *Vanity Fair*

"Magisterial sweep and terrific intensity . . . Most compelling is the way his own style swells and contracts with his subject matter, blithely metaphorical in praising Bellow, earnest and lucid in sorting out Jonathan Franzen or Zadie Smith, sarcastic in attacking Rushdie."

—*Publishers Weekly*

"[A] provocative gathering of recent reviews by the stylish critic and novelist . . . Wood's charming, admirably detailed tribute to 'Saul Bellow's Comic Style' is, as they say, worth the price of admission. . . . A miscellany, then—and an unusually rich and satisfying one."

—*Kirkus Reviews*

"Mr. Wood is recklessly committed to literature, and brave enough to risk ridicule by pushing every thought to the limit. . . . [His] kind of open-eyed and sympathetic reading is how criticism justifies its existence."

—Adam Begley, *The New York Observer*

"What Marianne Moore once said of Hugh Kenner—'Fearless, he can be too fearless, but we need him'—may be said equally of Wood. It is the excess, the polemical drive, that makes him exhilarating to read, often to be instructed by, sometimes to argue with."

—William H. Pritchard, *The New York Times Book Review*

"Wood writes with such felicity and zeal that one feels neither the inclination nor the possibility of disagreeing with him. . . . [His] enthusiasm provides such an attractive alternative to the truculence of Dale Peck, and the bloodlessness of 'in-house' academic criticism."

—Robert McFarlane, *The Times Literary Supplement*

"A collection of literary essays of the highest quality."

—*The Buffalo News*

"Penetrating insight . . . Wood's enthusiasm for writers is infectious."

—*San Jose Mercury News*

"The most incisive literary critic of our time . . . .Intriguing."

—*The Washington Times*

THE IRRESPONSIBLE SELF

ALSO BY JAMES WOOD

The Book Against God

The Broken Estate: Essays on Literature and Belief

The Irresponsible Self

ON LAUGHTER AND

THE NOVEL

❧

James Wood

PICADOR
FARRAR, STRAUS AND GIROUX
NEW YORK

www.picadorusa.com

Picador® is a U.S. registered trademark and is used by Farrar, Straus and Giroux under license from Pan Books Limited.

For information on Picador Reading Group Guides, as well as ordering, please contact the Trade Marketing department at St. Martin's Press.
Phone: 1-800-221-7945 extension 763
Fax: 212-677-7456
E-mail: trademarketing@stmartins.com

These essays have previously appeared, in slightly different form, in *The New Republic, The London Review of Books, The New Yorker,* and *The Times Literary Supplement.*

Designed by Jonathan D. Lippincott

Library of Congress Cataloging-in-Publication Data

Wood, James. 1965–
    The irresponsible self : on laughter and the novel / James Wood.
        p. cm.
    ISBN 0-312-42460-4
    EAN 978-0312-42460-2
    1. Fiction—19th century—History and criticism. 2. Fiction—20th century—History and criticism. 3. Comedy. I. Title.

PN3352.C6W66 2004
809.3'917—dc22   2003022955

First published in the United States by Farrar, Straus and Giroux

First Picador Edition: April 2005

D 10 9 8 7 6 5 4 3 2

For Glyn and Geraldine Maxwell

Contents

THE IRRESPONSIBLE SELF

Introduction: Comedy and the Irresponsible Self

֍

I

Comedy, like death and sex, is often awarded the prize of ineffability. It is regularly maintained that comedy cannot really be described or explained, that to talk about it is merely to do it noisy harm. Particular derision is reserved for the formal criticism of comedy, which seems to most sensible people like an unwitting bad joke, since nothing is funnier than solemnity about laughter. But the people who resist the intrusion of criticism into comedy are often the same people who claim that a poem or music or the idea of beauty can't really be talked about either.

Such people seem to fear too much self-consciousness, or to have too little faith in words, and in particular too little faith in the possibilities of exegesis. Actually, much comedy is explicable, exhaustively so; what can be a little absurd are theories of comedy—so plentiful in modern times—though that did not deter Schopenhauer, Baudelaire, Meredith, Bergson, or Freud. Since I obviously believe in criticism's capacity to talk about many things, I will offer for critical discussion a joke—or, really, a witty reply. One London lunchtime many years ago, the late poet and editor Ian Hamilton was sitting at his usual table in a Soho pub called the Pillars of Hercules. The pub was where much of the business of Hamilton's literary journal, *The New Review*, was conducted. It was sickeningly early—not to be at work, but to be at drink. A pale, haggard poet entered, and Hamilton offered him a chair and a glass of something. "Oh no, I just can't keep drinking," said the weakened poet. "I must give it up. It's doing terrible things to me. It's not even giving me any pleasure any longer." But Hamilton, narrowing his eyes, responded to this feebleness in a tone of weary stoicism and said in a quiet, hard voice, "Well, none of us *likes* it."

I think Hamilton's reply is very funny; and so did *The New York Times*, which reproduced it in its obituary of Hamilton, but mangled it by failing to italicize "likes." That such a mangling is instantly felt as damage suggests that the joke is indeed explicable—for we instinctively know that the comedy of the reply inheres in that wearily stressed verb "*likes*." So why is it funny? There is comedy in the inversion of the usual idea that drinking is fun and voluntary. In Hamilton's reply, drinking has become unpleasant but unavoidable, one of life's burdens. The cynical stress on "*likes*" gives the reply a sense of weary déjà vu: it sounds as if Hamilton is so obviously citing a truism that it is barely worth saying it aloud. It is always funny when singular novelty is passed off as general wisdom, especially when it is almost the opposite of the truth.

The joke simultaneously plays on the inversion of drinking as good fun while playing off the grim truth of alcoholism, which of course is indeed a state in which drinkers may not much like alcohol but cannot release themselves from it. Against those two worlds—the world of ordinary, pleasant, voluntary drinking, and involuntary alcoholic enslavement—Hamilton's reply proposes a stoical tragicomic world, populated by cheerful but stubborn drinkers doing their not very pleasant duty. The joke seems to me to open, in a moment, a picture at once funny and sad.

Hamilton's comic stoicism also creates, like much comedy, an alternative community. Instead of asserting his difference from the poet ("Well, so be it, but *I* still like drinking"), Hamilton effectively says, "Well, so be it, but we're all in the same boat, and none of us is having a good time." Hamilton's reply barely offers the poet the chance of resigning from this community; we are all stuck in it: it is the price of adulthood (or literary adulthood). At the same time, the joke can only work if it rests on the idea of a normative community, the ordinary world in which people enjoy drinking and are free to drink or not to. Mildly rebellious, the joke is also oddly forgiving, because Hamilton offers himself as the weary, downtrodden example of what living in this alternative community will do to you, and offers the alternative community as the *real* normative one. The beauty of the quip is that it seems at first to assert a superiority, only, on closer inspection, to offer a helpless commonality.

I like Hamilton's joke, too, because it arises gently from its context, out of a natural exchange, and in so doing offers us access, albeit fleeting, to the character of the man who made it. It is unflashy; it is not an obviously great or crushing *mot*. It represents the opposite of those forced moments when someone says "Do you want to hear a joke?"—at which point most of us freeze, alarmed that we won't get the punch line, and nervously aware that we are now inhabiting a "comic moment." In literature, there are novels that have the feel of Hamilton's quip—novels in which a mild tragicomedy arises naturally out of context and situation, novels which are softly witty but which may never elicit an actual laugh; and there are also "comic novels," novels which correspond to the man who comes up to you and says, "Have you heard the one about . . . ?" novels obviously very busy at the business of being comic. *Tristram Shandy*, for instance, is in multifarious ways a marvelous book, but it is written in a tone of such constant high-pitched zaniness, of such deliberate "liveliness," that one finds oneself screaming at it to calm down a bit. Dr. Johnson, a greatly tragicomic figure himself, found *Tristram Shandy* too eccentric to bear. The "hysterical realism" of such contemporary writers as Pynchon and Rushdie is the modern version of Sterne's perpetual excitements and digressions.

The subject of many of this book's essays—the implicit and not always explicit subject—is a kind of tragicomic stoicism which might best be called the comedy of forgiveness. This comedy can be distinguished—if a little roughly—from the comedy of correction. The latter is a way of laughing at; the former a way of laughing with. Or put it like this: at one extreme of comedy there is Momus, the ancient personification of faultfinding, reprehension, and correction, who appears in Hesiod and Lucian. And at the other extreme of comedy, in the area now called tragicomedy, is the "irresponsible self."

Not necessarily funny himself, Momus roots out absurdity and foolishness. He sees through you; he truffles for folly. Poor Coleridge, the tormented opium addict who had much to fear from being seen through, shudders, in the *Biographia Literaria*, at the horror of Momus's fabled desire to put a glass window in the breast of man so that his heart could be seen.

Momus, you might say, is the patron saint of satirists. The comedy of correction, which would include the Aristophanes of *The Clouds* and *The Wasps*, Leon Battista Alberti's allegorical comic tale *Momus* (written in the 1440s), Erasmus, Rabelais, some elements of Cervantes (though *Don Quixote* amiably contains many comic modes), Swift, Molière, and Flaubert's *Bouvard and Pécuchet*, is satirical in impulse, frequently violent and farcical, keen to see through the weaknesses of mankind, and essentially prenovelistic. *Bouvard and Pécuchet*, though written in the heyday of the novel, is the exception that proves the rule: it is actually much less like a novel than a treatise, written to prove how repetitively stupid we all are, by a writer whose comedy is often cruel, who was obsessed with the folly and vices of bourgeois idiocy, and who complained in a letter that he found the characters in *Madame Bovary* "deeply repulsive."

Flaubert was really a religious writer who transferred his devotion to aesthetics. He had the old religious impulse to scourge and check his characters. Indeed, the comedy of correction might be called religious comedy, since the ambition of total transparency, the desire to put a window in the human heart, strikes one as essentially religious. Kierkegaard sounds like Momus when he exults, in *Fear and Trembling*, that "a man sitting in a glass case is not so constrained as is each human in his transparency before God." That transparency received its memorably terrifying formulation when Jesus—who weeps but who never laughs in the Gospels—admonished us that to look on a woman with an adulterous heart is to have committed the act; we are known, through and through. Or if we are not fully known, as in Flaubert, there is a feeling that we should be. The few references to Yahweh's laughter in the Old Testament are all examples of laughing at, not laughing with: in Psalm 2, we are told that God will "laugh" at the heathen and "have them in derision"; and again in Psalm 37, that the Lord will "laugh" at the wicked man, "for he seeth that his day is coming."

Here, God is like Jupiter, who is described in both *Momus* and Erasmus's *The Praise of Folly* as looking down at heaven from a watchtower. Job's God is little different from Homer's gods: "And unquenchable laughter arose among the blessed gods / As they saw Hephaestus limping through the hall." Both Rabelais and Cervantes assume as funny such happenings as killing sheep, beating men to death, two men vomiting in each other's faces, a pack of dogs trying to mount a woman, and so on.

Most comedy before the rise of the novel is Aristotelian in nature. Aristotle argues in the *Poetics* that comedy arises from a perceived defect or ugliness that should not be so painful that we feel compassion, since compassion is the enemy of laughter. The Renaissance theorist of laughter Laurent Joubert, in his *Traité du ris* (1579), expanded on Aristotle by arguing that ugliness and the lack of strong emotion were crucial to comedy. We may feel sadness at witnessing something ugly, said Joubert, but in order for comedy to work we must in the end feel a pleasure at the lack of our compassion. Thus, when a man is stripped of his clothes, the sight of his genitals is shameful and ugly, and is yet "unworthy of pity," so we laugh. Secular or modern tragicomedy, the comedy of forgiveness, is almost the inversion of the Aristotelian idea. It is almost entirely the creation of the modern novel—with the huge exception of Shakespeare, whose role in the creation of the modern novelistic art of combined pathos and comedy is the subject of this book's first essay. If religious comedy is punishment for those who deserve it, secular comedy is forgiveness for those who don't. If correction implies transparency, then forgiveness—at least, secular forgiveness—implies deliberate opacity, the drawing of a veil, a willingness to let obscurity go free. In *Pride and Prejudice*, Elizabeth Bennet learns that laughing at is cruel (it is what her irresponsible father is always doing, not to mention the rebarbative Bingley sisters). Instead, she will laugh with Darcy, which entails being laughed at *by* him. For Austen, getting married—or, rather, falling in love—is the conversion of laughing at into laughing with, since each lover, balancing the other, laughs equally at the other, and creates a new form of laughter, a kind of equal laughter. Laughing with Darcy, and loving him, leads Elizabeth to realize that she was wrong to judge him as harshly as she did, that she may take many years to get to know him properly. It involves her in the deeply secular concession that, as Philip Roth has it in *American Pastoral*, "getting people right is not what living is all about. It's getting them wrong that is living." Her shallower, more easily satisfied sister "merely smiles" when she marries Wickham, says Elizabeth. But, she says, marrying Darcy, "I laugh."

Religious comedy, however slippery it may get—and few texts, technically speaking, are as slippery as *The Praise of Folly*—is fundamentally stable. There is the stability of didacticism, for one thing; the works of Alberti, Erasmus, and Molière, for instance, are edifying projects, conceived as lessons as well as entertainments. It is our task to extract what they preach. We can judge the stability of satire from the fixedness of its typology, the certainty of recognizing broad categories of human folly: hypocrisy, misanthropy, pomposity, foolishness, clerical dereliction of duty, and so on. In such comedy there is frequently the stability of allegory or fable, whereby a decoding of the story is implicitly promised; or there is the guarantee of retribution and formal moral closure. Molière offers perhaps the best example of this stability: the form of his plays tends toward the closure of punishment. The hypocritical Tartuffe is arrested by the king's men at the end; Monsieur Jourdain, the pompous would-be gentleman, is mocked and vanquished at the end of *Le bourgeois gentilhomme*.

It is true that this comedy always has the potential to spill over its borders—what Bakhtin celebrated in Rabelais as the "carnivalesque." It is true, too, that any neat division between religious and secular comedy would seem threatened by the apparent antireligiousness of writers like Erasmus and Rabelais. But the antireligiousness of premodern comedy is often closer to anticlericalism; as it were, the waste of religion is being mocked rather than its nutrition. Molière may have "corrected," in the character of Tartuffe, an atrociously hypocritical priest—and in turn been censured by the Catholic church—but the play is careful to separate Tartuffe's perversion of religion from its true practice. Cléante reminds Orgon, who is Tartuffe's infatuated and finally disillusioned host, that "you mustn't think that everybody is like him and that there aren't sincerely devout men left nowadays. Leave such foolish inferences to the free-thinkers, separate real virtue from its outward appearance." Hypocrisy, like blasphemy, is one of those modes of behavior that, in order to work, need the existence of the positive of which it is the distorted negative. It is an essentially stable category of thought. Or at least it is an essentially stable category when, as in Molière and Rabelais, it is heavily marked precisely as "hypocrisy." One of the wonders of the great Russian novel *The Golovlyov Family*, written in the 1870s by Saltykov-Shchedrin and discussed in this book, is that the apparently stable category of the hypocrite, a Russian Tartuffe, is put into the uncertain world of the novel rather than the theater. Whereas Molière is constantly telling us, in effect, "Gauge how false and hypocritical Tartuffe is by looking at the decent characters,"

Shchedrin says, in effect, "How do you know if Porphiry is a hypocrite if everyone else is hypocritical too?" As the novel progresses, so Porphiry, the Russian Tartuffe, mutates from a hypocrite into a solipsist or fantasist. He merges with his equally degenerate world; he is deprived of an audience. We are no longer theatergoers, confident that the hypocrisy we see onstage can be seen through; we are solitary novel readers, somewhat unsure of whether we are in the stalls or on the stage.

The comedy of what I want to call "irresponsibility" or unreliability is a kind of subset of the comedy of forgiveness; and although it has roots in Shakespearean comedy (especially soliloquy), it seems to me the wonderful creation of the late nineteenth- and early twentieth-century novel. This comedy, or tragicomedy, of the modern novel replaces the knowable with the unknowable, transparency with unreliability, and this is surely in direct proportion to the growth of characters' fictive inner lives. The novelistic idea that we have bottomless interiors which may only be partially disclosed to us *must* create a new form of comedy, based on the management of our incomprehension rather than on the victory of our complete knowledge: Svevo's Zeno is the cardinal example; Henry Green's butler, Raunce, is a softer representative. This kind of comedy is also found in Chekhov, Verga, Hrabal, Henry Green, Bellow, Nabokov, Joseph Roth, Tolstoy, Naipaul, Gogol, and Hamsun, many of whom are discussed in this book.

One way of looking at the "irresponsible self" in comedy is to examine the difference, in fiction, between reliably unreliable narration and unreliably unreliable narration. Generally, we know when an unreliable narrator is being unreliable because the author is alerting us, reliably, to that narrator's unreliability. (Swift works likes this.) But the modern novel brings us that wonderful character, the *un*reliably unreliable narrator, manipulated so brilliantly by Svevo and Hrabal and Nabokov and Verga. This category of storytelling can only work, can only be comic, if we think initially that we know more about a character than he knows himself—thus we are lulled at first into the comedy of correction—only to be taught that we finally know less about that character than we thought we knew at the outset; thus we are lulled into the comedy of forgiveness. Reliably unreliable narrators are often funny, playful, witty; but they don't move us as deeply as unreliably unreliable narrators. (It might be said that the comedy of correction may amuse us but it rarely moves us, because it does not intend to—this is true of a modern comedian of "correction" like Waugh—whereas the comedy of forgiveness has as one of its aims the generation of sympathetic emotion.) The short stories of Giovanni Verga appear to enact a comedy of correction—they seem at first terribly cruel stories—only to reveal that a complex literary art is being used to make the reader resist the comedy of correction and to supply instead his own tragicomedy of forgiveness. And Verga performs this magical task by manipulating an unreliable narration.

In Erasmus's *The Praise of Folly* (1511), two types of comedy, the old and the new, can be seen side by side—indeed, one can see the art of the novel push through for a second, and then retreat. The book's narrator, it will be remembered, is Folly herself, who, as she explains, is dressed in the traditional cap and bells of the licensed court fool. She is addressing an audience, and has come to praise herself. Isn't it the case, she asks, that the most foolish people are the happiest? Children and old people are the happiest of all, because they are saved from the tedium of life that afflicts the rest of us. Folly says that she keeps many marriages going because it is essential that husband and wife not know the truth about each other's faults. If one could look down on life, who would not see "how miserable and messy childbirth is, how toilsome it is to bring children up, how defenseless they are against injuries," and so on. Who would not commit suicide? But in fact, those who are most likely to commit suicide are those who have come closest to wisdom. By contrast, the foolish are happiest because they are blissfully unaware of life's hardships, and it is Folly herself who works this magic.

Erasmus pretty much invented the paradoxical encomium, in which the subject of the speech is also the speaker, and in which a narrator proposes her own foolishness as the best way to live. This is essentially unreliable narration, the smudged hermeneutics in which we learn to see what the narrator is failing to say about herself, how she is fallible in ways not known to her but obvious to us, and so on. Erasmus uses Folly's fallibility to avoid having his meanings pinned down; it is a form of literary escape, frolicsome in itself but also necessary in an age of religious censorship and retribution. Thus, if Folly is really foolish, what she proposes about life—despite its obvious wisdom—cannot be entirely wise. For instance, when Folly says that life is really just hardship and toil, we credit the unblinkered accuracy of the analysis. That is what life is like. Yet Folly proposes that in order to live happily one has to blinker oneself from this horror— blinker oneself from the accuracy of Folly's own analysis. So Folly is right, while offering to blind people to that rightness. Can she still then be right? This is the paradox of "foolish wisdom," familiar to us from the Fool in *King Lear*.

Erasmus makes his unreliable narration work most fruitfully for him when he reaches his true subject, the abuses of the contemporary church. Aren't those Christians, asks Folly, who "find great comfort in soothing self-delusions about fictitious pardons for their sins, measuring out the times in purgatory down to the droplets of a waterclock," aren't such people completely foolish? But aren't they very content? That is because Folly has come to their aid and made them foolish. If a philosopher, says Folly, were to point out how stupid all this religious observance is, how much happiness he would take away from ordinary ignorant believers! Likewise the theologians, who enjoy discussing such things as "whether God could have taken on the nature of a woman, of the devil, of an ass, of a cucumber, of a piece of flint." Folly praises those popes and priests who dress themselves in fine garments and enjoy the fruits of the world. How miserable the popes would be if they really had to imitate the life of

Christ, with its poverty and labor and *contemptus mundi*. This is funny, and also cleverly slippery.

Folly's very praise of such nonsense reveals its suspect quality more powerfully than if Erasmus himself were simply writing a tract against it. This is one of those moments where *The Praise of Folly* leaves its religious and satirical roots and, anticipating the techniques of the novel form, benefits enormously from its own literary complexity, ushering in a new kind of comedy.

However, the book begins to wobble, and it wobbles on just this fault line, between the old and the new, the religious and the secular. As Erasmus continues his mockery of clerical abuses and theological absurdity, so Folly's "praise" of such folly begins to recede, and we encounter several pages of straightforward, if highly entertaining, satire and mockery. Erasmus, as it were, begins to speak in his own voice. And he realizes this, making Folly quickly concede that she should stop talking so angrily about popes and priests "lest I should seem to be composing a satire rather than delivering an encomium." This is a literary uncertainty, the moment at which Erasmus either chooses not to or cannot maintain the consistency of the unreliable narrator, and diverts instead to the stability, the didacticism, of satire. Folly, *as a character*, is finally less important to Erasmus than the content of Folly's message. Old religious comedy asserts itself, and wins back ground from new, secular comedy; *The Praise of Folly* stops being slippery and jokey and gets a little self-justifyingly hard and angry.

These are junctions wherein one sees mixtures of the old and new comedy, the prenovelistic and novelistic: Erasmus offers one, and among novelists, Cervantes, Austen, and Sterne provide the best examples. In Cervantes there are the old elements of satire, correction, punitive violence, farcical shenanigans—Don Quixote and Sancho Panza vomiting in each other's faces, for instance—and even allegory; and there are also glimpses of a newer, more complicated, more internal comedy. Don Quixote's finally unknowable fantasy excites our compassion as much as it prompts our mockery at the end of the book. Sterne's characters are not fully realized creatures with interior lives—they are not quite novelistic, indeed at times they seem to belong to a long, banging satirical poem; Sterne gives Uncle Toby and Mr. Shandy their "hobby-horses," their "Cervantick" unitary obsessions, which makes them vivid single essences, bright blots of color. Yet Sterne's comic world sometimes breathes a very modern forgiveness, and there are moments of mingled tears and laughter which powerfully suggest a new kind of comedy.

Austen may be the most interestingly riven, the most transitional of all these writers. In her work, broadly put, there are the minor characters, who seem to belong to the theater, and who are theatrically mocked and "corrected" by the author in her old eighteenth-century satiric mode; and there are the great heroines of the books, the sole possessors of interior consciousness, heroic *because* they exercise their consciousness, who seem to belong to the newer world of the novel and not of the theater, and who are not mocked but gradually comprehended and finally forgiven (we forgive Emma even though we know, morally speaking, that we are not "supposed to").

II

I want to avoid overassertion. There are many kinds of comedy, of course. There are no straight lines, and no dead termini. Religious comedy does not just write its will to secular comedy and then expire. "Correction" does not somehow magically become "forgiveness" at some convenient moment in the nineteenth century, as the novel reaches its preeminence. When Beckett very funnily mocks the pedantry of Catholicism at the end of *Molloy*—"Does it really matter with which hand one asperges the podex?" "Is it true that the infant Saint-Roch refused suck on Friday?" "How long do we have to wait for the Antichrist?"—he sounds like Erasmus mocking the theologians in *The Praise of Folly*; there is the question of the essentially religious Flaubert; the thoroughly "unreliable" Hamsun is also saturated in Lutheran notions of punishment and disgrace; Kundera, who frequently invokes Rabelais, Diderot, and Cervantes, seems much more an antique comedian than a modern one, for all the Prague sex games. (Like Rabelais, he is robust rather than funny, and suggestive rather than moving.) Bergson's twentieth-century theory of comedy, which argues for "the absence of feeling that usually accompanies laughter," is almost indistinguishable from Rabelaisian practice. And if by "religious" one means the dream of transparency, the victory of knowing over the haze of unreliability, the existence of a stable system of human categorization and a certain odor of didacticism, then religious comedy continues to flourish well into an unreligious age. One finds this corrective strain still in political theater (Dario Fo, for instance, who is proud of his roots in commedia dell'arte), in dystopian allegory (Margaret Atwood, who can be bitingly and satirically funny), in the daily "corrections" of the tabloid press (who, precisely, need icons like Princess Diana and Mother Teresa so that they can have devils like Camilla Parker Bowles and Hillary Clinton), and in the kind of brisk social comedy that descends from Evelyn Waugh, Kingsley Amis, and Muriel Spark.

Against this, the comedy of irresponsibility is characterized by the mingling of emotions that Gogol famously called "laughter through tears." Perhaps the right word for this distinctive modern comedy is "humor." Freud distinguishes humor from comedy and the joke. He is particularly interested in "broken humor," which he defines as "the humor that smiles through tears." He argues that this kind of humorous pleasure arises from the prevention of an emotion. A sympathy that the reader has prepared is blocked by a comic occurrence, and transferred onto a matter of secondary importance. I discuss this humor in my essay on the great Czech writer Bohumil Hrabal. What Freud leaves dangling, and what one would want to add to his analysis, is that just because one's sympathy is blocked and transferred—Freud sounds rather Aristotelian here—it does not cease to be sympathy. On the contrary, sympathy is intensified by its blockage. Verga's stories act like this, as do Chekhov's.

This kind of comedy seems to me the creation of modern fiction (and by that I mean late-nineteenth- and twentieth-century fiction) because it exchanges typology for the examination of the individual, and the religious dream of complete or stable knowledge for the uncertainty of incomplete knowledge. Compare Joubert and Pirandello. Joubert, in his *Traité du ris*, argues that "empty promises of visual pleasure cause laughter" (in the words of his best modern commentator, Gregory de Rocher). If it is announced that we are to see a beautiful young maiden, and are introduced instead to a withered old hag, we laugh, especially if she is "dirty, smelly, drooling, toothless, flat-nosed, bandy-legged, humpy, bumpy, stinking, twisted, filthy, knotty, full of lice, and more deformed than ugliness itself." Pirandello, without explicitly referring to Joubert, seems to reply to him in his essay "L'umorismo." Suppose we see an old woman, says Pirandello, heavily made up and inappropriately dressed, in fashions more befitting a woman half her age. She at first seems comic, on the traditional Joubertian principle that incongruity and self-delusion are funny. (And they are.) But if we begin to try to enter the woman's head, if we try to merge with her—while acknowledging that we cannot utterly know her motives—our laughter turns to pity. We undergo a "perception of the opposite," and wonder if the woman is not herself distressed by her appearance and all the yearning to be young it represents. This mingled amusement and pity Pirandello calls humor. Pirandello saw humor as a modern invention, an enlargement of the old comic tradition. (Though it is fair to say that this is almost exactly Adam Smith's definition of "sympathy" in his *Theory of Moral Sentiments*; but then Smith, I think, was in advance of the novel's powers when he wrote his book. He was looking ahead, as it were, to something beyond him, to a form that did not yet quite exist.)

Pirandello's picture is valuable because it proposes that we try to become the old woman in our attempt to sympathize with her, while also suggesting that this may be an ultimately frustrated enterprise. Modern tragicomic fiction does not offer a guarantee of reliable knowledge; yet paradoxically, it continues to believe in the revelation of character, continues to believe that the attempt to know a character is worthwhile, even if it is beautifully frustrated. What has changed is the definition of "character," which is now much deeper than allowed for in premodern fiction. Henry James, reviewing *Middlemarch*, argued, unfairly, that George Eliot hemmed in her characters with too much authorial essayism—that she wanted to know them too well, in effect. He called for the fictional creation of characters "in the old plastic, irresponsible sense." I think by "old" James meant Shakespeare, the essential progenitor of the English novel; but by old he really also meant new—he meant his own kind of fiction, in which characters are free to contradict themselves without being corrected by the author, are free to make mistakes without fearing authorial judgment; that they are, "like people in real life, to be inferred by the reader," as Coleridge described Shakespeare's characters. In such fiction, the reader is not to be overly helped by the author. We must find out for ourselves how much we know of a character, and we may find that what we know is that we do not know enough (as we do not "know" why Isabel Archer returns to Gilbert Osmond).

Bergson said that one definition of comedy was watching people dancing to music through a window without our being able to hear their music. Bergson's idea of comedy belongs somewhat to the "corrective" school, to the world of Molière, of satire, and of mechanical farce. In the Bergsonian vision, the watcher has an advantage over the dancers. He comprehends them, sees how foolish they look and knows why they are dancing. He comprehends them because he is deprived of their music. His deprivation is his strength. But what if his deprivation was his weakness? What if that watcher did not *know* that the dancers were dancing to music? What if he had no idea why they were dancing? What if he felt no advantage over them, but felt, with mingled laughter and pity, that he was watching some awful dance of death, in which he too was obscurely implicated? (Camus offers as an example of the "absurd" seeing a man talking on the phone behind a glass partition. You wonder, he says, "why he is alive.") This alternative picture comes closest to my notion of the modern novel's unreliability or irresponsibility, a state in which the reader may not always know why a character does something or may not know how to "read" a passage, and feels that in order to find these things out he must try to merge with the characters in their uncertainty. Such a person is no longer the cruelly laughing Yahweh or Jupiter, and no longer the correctively laughing theatergoer, but simply the modern reader, gloriously thrown into the same mixed and free dimension as the novel's characters.

More than its predecessor, this book of essays was planned as a collection with a number of repeating themes. (And since it is largely a book of essays in appreciation, many about the secular and comic nature of modern fiction, it might, I hope, come to seem like the secular reply to the more religious proposals of *The Broken Estate*.) All of the essays were written between 1999 and 2003. I was lucky enough to select these topics, rather than have them always selected for me, because of my great fortune in editors, chiefly Leon Wieseltier at *The New Republic* and Mary-Kay Wilmers at the *London Review of Books*, who have sustained me in many different ways over the last decade. Most of the pieces appeared, in slightly different form, in one or the other of those two journals. Of the rest, three essays appeared in *The New Yorker* (Cervantes, Tolstoy, and J. F. Powers), and one in *The Times Literary Supplement* (Pritchett). I am very grateful to the literary editors at those publications.

The Saltykov-Shchedrin essay first appeared as an introduction to

The Golovlyov Family (New York Review of Books Classics). I am grateful to Edwin Frank, its editor.

It would only be just to give credit to those translators from whom I quote, usually anonymously, in these essays. Cervantes's translator is Edith Grossman; Joseph Roth's are Michael Hofmann and Joachim Neugroschel; Verga's is G. H. McWilliam; Hrabal's are Michael Henry Heim, Edith Pargeter, and Paul Wilson; Babel's is Peter Constantine; Svevo's are William Weaver and Mary Beth Brombert; *Anna Karenina*'s are Richard Pevear and Larissa Volokhonsky. I am aware, of course, of the hazards involved in writing about books at one remove from their originals, and know how much is lost; Nabokov liked to tell the jokey story, surely apocryphal, of how Herzen, after a few months in London, wrote to say how despised the poor were in that city—at least, to judge from the many times people angrily said the word "beggar" on the street. Readers will notice that the way I write about English and American prose style (in Bellow, Green, Zadie Smith, Jonathan Franzen, and so on) is quite different from the slightly warier, less localized approach of my writing about work in translation. Some will think me not wary enough; but if I am not wary enough, it is not because I do not understand the case for wariness, just that I am wary of excessive wariness, and warmed at least by the example of fine critics who themselves have written about work in translation—René Girard and V. S. Pritchett come to mind. In this fraught area, several translators—Michael Hofmann on Roth, Sverre Lyngstad on Hamsun, and G. H. McWilliam on Verga—have been helpful correspondents.

Don Quixote's *Old and New Testaments*

❦

The famous windmills Don Quixote mistakes for giants have something in common with the madeleine that makes Marcel's memory-buds salivate: they both occur conveniently early in very long books that are, in English at least, more praised than read. And Cervantes may resemble Proust in one further dimension. Both are comic writers, properly snagged in the mundane, whose fiction has too often been etherealized out of existence. Miguel de Unamuno, the relentlessly idealizing Spanish philosopher, considered *Don Quixote* a "profoundly Christian epic" and the true Spanish bible, and correspondingly managed to write about the novel as if not a single comic episode occurs in it. W. H. Auden thought that *Don Quixote* was a portrait of a Christian saint; and Unamuno's unlikely American supporter, Harold Bloom, reminds us that although "*Don Quixote* may not be a scripture," it nonetheless contains us all as Shakespeare does—which sounds more like religious lament than secular caution.

So it is worth reminding ourselves of the gross, the worldly, the violent, and above all the comic in *Don Quixote*—worth reminding ourselves that we are permitted the odd secular guffaw while reading this book. If all of modern fiction comes out of the knight's cape, then one reason might be that Cervantes's novel contains all major comic tropes, from the farcical to the delicately ironic, the trivial to the splendid. First there is the comedy of egotism. This is the "But enough about my work, what do you think of my book?" grand manner, brilliantly exploited by Tartuffe, or by Austen's Mr. Collins, who proposes to Elizabeth Bennet by listing all the ways in which he will benefit from marriage. Don Quixote is the great chivalric egotist, no more egotistical than when he appears to be most chivalrous, as when, after poor Sancho Panza has suffered several adventures with his master, including a beating by some drovers from Yanguas and being tossed in a blanket by a gang of men, Don Quixote has the nerve to tell his servant that these things are evil enchantments and therefore not really happening to Sancho: "Therefore you must not grieve for the misfortunes that befall me, for you have no part in them." This is the knight who, later in the book, finds he can't sleep and wakes his servant up, on the principle that "it is in the nature of good servants to share the griefs of their masters and to feel what they are feeling, if only for appearance's sake." No wonder that Sancho elsewhere defines a knight adventurer as "someone who's beaten and then finds himself emperor."

The egotist is never very good at laughing at himself, laughable though he often is. Cervantes has a marvelously undulating scene in which the knight and his servant are riding in the hills and are stopped by a fearfully loud noise. Both are made nervous by the sound. Don Quixote sets out to discover the source, and Sancho Panza weeps with terror; Don Quixote is moved by Sancho's tears. When they finally discover that the noise comes only from "six wooden fulling hammers," Don Quixote looks at Sancho Panza and sees that "his cheeks were puffed out and his mouth full of laughter, clear signs that he would soon explode, and Don Quixote's melancholy was not so great that he could resist laughing at the sight of Sancho, and when Sancho saw that his master had begun, the floodgates opened with such force that he had to press his sides with his fists to keep from bursting with laughter." At which Don Quixote gets cross with Sancho for laughing at him, and hits him with his pike, complaining: "In all the books of chivalry I have read, which are infinite in number, I have never found any squire who talks as much with his master as you do with yours." As so often in *Don Quixote*, the reader travels, in only a page or two, through different chambers of laughter: affectionate, ironic, satirical, harmonious.

Don Quixote is the greatest of all fictional enquiries into the relation between fiction and reality, and so a great deal of the comedy is self-conscious, generated when one or more of the characters seems to step out of the book and appeal either to a nonfictional reality or directly to the audience (the staple of pantomime performance and commedia dell'arte). The second book of *Don Quixote*, written ten years (1615) after the first (1605), throws irony on irony as the knight and his sidekick set out once again on their adventures, only to discover that they have become celebrities because a book about their escapades has appeared in the ten-year interim—the novel we have just been reading. Thus, Cervantes incorporates the fact of his own novel into its sequel. He delights in the epistemological hornet's nest into which Don Quixote and Sancho stumble in this second volume, as they assert their reality by recourse to a prior fiction whose culmination they are now enacting. But long before all these complexities, Sancho pleads with his master, in the first book, after being thrashed by the drovers from Yanguas: "Señor, since these misfortunes are the harvest reaped by chivalry, tell me, your grace, if they happen very often, or come only at certain times. . . ." Sancho winks at the audience, as if to say, "I know I'm playing a role, and so is my master." The awful poignancy of the novel is that the knight does not know this.

Sancho's request is the perfectly reasonable one that if violence is to be cartoonish, then the laws of the genre should be observed, and we should all be given fair notice—the banana skin seen in advance on the sidewalk, the large shadow cast by the prowling cat—that violence is on the way. And certainly many of the cartoon conventions do appear in Don Quixote. The two heroes are never, it seems, seriously damaged, despite the thrashings, beatings, tossings, and broken bones they suffer. They always peel their flattened silhouettes off the ground. There is slapstick, too: at one moment, after Don Quixote has been attacked by the shepherds whose sheep he has attempted to kill, he asks Sancho to peer into his mouth to see how many teeth have been knocked out. As he is doing so, Don Quixote vomits into his face. Sancho, when he realizes that this is vomit, not blood, promptly vomits back into his face. There is plenty of low comedy like this, including an inn that, like the cheese shop in the Monty Python sketch, is out of everything that is requested.

Nowadays, the violence and farce bore or repel, and indeed it can be tedious to wade through all the needlessly spilled blood: Don Quixote is pounded with a lance by a mule driver who beats him "as if he were threshing wheat"; "half an ear" is cut off by a Basque adversary; his ribs are crushed by the drovers from Yanguas; he is hit so hard by a mule driver that his mouth is bathed in blood; the shepherds knock his teeth out; and he is stoned by the convicts he tries to release. Vladimir Nabokov found it cruel, and never really reconciled himself to the novel. In a Tarantino-tainted age, when "reality" only ever seems to get the heavy sideburns of quotation marks, such violence seems less cruel than pointedly unreal, the guarantee of its unreality being the unkillability of its victims. But Cervantes's violence makes another point, too. It is powerfully anti-idealizing. It shows us how often the well-intentioned knight ends up inflicting his good intentions on others. Near the beginning of the book, Don Quixote runs into Andrés, a boy who is being whipped by his master. Certain that his chivalric duty is to free the oppressed, he sends the punitive master packing. Later, Andrés will turn up again, only to explain to

Don Quixote and his friends that everything turned out "very different from what your grace imagines." The master returned, of course, explains the boy, and flogged him all the harder, each time making a joke about how he was making a fool of Don Quixote. Andrés leaves, saying to Don Quixote that if he ever comes upon him again, even if he's being torn to pieces, "don't help me and don't come to my rescue."

This is the Quixote pattern. In another incident, Don Quixote attacks a group of monks accompanying a corpse. Convinced that the corpse is a knight whose death he must avenge, he charges at the poor monks, breaking the leg of a young man. Quixote introduces himself as a knight whose "occupation and profession" is to "wander the world righting wrongs and rectifying injuries." The young man tartly points out that this is hardly the case, since he was all right until Don Quixote came along and broke his leg, which will be "injured for the rest of my life; it was a great misadventure for me to run across a man who is seeking adventures."

Novel writing has an entrepreneurial element: to invent a central story which can function simultaneously as a plausible action and as an emblematic or symbolic one is akin to inventing a new machine or product, a patent that will run and run. Think of Chichikov traveling around Russia buying up "dead souls" (a title Gogol wanted kept secret while he was writing his novel, surely because he knew it would give away the clue to his "invention"), or of Bellow's Herzog writing his mental letters to great thinkers and public figures. These are grand concepts. In *Don Quixote*, a moderately prosperous Spanish gentleman, "one of those who has a lance and ancient shield on a shelf and keeps a skinny nag and a greyhound for racing," becomes possessed, through reading the fictions of chivalric adventures, by the idea that the knights-errant of folklore and fiction were real people; furthermore, it seems "reasonable and necessary to him, both for the sake of his honor and as a service to the nation, to become a knight-errant and travel the world with his armor and his horse to seek adventures."

When Cervantes invented Don Quixote's madness and propelled him out onto the Castilian plains to enact that madness, he set ticking a little hermeneutical clock by which, miraculously, we are still trying to tell the time. Don Quixote's misreadings—his determination to read fiction as reality—license our millions of readings of him because Cervantes kept the ambition of Don Quixote's journeying as wide and unspecific as possible. We know what Don Quixote thinks he is doing, but what is he really doing? What do his strivings represent? Does his misreading of the world represent the poignant comic battle of the unsullied Idea doing its best to exist in the brute world of Reality? Or for Idea and Reality should we read Spirit and Flesh? (Poor Sancho, in this schema, is always seen as the embodiment of Flesh.) Or Literature and Reality? Or is Don Quixote an absolutist artist, striving to shape the recalcitrant world into his vision of it?

That Don Quixote's adventures have been so idealized, not to say Christianized, says more about the idealizing tendencies of Christianity than about Cervantes's novel. It is as if those determined to see Don Quixote as some kind of saint or wild missionary of the spirit simply close their eyes to the mayhem and suffering he causes. But Andrés, the flogged boy, is right: Don Quixote's good intentions have a way of inverting themselves, of becoming opposites. Perhaps Cervantes was interested, then, not only in the pious triumphs of his knight but also in his pious defeats? And perhaps this interest, despite all that is said about Cervantes's Catholicism, has a secular, even blasphemous, bent? Dostoevsky, who was very interested in *Don Quixote*, surely saw this when he created the quixotic figure of Prince Myshkin, the Idiot, whose Christ-like actions have a way of contaminating the world around him. Prince Myshkin is not just too good for the world; he is dangerously too good.

When the young man complains to Don Quixote about his broken leg, the two fall into a kind of theological argument, really an argument about theodicy, about the ways in which we try to justify God's plan for the world. The young man is a skeptic. He alleges that the man whose corpse he is accompanying was killed "by God, by means of a pestilential fever." Don Quixote argues the conventional, orthodox position: "Not all things . . . happen in precisely the same way," he says, defending his decision to charge at the monks. For a brief, weird moment, it is as if Don Quixote is likening himself to God, to a God whose ways we cannot know, yet whose decisions seem to inflict incomprehensible suffering on us.

Cervantes's novel bristles with little blasphemous shards like this; it is why the novel is the great founder of secular comedy. In the novel, Don Quixote is often likened by his friends and acquaintances to a preacher, a missionary, a holy man. He himself argues that he is doing Christ's work. When he falls into conversation with a canon, the man in holy orders rebukes the knight for reading his books about chivalry, which are all folly and falsehood. He should instead read the Scriptures. But the great stories of knight-errantry are not fictions, replies Don Quixote. Who could deny, for instance, that Pierres and the fair Magalona really existed, for to this day one can see in the royal armory "the peg, slightly larger than a carriage pole, with which the valiant Pierres directed the wooden horse as he rode it through the air." The canon denies ever having seen this, but the damage is done. Blasphemy hangs like mirage heat. For how has Don Quixote just defended the existence of blatant fictions? By arguing from the existence of relics. And the logic is unavoidable: if mere fictions are proved real by arguing from relics, then religious relics, commonly used to prove the veracity of religion, may be fictions, too. This, in a Catholic country in the midst of Counter-Reformation fervency! Later, at the beginning of the second book, Don Quixote will argue that the legendary "giant Morgante," another folkloric figure, must have existed because we all believe— don't we?—that the biblical Goliath existed. Cervantes joins that select company of writers, like Milton, Montaigne, and Pierre Bayle, who delight in slipping blasphemy in through the tradesman's entrance while noisily welcoming divinity at the front gate.

This kind of teasing continues into the novel's second volume, in which Don Quixote and Sancho find themselves having to prove that they are the legendary figures they claim to be. It is a shame that many readers never get to the novel's stupendous second book, which is both funnier and more affecting than its first. A rough analogy of the action in the second book might go like this: Jesus Christ is wandering around first-century Palestine trying to convince people that he is the true Messiah. It is a difficult task, because John the Baptist, instead of preparing the way for the Messiah, has claimed that *he* is the true Messiah, and has gone and got himself appropriately crucified on Calvary. Since many people have heard of John's death and resurrection, Jesus finds himself being skeptically tested by his audience: can he perform this and that miracle? Moreover, when Jesus hears that John has been crucified on Calvary, he decides to prove his authenticity by changing his plans: he will not now be crucified on Calvary, but will instead travel to Rome to be eaten by lions. Tired, disillusioned, deeply saddened by the unexpected explosion of his greatest dreams, he sets out for Rome with his dearest disciple and right-hand man, Peter. But Peter, taking pity on him, gets together with some of the disciples and convinces Jesus that he should give up this Messiah lark, and should retire to somewhere nice, like Sorrento. Jesus meekly obeys, arrives in Sorrento, and immediately falls sick and dies, though not before renouncing all claims to divinity and announcing his convinced atheism.

The example of Old and New Testaments might be the easiest way to decipher the densely subtle games Cervantes plays in this second volume. Don Quixote and his servant are now literary celebrities because of the publication of Cervantes's first volume, and people want to meet them, put them to the test, pinch their veracity. Of course, the famous couple have no idea in what light they were depicted by Cervantes, so, in effect, people are laughing behind their backs. Since celebrities occasion mimicry, there is a rival Don Quixote now claiming that he is the real thing, and that our knight—i.e., Cervantes's—is a pretender. But in addition to all this, in the ten years between 1605 and 1615, Cervantes's novel did indeed—in the real world—inspire an imitation, a book named *The Second Volume of the Ingenious Knight Don Quixote de la Mancha*, by one Alonso Fernández de Avellaneda, about whom little is known. It appeared in 1614. Cervantes was already well into the writing of his second volume when he heard about Avellaneda's fraudulence; he decided to incorporate it into his own novel. In chapter 59, Don Quixote hears, through a bedroom wall, two men discussing Avellaneda's book. He is outraged, and quizzes the men about this imitation. When he learns that in Avellaneda's account Don Quixote travels to Saragossa, he decides to travel not to Saragossa (where he had indeed been intending to go), but to Barcelona, "and in this way I shall proclaim the lies of this modern historian to the world, and then people will see that I am not the Don Quixote he says I am."

Cervantes's great ironies are false horizons, one appearing after the other. Two fictional characters, in order to prove their "reality," must appeal to a prior fiction which was written by the same writer who has now created this second volume of fictional escapades. And these fictional characters must then argue with other fictional characters that they are Cervantes's characters and not Avellaneda's characters. So there is the novel we are reading (volume 2); there is the novel that first created these figures (volume 1); and there is a rival novel about similarly named characters. These three books merge to thoroughly rob "reality" of its empirical treasure. Reality is simpy another broken wall, apparently protecting nobody from skepticism's ravages.

Yet at the moment when Cervantes is at his most playful and selfreferential, Don Quixote and Sancho Panza are at their most real. This is the book's great paradox. The novel's second volume belongs to Sancho, who becomes wiser and funnier as the book progresses. His love for Don Quixote is tearfully manifest. And Don Quixote is fighting for his life—which, in a sublime irony, means that he is fighting for his fictionality (though he would not see it like this, of course). It is desperately important for Don Quixote that he is who he says he is, and that everyone believes him. If, in volume 1, Don Quixote was a copy of a copy—a man living out a literary fantasy after reading too much bad fiction—he becomes, in the second volume, a copy of a copy who is now responding to his own fictionality. When he gets a traveler, Don Alvaro Tarfe, to agree that he is the real Don Quixote and not Avellaneda's, and forces him to sign a certificate to this effect, we laugh but we also shiver at the awfulness of it. A certificate, the issuing of which negates the certificate; because, of course, Don Quixote does not prove his reality with his certificate. He merely proves—to us who knew it anyway—that he appeared in Cervantes's first volume. Italo Svevo was surely thinking of this moment when he had his comic hero, Zeno, get his doctor to sign a certificate of sanity. Zeno presents it to his father, who, with tears in his eyes, says, "Ah, then you truly are mad!" The reader, with tears in his eyes, says the same when Don Quixote flourishes his certificate.

A fantasy that seemed, in the novel's first volume, sometimes a lark, sometimes tedious, often unfathomable, becomes, in the second volume, something without which neither Don Quixote nor anyone else can live. All of us want Don Quixote to further his madness. We have come to believe in it partly because, as in Shakespeare, we are made to believe in a character's reality when he himself believes in it so strongly, and partly because we don't know precisely what "belief" entails anymore anyway. By the end of the book we have all become little Quixotes, reared and fed on a fictional account of a knight-errant's escapades. We are willing fantasists, now unsure of our ground.

It is a tremendous shock when Don Quixote decides to head for home, in order to retire from his adventuring and become a shepherd. It is an even greater shock when Don Quixote suddenly dies. He has a fever, is in bed for six days. The doctor's opinion is that despondency is killing him. He sleeps, awakes, and announces himself cured of his madness. He denounces "all the profane histories of knight errantry. . . ." Cervantes writes that those present, hearing this, "undoubtedly believed that some new madness had taken hold of him," one of the greatest comic sentences in the whole book. Don Quixote calls for Sancho Panza, and asks for his forgiveness for "making you fall into the error into which I fell, thinking that there were and are knights errant in the world." "Don't die, Señor," is Sancho's tearful response. Don Quixote makes his will, in which he leaves some money for Sancho, lives another three days, and then, "surrounded by the sympathy and tears of those present, gave up the ghost, I mean to say, he died."

The poverty of the language, its near clumsiness and refusal to plume itself up into magnificence, is deeply moving, as if Cervantes himself was overcome with wordless grief at the passing of his creation. Don Quixote has become his own fiction of himself, and cannot live without it. As soon as he renounces it, he must wither away. So in dying, he announces his own fictionality. Yet Sancho Panza remains, lives on. And who is Sancho? Earlier in the book, Don Quixote says of Sancho, admiringly, that "he doubts everything and he believes everything." Isn't this a fine description of the reader of this novel? Sancho is Don Quixote's reader, who lives on as the book's readers do, all-believing and all-doubting, made both faithful and skeptical by the novel's fidelities and skepticisms, happy inheritors of the knight's last will and testament.

Shakespeare and the Pathos of Rambling

❦

In the *Theaetetus*, Socrates is puzzled about how we make use of what we already know. Take a mathematician, he says. Such a person must already have in his head all the numbers he will work with. Yet when he counts numbers, he sets out, as it were, to learn from himself things that he already knows. The same, continues Socrates, is true of a scholar starting to read the same book for the umpteenth time. This is a paradox of redundancy, in which we have to unnaturally forget what we would naturally remember in order to learn something "new"—in some ways, a rather unnatural process.

Plato's simile suggestively describes how the flow of consciousness is depicted in fiction and drama. For one obvious element of the depiction of consciousness in literature is that it is paradoxically redundant. A flow of thought is invisible; it does not represent itself. The one thing we do not do with our minds is turn their contents into narratives, or even into unpunctuated monologues. Perhaps most of the time, as Nabokov complained about Joyce, we do not think in words at all. As soon as a fictional character thinks in any depth, the writer has to represent something which is not normally represented, and the character doing the thinking often has the air of

Socrates' mathematician, learning anew from himself something he would already know. The representation of consciousness in fiction hovers between a redundant remembering and a struggle against forgetting.

And this is literature's special burden, its special creation. For if the philosophical question is, How do we know ourselves? the literary question is always both the philosophical question of how we know ourselves and the literary-technical question of how we then *represent* knowing ourselves. The formal or technical redundancy I am talking about is clear enough when we look at the origins of the stream of consciousness, which lie in the dramatic soliloquy; and if we in turn look at the origins of the soliloquy, which lie in prayer. In Greek and Senecan tragedy, the moment when a character confides his thoughts or agonies or intentions to the audience often occurs at a moment of prayer or religious self-exhortation: the hero addresses a shrine, or makes a sacrifice, or calls on the gods to forgive or punish him (or punish his enemies), and the audience "overhears"—such is the convention—this self-statement. It is a little like reading the Psalms. Shakespeare's soliloquies retain that prayerful or religious quality of intention-making and self-exhortation: Edmund calling on the gods to stand up for bastards, or Lear calling to the gods, or Lady Macbeth's "Unsex me here," or her husband's final soliloquy ("Tomorrow and tomorrow and tomorrow"), which borrows from Psalm 90.

Of course, most of Shakespeare's soliloquies are addressed to the audience, so we become God by proxy, the Delphic oracle that never replies. Soliloquy may be seen, then, not merely as an address but as speech with an interlocutor who does not respond—as blocked conversation, and blocked intention. Again, this may flow from the idea of prayer, especially prayer as the frustration of wishes: for merely to speak to God is to be frustrated by his silence. This aspect of prayerful consciousness is obviously present in the novel in the form of the epiphany and solitary fantasy; what is Proust's madeleine but a secularized communion wafer, the Host by which the worshipper begins to examine himself?

But if soliloquy is often a kind of conversation with people who don't respond, then one might wonder: Why do heroes and heroines bother to speak to us nonresponders at all? Of course they "must," for the author's technical and literary reasons: because the reader needs to know things about them, and they need to know things about themselves. But beyond this technical demand, perhaps they "must" speak to us in this way for a more human and metaphysical reason: in some essential way, they are reminding the reader and themselves that they exist. Perhaps the metaphysical need arises, in part, from the author's literary-technical need?

Go back to Plato's idea of paradoxical redundancy. In life, people do not narrate their intentions and feelings as the soliloquy makes them do, speaking them out loud. In the soliloquy, the mind does not so much describe itself as describe itself as a narrator would, from the outside (as a narrator does, of course, in most novels). Shakespeare's contribution is that, while always a dramatist, he also prefigures the novel. For Shakespeare's world is not just one of soliloquies but also a soliloquizing world, in which people often speak at rather than to each other. In Shakespeare, the notion of the soliloquy as a blocked conversation is transferred to conversation itself between characters; you might say in fact that much conversation in Shakespeare is blocked soliloquy. Thus it is that Shakespeare explodes the traditional soliloquy even as he expands it, and essentially invents the stream of consciousness.

Shakespeare is a great developer of what might be called rambling consciousness, those moments when a character is allowed to drift, to go on mental safaris, to travel into apparent irrelevance, to be beside the point. It is through such rambling that absent-mindedness in the modern novel appears. In Shakespeare, these moments generally occur not in soliloquy but in conversation, when a character begins to produce a monologue. There is an

interesting moment, for instance, in *All's Well That Ends Well*
when Bertram is first introduced to the King of France. Instead
of receiving Bertram in the usual way and asking after him, the
king starts reminiscing about Bertram's father, whom he obviously
loved:

> Youth [he says to Bertram], thou bear'st thy father's face;
> Frank nature, rather curious than in haste,
> Hath well compos'd thee . . .
> I would I had that corporal soundess now
> As when thy father and myself in friendship
> First tried our soldiership! He did look far
> Into the service of the time, and was
> Discipled of the bravest. He lasted long,
> But on us both did haggish age steal on,
> And wore us out of act. It much repairs me
> To talk of your good father. In his youth
> He had the wit which I can well observe
> Today in our young lords . . .

Bertram tries to interject with various politenesses, but the king ram-
bles on self-involvedly for another sixty or so lines. Bertram thanks
the king for remembering his father so royally, and the king starts
again:

> Would I were with him! He would always say—
> Methinks I hear him now; his plausive words
> He scattered not in ears, but grafted them
> To grow there and to bear . . .
> "Let me not live," quoth he,
> "After my flame lacks oil, to be the snuff
> Of younger spirits, whose apprehensive senses
> All but new things disdain, whose judgments are
> Mere fathers of their garments, whose constancies
> Expire before their fashions." This he wished.
> I after him do after him wish too . . .

When a courtier reminds the king that he is loved, he ignores him and asks Bertram how long it has been since the death of the physician who was at the bedside of his old friend and thus is blamed by the king for letting him die. Six months, replies Bertram. "If he were living I would try him yet," says the king angrily. The king is a bit like Hotspur, who talks only to himself and who is reprimanded for "tying his ear only to his own tongue." The elegiac comedy of this scene arises from the prospect of a man so fiercely clinging to his past, and so self-involvedly ignoring his interlocutor. The king talks as if he is in conversation, but he is only in self-conversation, and happily contradicts himself, saying at the start that he sees the same kind of wit in the young lords as he did in his late friend, and ending by saying that he agrees with his late friend that the young are feckless, and he wishes he were in his grave.

Here we witness a character who may be mistaken but who is not inauthentic. Memory is amoral because in literature authenticity trumps morals. The self-use of memory allows a character to live in error, as it were, but always be forgiven, since what is important about memory is that it seems true to that character. Shakespeare's characters feel real to us in part because they feel real to *themselves*, take their own private universes for granted, and in particular their memories and pasts. Indeed, Shakespeare's characters manage to hold the paradox that they feel real to themselves but do not necessarily know themselves, which is the very paradox of consciousness, since I have no way of knowing that I do not actually know myself.

John Berryman noticed a passage in act 4 of *The Two Gentlemen of Verona* in which the clown, Launce, tells the audience about his dog, Crab. "Here we attend," writes Berryman, "for the first time in English comedy, to a definite and irresistible *personality*, absorbed in its delicious subject to the exclusion of all else, confused, and engaging." Launce upbraids Crab for pissing in a gentleman's hall and recalls that the gentleman ordered that poor Crab be whipped. Launce tells us that he went to "the fellow that whips the dogs" and told him that it was not Crab that pissed but Launce himself. Thus Launce was whipped from the hall. "How many masters would do this for his servant?" asks Launce of his dog, and develops the question:

> Nay, I'll be sworn, I have sat in the stocks for puddings he hath stol'n, otherwise he had been executed; I have stood on the pillory for geese he hath kill'd, otherwise he had suffer'd for't. Thou thinkst not of this now. Nay, I remember the trick you serv'd me when I took my leave of Madam Silvia. Did not I bid thee still mark me and do as I do? When didst thou see me heave up my leg and make water against a gentlewoman's farthingale? Didst thou ever see me do such a trick?

How finely, in this passage, we are really eavesdropping on a man who is not talking to us but talking to his dog ("Thou thinkst not of this now"). Of course, Launce is really talking to himself, too. Again, we see how Shakespeare dares to fill the soliloquy with a character's apparent irrelevances. And one of these "irrelevances" is a character's determination to persist with analogy or metaphor, as Launce does, seemingly only to please himself—his little conceit that he has become his dog's servant. Again and again in Shakespeare's soliloquies the dramatist repeatedly "risks" letting his characters use metaphor for their own ends, lets them develop their figures of thought and speech as *they* might develop them. We know that Launce is babbling to himself in part because he is pressing his (i.e., Shakespeare's) analogy to such "selfish" length.

In a soliloquizing world, like Shakespeare's, in which characters often speak at each other while mistakenly supposing that they are talking with · them, the distinction between private and public thought collapses. Both are failed privacies. What we say to ourselves is often quite similar to what we say to each other, because we have forgotten about the distinction. Sterne, Dickens, Chekhov, and sometimes Joyce seem to me the great developers of this insight. Consider, for example, a moment in one of Chekhov's earliest stories, "The Steppe." A little boy, Yegorushka, is going to a new school, and he has hitched a ride with two men, a wool trader named Kuzmichov and a priest called Father Christopher. At the beginning of the journey, as they leave the boy's home village, they pass the cemetery in which the boy's father and grandmother are buried:

> From behind the wall cheerful white crosses and tombstones peeped out nestling in the foliage of cherry trees and seen as white patches from a distance. At blossom time, Yegorushka remembered, the white patches mingled with the cherry blooms in a sea of white, and when the cherries had ripened the white tombs and crosses were crimson-spotted, as if with blood. Under the cherries behind the wall the boy's father and his grandmother Zinaida slept day and night. When Grandmother had died she had been put in a long, narrow coffin, and five-copeck pieces had been placed on her eyes, which would not stay shut. Before dying, she had been alive, and she had brought him soft poppy-seed bun rings from the market, but now she just slept and slept.

This is a form of stream of consciousness, which captures not only how a small boy thinks but how all of us think, with useless banality, about the dead: "Before dying, she had been alive . . . but now she just slept and slept." Joyce admired Chekhov, and little Yegorushka's drifting thought perhaps reminds us of Dignam's memory of his dead father in *Ulysses*:

> His face got all grey instead of being red like it was and there was a fly walking over it up to his eye. The scrunch that was when they were screwing the screws into the coffin: and the bumps when they were bringing it downstairs. Pa was inside it and ma crying in the parlour and uncle Barney telling the men how to get it round the bend. A big coffin it was, and high and heavylooking. How was that? The last night pa was boosed he was standing on the landing there bawling out for his boots to go out to Tunney's for to boose more and he looked butty and short in his shirt. Never see him again. Death, that is. Pa is dead. My father is dead. He told me to be

a good son to ma. I couldn't hear the other things he said but I saw
his tongue and his teeth trying to say it better. Poor pa. That was
Mr Dignam, my father. I hope he is in purgatory now because he
went to confession to Father Conroy on Saturday night.

Chekhov, I think, does it better than Joyce, who cannot resist an
element of the literary ("A big coffin it was, and high and heavylook-
ing"; "Pa is dead. My father is dead") and a slight tinge of the stock-
comic—the Irish drinker telling his son to be good to his mother
and going to confession just in time. Chekhov risks greater banality,
and so wins a greater naturalness from his little boy. But what is really interesting is what happens after Yegorushka has had his memory of his grandmother. A page later, Yegorushka cries because he
misses his mother, and Father Christopher comforts him. "Never
mind, son," says Father Christopher. "Call on God. Lomonosov
once travelled just like this with the fishermen, and he became famous throughout Europe. Learning conjoined with faith yields fruit
pleasing to God. What does the prayer say? 'For the glory of the Creator, for our parents' comfort, for the benefit of the church and
country.' That's the way of it." Well, of course Father Christopher is
not comforting the boy at all; he is entirely self-involved, in a way we
are familiar with from Chekhov's later work, especially his plays. He
is speaking his mind, literally. It is a stream of consciousness. And he
speaks in the apparently arbitrary manner that the boy thinks in, that
is to say, aimlessly.

But what is the function of aimless thought? There is a marvelous
example of the authenticity of random memory in *Henry IV, Part 2*.
In a famous scene in the tavern at Eastcheap, Mistress Quickly is trying to get Falstaff to pay his debts. He feigns not to remember that
he has borrowed money from her, and she launches into a tirade, in
an attempt to remind him:

Thou didst swear to me upon a parcel-gilt table, sitting in my Dol-
phin chamber, at the round table, by a seacoal fire, upon Wednesday
in Wheeson week, when the Prince broke thy head for liking his fa-

ther to a singing-man of Windsor, thou didst swear to me then, as I was washing thy wound, to marry me and make me my lady thy wife. Canst thou deny it? Did not goodwife Keech, the butler's wife, come in then and call me gossip Quickly? Coming in to borrow a mess of vinegar, telling us she had a good dish of prawns, whereby thou didst desire to eat some, whereby I told thee they were ill for a green wound? And didst thou not, when she was gone downstairs, desire me to be no more so familiarity with such poor people, saying that ere long they should call me madam? And didst thou not kiss me and bid me fetch thee thirty shillings? I put thee now to thy book oath. Deny it if thou canst.

This moment is so lively and funny in part because we seem to see how a mind works: it is continually remembering *more*, and most of it is useless information. But useless to whom? Useless to those around her, yet who is Mistress Quickly reminding here? Is it Falstaff, or is it not, really, herself? Yet what are we to make of the many irrelevances, the seacoal fire, the wife with her dish of prawns, and so on? The irrelevance is funny because the Mistress is unwittingly writing a kind of parody of narrative, adding more and more detail, more verisimilitude. This in turn shows us that the mind is not actually knowable even as it is at its most characteristic, its most expressive, precisely because it *exceeds narration*. The spectacle of the Mistress's tirade suggests that if the mind were allowed to narrate itself, it would produce a narrative that simply never stops.

Mistress Quickly uses detail as if she were constructing a narrative, seeking to create verisimilitude. In a sense, she is; she is trying to persuade Falstaff that he was there. But this involves her in the recitation of many details which she must already know, but which, in the telling, appear for the first time as *recited details*, appear for the first time in a narrative, however haphazard and rambling that narrative is. So she is in the paradoxical position of convincing herself, like Socrates' mathematician, of what she already knows.

Thus a certain desperate quality attaches to the Mistress's defiant challenge to Falstaff, "Deny it if thou canst." It is not just that the

Mistress is saying to the assembled company that she is speaking the truth and Falstaff isn't; it is that she is saying that what *she* remembers, what she experiences, is real, is as real as the great fat seigneurial slab of reality who sits in front of her. "Deny it if thou canst." Well, Falstaff can deny it, and outrageously does, but we cannot, and do not. Even if every detail is beside the point, even if it were subsequently proved that the Mistress made it up, we cannot deny what is so true to a character. Perhaps this is what Henry James meant when he talked about the "irresponsibility" of characters. Characters are irresponsible, art is irresponsible when compared to life, because it is first and foremost important that a character be real, and as readers or watchers we tend to applaud any effort made toward the construction of that reality. We do not, of course, indulge *actual* people in the world this way at all. In real life, the fact that something seems real to someone is not enough to interest us, or to convince us that that reality is interesting. But the self-reality of fictional characters is deeply engrossing, which is why villains are lovable in literature in ways that they are not in life.

Mistress Quickly's randomness of thought is what makes her a comic and forlorn character at this moment. But one is still puzzled by the idea of truly random thought. For when thought is random and detail is recalled for no obvious reason, then remembered detail has no obvious metaphysical superiority, or privilege, over what has actually been forgotten. One of the reasons that random thought *is* random is that it is treading over what is forgotten, over the corpses of thoughts. Thought becomes a little like the old fiendish punishment that used to be handed out in English boarding schools, in which the victim had to color in every other square on a piece of graph paper. There is no necessary difference between a colored square and one left blank.

The delicate question then becomes, What is the status of irrelevant detail? Is it remembered data or forgotten data? Is it the very definition of the self, or everything but the self? Are absent-mindedness and present-mindedness the same thing? As Augustine points out in the *Confessions*, memory is partly convincing yourself of what you already really knew all along; and the representation of consciousness, the speaking-aloud of consciousness, is a further redundant self-convincing. We are always forgetting things until the moment we actually remember them. And at that moment are we really recalling them, or merely paying a kind of tribute to their actual forgettability? Likewise, there is no such thing as forgetting, because one doesn't really know *when* one has forgotten something; by definition, it has disappeared. Mistress Quickly's irrelevances, like those of her fictional heirs in Chekhov and Joyce, are sad and funny because they have the aspect of remembered detail but the status of forgotten detail.

How Shakespeare's "Irresponsibility"
Saved Coleridge

❧

I

The English are ecclesiastical but rarely metaphysical; they think in churchyards. Elegy and practicality are the English modes, complementary rather than antagonistic, for elegy can be seen as practical mourning, a way of composing the laurels. Metaphysics, by contrast, is a mere burr of thought, an adhesion to be plucked off the sturdy English garment and flicked back into the dark thicket whence it came. Schopenhauer noted that "whenever anyone in England wishes to describe something as very obscure or indeed as totally unintelligible, he says it is like German metaphysics." Perhaps he was thinking of Thomas Gray, the elegist of churchyards, who once complained: "Must I plunge into metaphysics? Alas, I cannot see in the dark; nature has not furnished me with the optics of a cat."

Samuel Taylor Coleridge is the great English turncoat. He was burred in thought. Amid stolid Englishness, he was a traveling temerity—mobile, metaphysical, Germanic yet Englishly Protestant, the victor of systems. He loved, as he put it in a letter, to "conundrumize." His prose work—his lectures on Shakespeare of 1818, the *Biographia Literaria* (1817), his copious notebooks and marginalia, and his late theological work, collected in *Aids to Reflection* (1825) and the posthumous *Confessions of an Inquiring Spirit*—is a junction box of inheritances, full of magical combinations: Lessing and Kant and Schlegel, Bacon and Hartley and Locke. His prose is many-roomed, extraordinarily hospitable to all he had learned, in his great reading, from the English poets, above all Shakespeare and Milton: that is to say, although he can subdue words whenever he wants, he also lets them muster their palpabilities on the page, *as words*, letting them trail their etymologies like invisible hems. (His modern rival, in this regard, is Virginia Woolf, whose father gave her Campbell's life of Coleridge to read when she was a teenager.) It is a dragging and dense style, sometimes obscure, with voluminous sentences that stretch like library corridors. He called this, in a typically lovely phrase, a prose that had "the hooks-and-eyes of memory." (Woolf wrote of using language "with roots.") At the same time, Coleridge is always bounding into simile and metaphor, and his use of the metaphorical often glints epigrammatically—as for instance when he wrote that "Swift was the soul of Rabelais dwelling in a dry place."

Fittingly, his own scattered influence is hard to collect. Though some have suggested Hazlitt as the influence on Keats, it was probably Coleridge who gave the young poet his idea of "negative capability," for Keats, before writing his famous letter, had read the *Biographia*, with its similar advocacy of what Coleridge called the "negative faith" that free drama requests of us. His criticism of Shakespeare has been surreptitiously influential: it is both intensely practical, grounded in texts and textual emendations ("practical criticism" is Coleridge's phrase, from the *Biographia*), and intensely theoretical. His radical yet commonsensical Protestant approach to biblical criticism, which proposed reading the Bible as if it were like any other great text, influenced Matthew Arnold and subsequent Anglican theology. And he clearly had an effect on Melville, his true colleague in language, who read the *Biographia* in February 1848, before writing *Moby-Dick*. Both writers loved Sir Thomas Browne, the seventeenth-century essayist, for his loitering speculations and thronged lexicon. Both indulged in what Melville called "philosophical ripping," boisterous monologues of speculation and association. Both were drawn, in their reading of Shakespeare, to a kind of amoral self, to Shakespeare's villains and fools and madmen, finding in those characters what Melville called "things which we feel to be terrifically true . . ." And of course both were in love with, indeed captives of, a kind of irresponsibility of metaphor, tending to see the world as a transit of likenesses.

Coleridge's metaphors and similes accompany him as a kind of code, a shadow from which we can read the hour of his life. Here he is in Bristol, a young revolutionary, being hissed at during a political lecture. "I am not at all surprised," shouts Coleridge over the crowd, "when the red hot prejudices of aristocrats are suddenly plunged into the cool waters of reason, that they should go off with a hiss!" And here is Coleridge giving way to characteristic self-pity: "I am in stirrups all day, yea, and sleep in my spurs."

Yet as in Melville's case, his metaphorical power has a life of its own, and acts in a contradictory manner, turning lament or complaint into its opposite, sheerly by existing as literary exuberance, and literary art. This is the irresponsibility I refer to, in which metaphor always goes beyond itself, often turning back on itself dialectically, turning negatives into positives and positives into negatives. For instance, Coleridge suffered terribly on his long voyage to Malta in 1804, but was able to summon the wit to complain, metaphorically, that his bed did everything but enable him to sleep in it: the bed was "like a great Genius apprenticed to a wrong trade." Poetry has died in me, wrote Coleridge in 1801: "I was once a Volume of Gold Leaf, rising and riding on every breath of Fancy—but I have beaten myself back into weight and density, and now I sink in quicksilver, yea, remain squat and square on the earth." Five years later, he again complained that he had got lost in "the unwholesome quicksilver mines of abstruse Metaphysics." The reader wonders if these mines were either so unpleasant or so antipathetic to the spirit of poetry if they spurred on Coleridge to turn them into such happy metaphor . . .

What was Coleridge like? Richard Holmes's great biography has given us the best portrait. He was both wild and saturnine, inspired and arrested. From young radical to old conservative—a journey on which he was accompanied by Wordsworth and Southey—Coleridge was always an overwhelming talker and extemporizer. His lectures, such as we have them, are not written texts but aural showers, gathered by certain loyal listeners in notebooks and published posthumously. The *Biographia* was dictated to a friend over the summer of 1815. We see him pounding roads (Hazlitt noticed that he walked from one side to the other), messy with metaphysics, wayward, vulnerable, impossible. A friend said that if he were richer, he would pay Coleridge five hundred pounds a year to dine with him twice-weekly. He was big and shambling, physically careless, with dark eyes and a voluptuous mouth. He was large-hearted but irresponsible, a negligent husband and intermittent father. In his middle years, he moved from one friend's house to another, promising to stay a few weeks and then installing himself for months, sleeping on sofas and housing himself in with hundreds of books and papers. Projects and proposals flowed from him: he wrote a ninety-page Greek grammar for his son, dreamed of establishing an observatory, founded, edited, and wrote most of a weekly paper, *The Friend*, for eighteen months (in 1810 and 1811), and spent several years discussing religious symbolism with Hyman Hurwitz, the director of the Hebrew Academy for Jews in Highgate.

II

But Coleridge was weak, too, and his writing, especially his criticism, represents a long struggle with his terrible rudderlessness, an entangled struggle with his own weakness, which he would elaborate into a philosophy and a theology of self-consciousness. This immense, perforated organum of allusion and enigmatic suggestion is powered by, and ceaselessly returns to, the question of the self, and how to escape it, sacrifice it, redeem it, and finally know it.

Coleridge returned from Germany in 1800, his mind full of Kant and Lessing. The great spurt of poetic activity that produced the poems chosen for the *Lyrical Ballads* was over. He had already decided that "abstruse researches" had killed the poetic instinct in him, and he was veering toward a peculiar combination of piety and self-pity, each feeding off the other. His poems repeatedly take this shape—a trough of plaint rising to an aeration, in which the poet reminds himself and his readers of "truth in Christ" ("Reflections on Having Left a Place of Retirement"), or that God is the "Great universal Teacher!" ("Frost at Midnight"). In his moving poem "To William Wordsworth," written in 1807, the night after hearing his friend read aloud all thirteen books of *The Prelude*, Coleridge reflects on Wordsworth's greatness, and then considers his own thin powers ("And genius given, and knowledge won in vain")—but then, Lear-like, reproaches himself—"That way no more!"—for wandering back onto such an "unhealthful road," and for plucking "the poisons of self-harm."

These poisons were both figurative and literal, of course. Coleridge had been suffering terrible pain and intestinal storms for several years. He thought these were brought on by delicate nerves. In January 1801 his health had collapsed—swollen joints, rheumatic fevers, an enlarged testicle—and he had dosed himself heavily with opium. This was probably the beginning of serious addiction. The opium seized his insides, causing constipation. On his voyage to Malta in 1804, according to Richard Holmes, Coleridge suffered the humiliation of having strenuous enemas administered by the ship's officers. Severe addiction lasted a long time, from 1804 until 1816, when a friend persuaded Dr. James Gillman to take a distinguished addict into his home. The addict, warned the friend, needed the su-

pervision of a doctor to ensure that he would follow a regulated plan
of withdrawal. Typically, Gillman expected to have Coleridge for a
few months in his house, but Coleridge was Gillman's guest for sixteen years, until his death in 1834.

The servitude of this addiction prompted an awful self-reckoning
for Coleridge. Opium, and the behavior it encouraged or accompanied, lost Coleridge the respect and alliance of the man he most
revered, Wordsworth. By 1809 Wordsworth, who had seen Coleridge effectively abandon his wife and children, had seen Coleridge
move from temporary house to house, had seen the nectary of
Coleridge's lyric gifts dry into tendrils of metaphysics, decided that
he must warn his more naïve friends against letting Coleridge into
their houses. He wrote to Thomas Poole that Coleridge "neither will
nor can execute anything of important benefit either to himself, his
family or mankind." Coleridge heard that Wordsworth had inter-
vened against him, and went to pieces. His notebooks, as Holmes
quotes from them, are painful to read. Again and again, in the direst
anguish, he returned to the thought that Wordsworth has "no Hope
of me!"

A contrasting diptych might be made of the temperamental dif-
ferences between Wordsworth and Coleridge. The former, relatively
unbookish, autonomous, calmly propulsive, a natural genius, self-
measuring and self-measured, a little priggish, convinced, as he put it
in *The Prelude*, that he was "chosen" to be a great poet. The latter,
book-bound, helpless and social, combustible and stalled, an unnatural genius, self-invigilating and self-exceeding, desperately devout,
cast out of poetry's choosing by his manic interest in philosophical
thought, and absolutely in love with Wordsworth, with the man and
with his flowing lyric potency. His response to Wordsworth's alien-
ation was the *Biographia*, which lovingly explicated Wordsworth's
poetry. Yet in 1817 Henry Crabb Robinson reported that the book
had given Wordsworth no pleasure: "The praise is too extravagant
and the censure inconsiderate."

But the deeper pain of addiction, to judge from Coleridge's writings, issued from the apprehension of the weakness of his will. Coleridge found himself utterly conquerable. Again and again he writes of this. In a long letter to John Morgan, written in 1814, he laments that "by the long long Habit of the accursed Poison my Volition (by which I mean the faculty *instrumental* to the Will, and by which alone the Will can realize itself—its Hands, Legs, & Feet, as it were) was compleatly deranged, at times frenzied, dissevered itself from the Will, & became an independent faculty." He continued: "What crime is there scarcely which has not been included in or followed from the one guilt of taking opium? Not to speak of ingratitude to my maker for the wasted Talents; of ingratitude to so many friends who have loved me I know not why; of barbarous neglect of my family." He called opium "this *free-agency-annihilating* Poison," and often stressed that he had not freely gone to it for pleasure, but had been *driven* to it "by cowardice of pain, first of mental pain" and then "of bodily Pain."

Opium, which caused terrible dreams, had given Coleridge a particular fear of sleep, of dreaming, and perhaps of the untethered life of memory itself: in a word, of the unconscious. "The Pains of Sleep," an agonizing poem written in 1803, describes nights of "fiendish dream" and "the unfathomable hell within." Coleridge pictures the will caught in a kind of cleft, "burning" to do the right thing, but "still baffled": "To know and loathe, yet wish and do!" A year later, on the Malta voyage, he confided to his notebook that he feared sleep as "a pandemonium of all the shames and miseries of the past life from earliest childhood all huddled together." Memory had become the ticking of a bad conscience for Coleridge, and dream the emblem of a soiled vitality.

Not surprisingly, perhaps, it was at this very moment, while the will was in shabbiest abeyance, that Coleridge began to formulate a coherent theory of the will, and its relation to memory and control. It is not too neat to say that his interest in the will bloomed at the instance of its actual collapse, and that its central importance was then developed theoretically in inverse proportion to his own lack of will.

It was in 1801 that Coleridge, with the help of Kant, first began to throw off his youthful interest in the associationism of David Hartley, who, adapting Locke, had argued for the importance of the impact of physical sense-impressions, and had seen the mind as a passive screen on which experience threw its defining pigments. Coleridge started to insist that a free will was an essential component of the self, and that Hartley's theories made the self a creature of mechanical effects. In the *Biographia*, he wrote that under Hartley "our whole life would be divided between the despotism of outward impressions, and that of senseless and passive memory." This would be mere "lawlessness."

Kant offered Coleridge a way of making the self both passive and active. On the one hand, the world is phenomenal: we gather and order the phenomena of perception. Coleridge called this the faculty of understanding, and in the *Biographia* it becomes, roughly, the "primary imagination." On the other hand, said Kant, the world was noumenal: there were transcendent things-in-themselves, unknowable, and this domain is grasped by the practical reason or will. This practical reason asserts itself not by argument but by command and precept; it is how we believe in God. Coleridge bent and expanded Kant's category, stripping it of its philosophical restraint and making it something closer to free will, and at other times closer to the decisive and controlling activity of the imagination. Coleridge called this faculty "reason" (in the *Biographia* it is, roughly, the "secondary imagination"), by which he did not mean the Enlightenment virtue of universal and necessary rationality, but instead a more Kantian organ, something that "sees invisible realities or spiritual objects."

This great effort of comprehension had its roots in Coleridge's sickness. The *Biographia* is an extraordinary work not least as the record of an exploding consciousness. But it is moving in part because of the spectacle it offers of a self willing itself to have a will. He writes there that "I know myself only through myself." The *Biographia*, necessarily trapped within this self-searching, pulls in opposite directions, toward the self and, in horror, away from it. It is as self-evading as it is self-observing. There is a remarkable passage at the end of chapter 6 when Coleridge, having dismissed the "lawlessness" of Hartley's associationism, concludes nevertheless that memory is endless, and that "all thoughts are in themselves imperishable," and that God might well "bring before every human soul the collective experience of its whole past existence." With mounting horror, Coleridge continues: "And this, this, perchance, is the dread book of judgement, in whose mysterious hieroglyphics every idle word is recorded!" Perhaps, says Coleridge, none of our past acts can be loosened from the chain of memory, a chain "to all whose links, conscious or unconscious, the free will, our only absolute *self*, is coextensive and co-present." But then, having stared at the horrid infinity of memory, Coleridge simply turns away from it, in a gesture similar to the Lear-like moment in his poem "To William Wordsworth," and announces: "But not now dare I longer discourse of this, waiting for a loftier mood, and nobler subject, warned from within and without, that it is profanation to speak of these mysteries."

So against the palpable fear of a limitless and arraigning memory is posed the free will, and the will's capacity to cure itself, which has now been elevated into "our only absolute *self*." Six years later, De Quincey, in *Confessions of an English Opium-Eater*, would agree with Coleridge that memory is the dread book, and would utter the strikingly Freudian thought that "there is no such thing as forgetting." Yet De Quincey celebrates opium as Coleridge never does, swimming in the azure of its visions, waters that for Coleridge were green and drowning. Coleridge seems to need to resist De Quincey's happier drift, De Quincey's surrender to the magical utopianism of opium dreams, and this means, in some respects, resisting the drift of consciousness. A will exists, insists Coleridge, "whose function it is to control, determine, and modify the phantasmal chaos of association." It is surely clear that Coleridge is talking not merely about Hartley here, but about the chaos of free consciousness itself. Even as Coleridge enacts a stream of consciousness, and enacts a considerable feat of memory (recall that he dictated the *Biographia* to a friend, so the entire book is a kind of Sternean performance), he warns against that enactment. For what is stream of consciousness, really, but a stream of association? Sterne had made this clear enough in *Tristram Shandy*, a novel deeply admired by Coleridge.

So it is that Coleridge alights on his lovely image of the self winning its way against a counterflow, just as a water insect "*wins* its way up against the stream, by alternate pulses of active and passive motion, now resisting the current, and now yielding to it in order to gather strength and a momentary fulcrum for a further propulsion. This is no unapt emblem of the mind's self-experience in the act of thinking." But what this emblem perhaps evades is that in the case of the self, and especially in the case of Coleridge's self, the countercurrent against which we struggle is not provided by nature, does not mysteriously or naturally come from outside, but is produced *by the self*. The self *makes its own obstacles*, which it must then surmount. Yet this surmounting is then likely to throw up fresh obstacles. It can be put this way: the self medicalizes itself, or, in the classical term, mithridatizes itself—healing itself by poisoning itself, poisoning itself by healing itself: exactly the dynamic of Coleridge's opium-taking.

III

Generally, the great pathos, tension, and comedy of Coleridge's work is that he commits the sins he warns against—and commits them while in the act of warning against them. It is why he is so likable a Christian, despite his orthodoxy. His piety shares its borders with a rogue state. His devoutness is a brave face, not self-exhortation so much as self-accusation. It is a comic struggle. A local example is found, as I suggested earlier, in his joyous use of digressive metaphor, and his simultaneous awareness that such digression must be bridled. Coleridge, of course, who happily called himself a "philoparenthesist," or lover of parentheses, does not bridle himself, but merely produces further digressions about how he should not digress. In one of the letters from Germany that appears in the *Biographia*, he discourses wildly on German and Latin etymology, and then reproaches himself: "Now I know, my gentle friend, what you are murmuring to yourself—'This is so like him! running away after the first bubble, that chance has blown off from the surface of his fancy; when one is anxious to learn where he is and what he has seen.' " Like Melville, Coleridge uses metaphor to describe and censure his own volubility; then metaphor, being itself a species of volubility, an extender of discourse with a free life of its own, becomes merely an exhibit in the case against itself.

Coleridge lacked Melville's atheistic instincts, yet in a somewhat similar way to Melville he was always being thwarted by his own fertility. He had an immense desire for unity and wholeness, and writes often about the harmonization of discordant opposites: it is his very definition of the imagination and its power. Yet his own speculative powers and drives always caused that unity to undergo a splitting, which only made the need for a harmonious solution more pressing.

One way in which Coleridge sought to find a harmonious reconciliation of opposites—a way, as it were, of taming the irresponsibility of the self—was by turning to God. If Coleridge first asked that the self know itself, he next asked that the self redeem itself. These were not abstract questions for Coleridge. He fervently believed that "Know Thyself" was both the great demand of philosophy and the great demand of God; he liked to quote Juvenal, "From heaven descended the 'Know Thyself.'" The problem is not simply that it is hard to know oneself but that conscious self-knowledge may make the self harder to see, obscure the cleanliness of the self. For conciousness is irresponsible. Paradoxically enough, conscious self-knowledge makes conscious self-knowledge harder. Coleridge knew this: "Do you know your knowledge?" was one of his teasing questions.

And conscious self-knowledge makes very difficult that longing for stability and order that Coleridge seems, religiously, to desire— "the only absolute self," the "very and permanent self." At the end of his *Confessions of an Inquiring Spirit*, he writes that Christianity lets "the unsubstantial, insulated self pass away as in a stream," an orthodox enough formulation. But where is "the only absolute self" to be found? Coleridge could hardly be optimistic, despite all the theoretical exhortation, about the absoluteness of his own self. His life had been a convoy of shames, his free will flabby and weak. So he must offer himself up for redemption, to be saved. Coleridge had a deep sense of his sinfulness and a firm belief in original sin. Thus he writes, again in perfect orthodoxy, "To conquer ourselves is the only true knowledge." Yet isn't this an awfully long way from the "Know Thyself" which Coleridge dreamed of as the path to redemption? This, in Christian sacrifice, is more like self-obliteration. It seems, then, that for Coleridge, philosophical redemption ("Know Thyself") was at loggerheads with religious redemption ("Conquer Thyself"); conscious self-knowledge (the philosophical path) was contradicted by unconscious knowledge (the religious path). Thus Coleridge proceeded, attempting at once to escape, conquer, save, and know himself.

IV

In one area, however, Coleridge absolutely triumphed, and with an interesting lack of struggle. This was in his literary criticism, and in particular in his writing on Shakespeare. For here we find that there is a peaceable recurrence of many of the terms that are at war in his philosophy and theology of the self, now applied with perfect ease and equanimity to literature. Or more exactly, the terms that clog Coleridge's drama of the self become freeing when applied to the drama of fictional selves. His idea of "negative faith," which is expounded in the *Biographia*, is really no more than the idea that true drama subdues us by its own free force. Negative faith "permits the images presented to work by their own force, without either denial or affirmation of their real existence by the judgement." In other words, the supervening will or judgment is quieted, is lulled into a kind of sleep, and a sort of willing passivity overcomes the watcher. What was such a menace to the self theoretically is here a strategy of dramatic power.

In a lecture from 1818, Coleridge makes this even clearer. The point about literary works, and especially drama, he says, is that we are watching fictional representations. "The true pleasure we derive from theatrical performances arises from the fact that they are unreal and fictitious." In this world, dramatic illusion is most like dreaming, says Coleridge. In sleep, we undergo "a suspension of the voluntary and therefore of the comparative power. The fact is that we pass no judgment either way—we simply do not judge them to be unreal— in consequence of which the images act on our minds, as far as they act at all, by their own force as images."

Illusion is like sleep (clearly this is yet another formulation of the "willing suspension of disbelief"), and differs from it, says Coleridge, only in degree, rather than in kind. In sleep, we pass into dream with "a sudden collapse into this suspension of Will"; "whereas in an interesting play" we are brought gradually to this

point by poet and actors, "and with the constant and positive Aid-
ance [i.e., aid] of our own Will. We *chuse* to be deceived." We place
ourselves in a state in which "the Images have a negative reality," and
anything that gets in the way of this negative reality breaks the illusion—in other words, wakes us up.

So: our will is watchful, and may be roused by incredible work,
but is apparently content to doze in the perfume of its own suspension. Notice that Coleridge is aiming for a theory of illusion in
which we choose, by an act of will, to suspend the will. Thus he
achieves in literary criticism what he could not achieve in his writing
about the self: a paradoxical harmonization of apparent opposites. In
his writing about the self, Coleridge always seeks more will, and is
in danger of its suspension; in his criticism, he seeks less will, and
cherishes its suspension.

Why is he able to escape, in literary criticism, what oppresses him
so strongly in his philosophical writing? I suggest that he is able to
escape because he is able to escape himself, and able to escape religion, or God. He leaves himself and literally suspends himself in
other selves, the characters that the ideal dramatist creates. And this
ideal, of course, the writer who preeminently enables this escape,
was that delightfully unreligious, or prereligious, almost pagan dramatist, Shakespeare.

Coleridge's sense of the way we can drift in imagination is striking, and makes him a brilliant analyst of the way Shakespeare lets his
characters drift in soliloquy and solipsism. In a marginal note on one
of Sir Walter Scott's novels, Coleridge censures Scott for trying to
create a delightful, rambling character like Mistress Quickly and
muffing it. Scott's character is too busy expressing strong authorial
opinions, and is not irresponsible or freely discursive enough. "It is
the weak memory that is discursive not the strong feeling," is his
shrewd comment.

Coleridge has a very astute eye for the freedom of Shakespeare's
characters. Repeatedly he defends Shakespeare's heavy use of puns,

conceits, similes, and metaphors against those who, like Dr. Johnson, would censure them as unnatural or forced. Coleridge argues that, on the contrary, Shakespeare's greatness lies in this. Prospero's commandment to Miranda, for instance, that she advance "the fringèd curtains of her eyes" is not absurd, he maintains, for it is precisely the stagy, melodramatic language Prospero would use. Coleridge, unsurprisingly, defends the freedom of metaphor.

In the long, drifting, metaphorical soliloquies that Shakespeare's characters use, Coleridge sees a very emblem of the way the imagination drifts. This drifting imaginative power sounds almost like Bakhtin: in defending Shakespeare's conceits, writes Coleridge, we must allow for an effort of the mind, which is attempting to describe what it cannot describe, and this is the attempt "to reconcile opposites and qualify contradictions, leaving a middle state of mind more strictly appropriate to the imagination than any other, when it is, as it were, hovering between images. As soon as it is fixed on one image, it becomes understanding; but while it is unfixed and wavering, between them, attaching itself permanently to none, it is imagination." Leaving aside the accuracy of this description, what is striking is that Coleridge makes Shakespearean soliloquy, and Shakespearean metaphor within the soliloquy, the very definition of the imagination.

So it is not surprising that Coleridge, like Melville, is drawn to those characters who are, in a sense, most "irresponsibly" free— Shakespeare's malefactors and evil theorists, his comics and fools and madmen, like Iago and Lady Macbeth, Hamlet, Lear, and Othello. Coleridge observes that Shakespeare often uses such characters to speak general, even wise, truths. In *Table Talk*, he is reported to have said that "it is worth while to remark the use which Shakespeare always makes of his bold villains as vehicles of expressing opinions and conjectures of a nature too hazardous for a wise man to put forth directly as his own." He notices this about Iago, for instance, and calls him "a bold partisan for truth"; and argues that Lady Macbeth is not simply evil: her conscience is not dead, but is "continually smarting within her." He always argued that the much mocked Polonius should not be acted as a fool, but as a wise man who possessed wisdom no longer useful to the court around him: "the personified memory of wisdom no longer possessed." Regan and Goneril were Shakespeare's only "pictures of the unnatural," and as a result they are almost faceless and characterless to us.

"In thus placing these profound general truths in the mouths of such men as Cornwall, Edmund, Iago etc, Shakespeare at once gives them utterance, and yet shows how indefinite their utterance is." This is what I mean by Coleridge's appreciation of the irresponsible or amoral self. He lacked Dr. Johnson's moral shudders, his desire to rewrite Shakespeare. Instead, he likes the irresponsibility of Shakespearean creation, and delights in the bottomlessness of Shakespearean characters—that they, "like people in real life, are to be inferred by the reader."

He was fascinated, as every reader is, by Shakespeare's invisibility, by his selflessness; and that fascination is marked by Coleridge's own inability to escape himself. Thus he writes in one lecture: "Yet with all these unbounded powers, with all his might and majesty of genius, he makes us feel as if he were unconscious of himself." Shakespeare achieves what Coleridge never could, unconsciousness. Yet Coleridge was obsessed with the defense of Shakespeare's conscious intentions. In his discussion of Shakespeare's conceits and puns, he always stresses that Shakespeare *intended everything* he did, that he never erred, and that it is our job as readers to credit Shakespeare with inerrant intentionality. The famous formulation occurs in the seventh lecture from 1811: Shakespeare "never introduces a word, or a thought, in vain or out of place . . . [The plays form] a most perfect, regular, and consistent whole."

Thus Coleridge, always searching for an organic reconciliation of opposites, finds the deepest reconciliation in Shakespeare—who miraculously manages to be the great poet of intention yet also the great poet of will-lessness and unconsciousness; a dramatist whose impeccable sense of illusion requires that we will the suspension of our own wills; and whose characters, as embodiments of the imagination itself, move freely between fixities and travel into an irresponsible freedom, turning negatives into positives by speaking "indefinite," unspeakable truths.

It is often remarked that the *Biographia Literaria* announces a theoretical chapter on the imagination but never provided it; surely, instead, Coleridge found it in Shakespeare.

Dostoevsky's God

❦

I

The world of "the slap"—everyone knows that this is Dostoevsky's world, his "underground" world of humiliations, affronts, jousts, and slights. When, in *The Possessed* (1872), the repulsive revolutionary Peter Verkhovensky visits Kirilov to tell him that he has murdered Shatov, and Kirilov says, "You've done this to him because he spat in your face in Geneva!" we know we are deep in the underground, profoundly enwebbed, and we know that this spider's psychology is something new in literature.

Consider a few scenes. The narrator of *Notes from Underground* (1864), the underground man, is one day in a tavern when a powerful soldier, an officer, blocked by the narrator, picks him up and moves him out of the way. The narrator is humiliated to have been treated so lightly, and cannot sleep for fantasies about how he will avenge himself. The officer walks every day down the Nevsky Prospect. The narrator follows him, "admiring" him from a distance. He decides that he will walk in the opposite direction and that when the two men meet, he—the narrator—will not give an inch. But day after day when the moment of physical encounter arrives, he weakens, and moves out of the way just as the officer strides past. At night he wakes up obsessed with the question "Why is it invariably I who swerves first? Why precisely me and not him?" Eventually, he does manage to hold his ground, the two men brush shoulders, and the narrator is in ecstasies. He goes home singing Italian arias, feeling properly avenged. The satisfaction, of course, lasts only for a day or two.

In *The Eternal Husband*, a brilliant novella published in 1870, a cuckolded husband, Pavel Pavlovich, whose wife has recently died, travels to Petersburg in order to torment his wife's former lover, Velchaninov. He does indeed torment the lover, not least because the lover does not know for sure if the husband ever discovered the affair. Pavel Pavlovich visits Velchaninov's apartment again and again, teasing and punishing him by withholding the real secret. Does he know of the affair? Yet in typical Dostoevsky fashion, revenge curdles into a sour love. It transpires that the cuckolded husband is really in love with his wife's former lover. He cannot leave him alone, and his "torture" of him oscillates wildly between expressions of admiration, cringing humility, and savage resentment. The former lover decides that the husband came to Petersburg in order to kill him. He came to Petersburg because he hated him. But, decides the lover, the cuckolded husband loves him too, "out of spite"—"the strongest kind of love." When, at the end of the book, the two finally part, the former lover holds his hand out; but the husband cringes away from it. The lover, with derision and insane pride, says, "If I, if *I* offer you this hand here . . . then you might well take it!"

And finally, a scene from *The Brothers Karamazov*, written in the last years of Dostoevsky's life (1878–1881). Fyodor Pavlovich, the old head of the Karamazov family, a clown, buffoon, and malefactor, is about to enter a dining room at the local monastery. He has already acted scandalously in the cell of the saintly old monk, Father Zosima. Fyodor decides that he will act scandalously in the dining room too. Why? Because, he thinks to himself, "It always seems to me, when I go somewhere, that I am lower than everyone else and that they all take me for a buffoon—so let me indeed play the buffoon, because all of you, to a man, are lower than I am." And as he thinks this, he remembers being asked once why he hated a certain neighbor, to which he had replied: "He never did anything to me, it's true, but I once played a most shameless, nasty trick on him, and the moment I did it, I immediately hated him for it."

There is a dark novelty in all this, for sure, but what does it consist of? It is not merely that such characters are, as Dostoevsky believed the Russian soul to be, very "broad," capable of confusing and unpredictable swervings, full of abysses. Nor is this simply a display of what Stendhal called, in *The Memoirs of a Tourist*, the modern emotions—"envy, jealousy, and impotent hatred" (Stendhal, after all, is a mere gardener in Dostoevsky's underground, a genial above-grounder by comparison); nor only what is commonly called *ressentiment*. Rousseau may have come closest when he talks of the new inwardness being the replacement of old categories such as virtue and vice with the modern malaise of *amour-soi* and *amour-propre*. For clearly pride and the deformations of pride are unwashable habits for all but the holiest of Dostoevsky's characters. The underground man, the cuckolded husband, and Fyodor Karamazov all seem to act in ways that are against their interests, and what marks their newness, their modernity, as fictional characters is that they do so again and again without cease, and do so, as it were, theoretically: they act like this because their interest is the maintenance of their pride. (By "theoretical" I mean not that Dostoevsky's interest in psychological oddity is abstract but that it is philosophical; *The Eternal Husband* has indeed a whole chapter of psychological exegesis entitled "Analysis.")

When we think of typical Dostoevskian action we surely think of a bewildering mixture of haughtiness and humility, coexistent in the same person, each element oddly menacing. The underground man, that antibourgeois banshee, alternately ingratiating and screaming with fury; Peter Verkhovensky, hateful and dominating to his subordinates but sheepish and adoring with his hero, the child rapist Stavrogin. And Smerdyakov, the real killer of Fyodor Karamazov, an illegitimate servant who is horrible to his adoptive father but slyly humble before the Karamazov men. And it is not only the menace of pride but the comedy of pride that reverberates throughout Dostoevsky, though comedy is not always associated with Dostoevsky's name. Nothing is funnier in *The Possessed* than the proud, weak governor, Andrei von Lembke, who is being manipulated by Peter Verkhovensky. As the local mayhem mounts, the governor loses control. He shouts at a group of visitors in his drawing room, "That's enough!" and marches out, only to trip on the carpet. He stands still for a moment, looks at the carpet, says aloud, "Have it changed!" and walks out.

Dostoevsky shows us that pride and humility are really one. If you are proud you almost certainly feel humbler than someone in the world, because pride is an anxiety, not a consolation. And if you are humble you almost certainly feel better than someone in the world, because humility is an achievement, not a freedom, and the humble have a way of congratulating themselves for being so humble. Pride, one might say, is the sin of humble people and humility is the punishment for proud people, and each reversal represents a kind of self-punishment. Thus Fyodor Karamazov enters the dining room ready to abase himself *because* he disdains everyone else. This sort of logic is hard to find, or hard to find as an explicit psychology, in novelists before Dostoevsky. One has instead to consult the religious weepers and gnashers—Ignatius of Loyola, say, or Kierkegaard—to find anything like it.

But Fyodor enters the dining room, as the underground man walks toward the officer, and as the cuckolded husband comes to Petersburg, for another reason: because he needs other people in order to confirm himself. The underground man admits this; he calls himself "a retort man," a man who comes "not from the bosom of nature but from a retort." This "dialogism" was most influentially noticed by Mikhail Bakhtin, who posited it as the fundamental principle of Dostoevsky's work. As he writes in *Problems of Dostoevsky's Poetics*:

> What the underground man thinks about most of all is what others think or might think about him; he tries to keep one step ahead of every other consciousness, every other thought about him . . . At all the critical moments of his confession he tries to anticipate the possible definition or evaluation others might make of him . . . interrupting his own speech with the imagined rejoinders of others.

Thus in Dostoevsky the many pairings, or doublings, in which one character revolves around another, and each is murderously dependent on the other: Peter Verkhovensky and Stavrogin, Raskolnikov and Svidrigailov, Ivan Karamazov and Smerdyakov, Velchaninov and Pavel Pavlovich. In Fyodor's case—and perhaps it is the case with any colossal egotism—other people appear to have become himself. He dislikes his neighbor because of something that he, Fyodor, did to him: "I once played a most shameless, nasty trick on him, and the moment I did it, I immediately hated him for it." Clearly Fyodor longs—however buried the original religious sentiment—to punish himself because he hates himself. But since other people have merged with himself, he punishes himself by punishing other people, hates himself by hating other people.

And this leads to a Sisyphean repetition of behavior. Self-punishment means being condemned to reenact scandal after scandal without cease, because each self-punishment has become indistinguishable from sinning. The sin itself has become the punishment for that sin, and each sin, being another act of outrage, just opens the wound again. Clearly there is no way that Fyodor Karamazov could ever stop behaving badly to his neighbor, since there is no logic by which he could possibly begin to feel warmly toward him. He would have to like himself, and that is surely not going to happen.

One can go further than the thoroughly unreligious Bakhtin, subtle as he always is. The really remarkable aspect of Dostoevsky's celebrated psychology is surely that it is deeply sophisticated and wise in theoretical and human terms, but can only be finally understood in religious terms. His characters, even the very godless ones like Fyodor Karamazov, live under the mottled shadow of religious categories. They are the most complicated modern, secular agglomerations of unconscious motivation and conscious masquerade ever created, and yet there is nothing in Dostoevskian motivation which cannot be also found in the Gospels. They are humbly proud and proudly humble (Mary Magdalene). They sin in order to punish themselves, and know in advance that they will do so (Peter). They doubt in order to be reassured (Thomas). They betray in order to love (Peter, Judas).

Above all, their actions are comprehensible only and finally as efforts to confess, to reveal themselves, to be known. A tiny scene in *The Brothers Karamazov* comes to mind. Katerina Ivanovna, Dimitri Karamazov's fiancée, has taken Grushenka's hand and is kissing it. Grushenka is Dimitri's mistress. Unexpectedly, she extols Grushenka, who appears to bask in the praise. Grushenka takes Katerina's hand as if to reciprocate—and then unexpectedly drops it. "And you can keep this as a memory—that you kissed my hand and I did not kiss yours." Katerina calls her a slut, and has her ejected from the house. Once one has gone through all the "psychological" explanations, once one has burrowed into all the corridors of dialectic, a stubborn inexplicability remains. Why act like this? What is furthered? Grushenka seems to want to annihilate herself. The only explanation is religious. Grushenka, like so many Dostoevsky characters, wants to be *known*, even if she is not aware of it. She wants to reveal herself in all her dirtiness, her baseness, wants to reveal herself as hateful, proud, bitter, little. She wants to confess, and to be called a slut. The underground man desires, really, not to avenge himself but to *reveal* himself to the officer. Because, after all, to let people know what you think of them is also to let them know what you think of yourself. This is the crucial point at which secular psychology meets religious mystery. *The Brothers Karamazov*, which would be the consuming work of Dostoevsky's last years, is precisely concerned with the feebleness of psychological explanation in the face of the oddity and extremism of religious motivation.

I I

The final volume of Joseph Frank's magnificent biography opens in 1871, as Dostoevsky returns to Russia after four years abroad. Frank touches quickly upon the earlier years: Dostoevsky's involvement with radicalism and socialist utopianism in the 1840s, which had led to his arrest in 1849 and his mock execution (apparently a little joke of the tsar's) at the Peter and Paul fortress; his penal servitude in Siberia, from 1850 to 1854: the writing of *Notes from Underground* and *Crime and Punishment* (1866), and the dictation, in one month, of *The Gambler*, to a stenographer, Anna Grigorievna, whom he married in 1867. Frank repeats the emphasis he has made in earlier volumes, on the centrality in Dostoevsky's life of his four years in Siberia. He was doubtless never an atheist—Belinsky had said years before that whenever he mentioned Christ, the expression on Dostoevsky's face changed, "just as if he were going to cry"—but he became a devoted reader of the Gospels in Siberia. A copy of the New Testament lay under his pillow for four years. In the prison camp he felt that he discovered the essence of the Russian peasant, and this knowledge funded his later religious nationalism and xenophobia. The Russian sinner, he declared years later, knows that he has committed wrong, while the European is untroubled by his sin, and indeed accepts it as justified. "I think that the principal and most basic need of the Russian people is the need for suffering, incessant and unslakeable suffering." Yet the Russian attempt at self-restoration will be "always more serious than the former urge to deny and destroy the self." In *The Brothers Karamazov*, he will have Dimitri, charged with murdering his father and facing twenty years of hard labor, exclaim in prison to his brother Alyosha: "It's impossible for a convict to be without God . . . And then from the depths of the earth, we, the men underground, will start singing a tragic hymn to God, in whom there is joy! Hail to God and his joy! I love him."

But if Dostoevsky had changed, so had Russia when the novelist and his much younger wife returned in 1871. The serfs had been liberated ten years before, and Russian radical thought, which in the 1860s had followed Chernyshevsky's idea of "rational egotism," and which had exploded into the violent ruthlessness of Bakunin and Nechaev (the model for Peter Verkhovensky), was becoming gentler and broader. Political thought was still divided between the generally conservative Slavophiles and the more radical Westernizers, between those who felt, like Dostoevsky, that Russia needed to offer its own solutions to its own problems and those who, like Turgenev, saw Europe as the beacon that would illuminate a backward nation.

But in the last decade of his life Dostoevsky discovered that Russian radicalism was not only the secular Westernizing kind. There was a new strain, which, while never exactly Christian, seemed sympathetic to certain Christian values. These were people who, without Orthodox faith, were yet willing to suspend themselves in the oil of the religious. Some of the populists, for instance, began to see the rural Russian way of life as treasurable, unique. Dostoevsky, who was conservative but never ideologically pinioned in one place, was not automatically anathema to these new, Christianized radicals. Both Dostoevsky and some of the populists began to envision the transformation of society along the principles of Christian love, charity, and selflessness. This was keenly pleasing to Dostoevsky. Once, perhaps, he had believed in the socialist eschatology of a graspable earthly utopia. But his reading of the Gospels had encouraged him to believe that socialism was a kind of blasphemy, an earthbound mimicry of an inimitable divine mission. Socialism "is also Christianity, but it proposes that it can succeed with reason," he wrote in his notebooks in the early 1870s. Christianity—and here Dostoevsky and Kierkegaard converge—was not reasonable. It was perhaps a kind of lunacy. It existed not on the bread of reason but on the yeast of faith. The true Christian transformation, Dostoevsky believed, would happen at the end of time, and not by human will. The true Christian, said Dostoevsky, would say to his brother: "I must share my possessions with my brother and serve him in every way." But the "communard" only "wants to take revenge on society while claiming to appeal to higher goals."

Those unfamiliar with Frank's earlier volumes may be surprised to find how devoted a husband and father Dostoevsky was. After his death, his wife modestly blacked out the erotic yearnings he expressed in his letters to her. From the status accorded the suffering child in his work, one might well infer that he was a loving father. But Dickens (whom Dostoevsky of course deeply admired) used children in rather similar ways in his novels, and still managed to abandon his wife and children. Frank writes movingly of the pain felt by both parents when their three-year-old son, Aleksey (Alyosha), died from a prolonged epileptic fit in 1878. The couple could not return to the apartment in which he had died. Dostoevsky, wrote Anna in her reminiscences, "was crushed by this death. He had loved Aleksey somehow in a special way, with an almost morbid love." In *The Brothers Karamazov*, of course, the avowed hero is the saintly Alyosha (the diminutive of Aleksey), and Ivan's great image of senseless suffering is the child in pain.

Dostoevsky, perhaps, already looked crushed. A few years before, in 1873, when he was made editor of *The Citizen*, a weekly journal, a twenty-three-year-old member of the journalistic staff, Varvara V. Timofeyeva, had described Dostoevsky: "Very pale—with a sallow, unhealthy paleness—who seemed tired and perhaps ill . . . with a gloomy, exhausted face, covered like a net, with some sort of unusually expressive shadings caused by a tightly restrained movement of the muscles." He told Varvara that "the anti-Christ has been born

. . . and is *coming*." And he spoke of the Gospels: "So much suffering, but then—so much grandeur . . . It's impossible to compare it with any well-being in the world!"

Frank's account of this last decade is really a story of unworldliness, for all that these are the years when Dostoevsky became a social "prophet." Until the publication of *The Brothers Karamazov*, whose monthly installments "held all of literate Russia spellbound," Dostoevsky was most famous for his *Diary of a Writer*, a monthly publication of sixteen pages in which he gathered together stories, polemics, replies to his critics, and journalistic commentary on Russian news items such as the latest sensational court case. In the diary, he developed his growing Russian nationalism, in which he saw Russia messianically rescuing the rest of the world by bringing about the union of all Slavs, a mere prelude to a worldwide reconciliation of all humans under Christ, a Christ kept truly alive only by the true church, the Orthodox church. There was wild anti-Europeanism, anti-Catholicism, and anti-Semitism in this journalism.

Yet for all this, the practical political remedy was becoming more and more ethereal—more religious. Even as Dostoevsky immersed himself in the debates of his country, his politics were thinning into Christological mist. He would tell querulous correspondents, again and again, to turn to Christ, to pray, to love one another, to ask for forgiveness. He pondered more and more deeply the life and teaching of Saint Tikhon Zadonsky, a mid-eighteenth-century Russian monk who influenced his portrait of Father Zosima in his last novel. Tikhon taught, in Frank's words, "that humankind should be grateful for the existence of temptation, misfortune and suffering because only through these could humans come to an acknowledgement of all the evil in their souls." (Frank speculates plausibly enough that Dostoevsky may well have taken these words to be a response to the problem of Job, with whose story Dostoevsky had been obsessed from an early age.) Inwardly, Dostoevsky was preparing himself for the religious transfiguration for which he argues so movingly in his last great novel. For his fifty-eighth birthday, in 1879, Anna gave him a large photographic reproduction of Raphael's Sistine Madonna. "How many times [have] I found him in his study in front of that great picture," she later wrote, "in such deep contemplation that he did not hear me come in."

III

The Brothers Karamazov, for all its "dialogism," represents a vast Christian exhortation. In *The Possessed*, one of the revolutionary socialists, Shigalev, announces his plan of social transformation. To our ears it is a nightmare out of Orwell. One-tenth of humanity will have unlimited freedom and unrestricted powers over the remaining nine-tenths. These unfortunates must give up their individuality and be turned into a herd of identicals. Peter Verkhovensky, of course, exclaims that Shigalev has "invented equality," an equality in which "everyone belongs to all the others, and all belong to everyone. All are slaves and equals in slavery." To this horrid vision, *The Brothers Karamazov* again and again poses a true Christian equality, in almost identical language (this similarity oddly missed by the omnivorous Joseph Frank): Father Zosima tells his fellow monks that they are "guilty before all people, on behalf of all and for all, for all human sins." Later in the novel, when Dimitri Karamazov is falsely accused of killing his father, he offers himself as a scapegoat. He accepts punishment, he says, because he wanted to kill his father and might well have killed him, and is therefore willing to be "guilty before all." The forced enslavement and forced equality of Shigalev's protocommunism has been replaced by the willing enslavement and ecstatic equality of Christian penitence.

The Brothers Karamazov, of course, tells the story of the unstable and passionate Karamazov family, gentry in a miserable provincial town dominated by a monastery. The hated patriarch, Fyodor, is murdered, and suspicion falls on Dimitri, who had visited the house at the time, and who had emerged covered in blood and apparently three thousand rubles richer. In fact, Fyodor was killed, as we discover late in the book, by his atheistic, skulking servant, Smerdyakov, who is a kind of devil figure. But each of the three brothers, Dimitri, Ivan, and Alyosha, had at one time imagined the murder of his father. Dimitri had attacked Fyodor and had several times threatened to kill him; Ivan, an atheist who believes that in a world without God and immortality "everything is permitted," appears to countenance killing Fyodor when he meets the murderous Smerdyakov and informs him that he will be away from the house for a certain period. Certainly Smerdyakov takes Ivan's comment to be an official approval. Even saintly Alyosha, who had been a monk in training at the monastery, admits that he has imagined murder.

The novel, like *Macbeth*, explores the sense that to have imagined a crime is to have already committed it. Macbeth, after all, is changed—his mind is "full of scorpions," as Shakespeare has it—at the moment he hears the witches' prophecy. Nothing can be the same again. Both works of art live under the shadow of Christ's unfair, even repulsive, admonition that to have looked on a woman with an adulterous heart is to have committed the act. It could be said that all of Dostoevsky's characters, in their febrile determination to turn ideas into action, behave like people who have heard Christ's warning, who deeply believe it, and yet are deeply evading it. The novel seems to come to the conclusion that indeed, as Father Zosima puts it, all are guilty before all. Dimitri, who is fallen, noble, Christ-obsessed, and who has the zeal of the converted sinner, accepts this guilt, and though he professes his actual innocence of the crime, goes willingly to be punished for it.

Yet are not some more guilty than others? Dostoevsky firmly believed that without faith in God and belief in immortality, nothing restrained man's worldly behavior. Without God, everything is permitted. This is an obviously flawed conclusion, since a glance at world history shows that *with* God everything already has been permitted. (The Crusades, the Inquisition, burnings at the stake, wars, Christian anti-Semitism, and so on.) Gibbon famously thought that the conclusion might go the other way—that a world without religions might well have been a sweeter place. But Dostoevsky had already written a novel, *Crime and Punishment*, which demonstrated what might go wrong in a man without the Gospel, and here he is at it again in *The Brothers Karamazov*. For although Dimitri and Alyosha have imagined Fyodor's death, and are in some respects "guilty," it is the atheist Smerdyakov, who borrowed the atheist Ivan's teaching that "without God everything is permitted," who actually killed the old man. And Smerdyakov is really Ivan's twisted double. Ivan, who has his own nobility, would never have killed his father, but in a sense his idea did the deed, via Smerdyakov. An idea is the killer. Atheism did it.

The Brothers Karamazov is a book in love with, and afraid of, ideas. In the end, I think, it proposes the peace of a realm beyond ideas: paradise. This is best seen in the most famous chapter, Ivan's "Legend of the Grand Inquisitor." Just before he tells this story to the believer Alyosha, Ivan attacks God for allowing to exist a world in which children suffer. Ivan is one of those atheists who stand on the rung just below faith; he is an almost-believer, and Dostoevsky clearly admires him. In such a man, unbelief is very close to belief, just as in many of Dostoevsky's other characters, love is close to hate, punishment to sin, and buffoonery to confession. Religion, Ivan says, tells us that in a future paradise the lamb will lie down with the lion, that we shall live in harmony. But "if everyone must suffer in order to buy eternal harmony with their suffering, pray tell me what have children to do with it . . . Why do they get thrown on the pile, to manure someone's future harmony with themselves?" He continues: "I absolutely renounce all higher harmony. It is not worth one little tear of even that one tormented child. They have put too high a price on harmony; we can't afford to pay so much for admission. And therefore I hasten to return my ticket."

He gets Alyosha, the true Christian, to agree with him. If one could build "the edifice of human destiny with the object of making people happy in the finale, of giving them peace and rest at last, but for that you must inevitably and unavoidably torture just one tiny child . . . and raise your edifice on the foundation of her unrequited tears—would you agree to be the architect of such conditions?" Alyosha says he would not. But, replies Alyosha, there is Christ, who can "forgive everything, forgive all *and for all.*"

To which Ivan responds with his now famous legend. It, and the preceding chapter, are deservedly revered. The writing here has the ferocity, the august vitality, the royal perspective, of scriptural writing. It is, truly, a visited prose. In the legend, Christ is upbraided for allowing humans too much freedom. Humans do not want freedom, says the Inquisitor to Christ; humans are afraid of freedom. They want, really, to bow down to an idol, to subject themselves. They have no desire to live in the freedom to choose between good and evil, between doubt and knowledge.

In these two chapters, Dostoevsky mounts perhaps the most powerful attack ever made on theodicy (the formal term for the effort to justify God's goodness in a world of evil and suffering). In particular, Dostoevsky challenges the two chief elements of theodicy: that we suffer mysteriously on earth but will be rewarded in heaven; and that evil exists because freedom exists—we must be free to do good and evil, to believe in God or not to believe in him. Any other existence would be robotic, unimaginable. In this scheme, Hitler *must* be "allowed" to exist, since we must be free to inhabit every human possibility, good and evil. To the first defense, Ivan says that future harmony is not worth present tears. And to the second—to my mind even more devastating—Ivan says, in effect, "Why is God so sure that man even wants to be free? What is so good about freedom?" After all—Ivan does not say this, but it is implicit—we will probably not be very free when we get to heaven, and heaven sounds like a nice place. So why are we all so ragingly and horribly free on earth? If there are no Hitlers in heaven, why should it have ever been necessary for there to be Hitlers on earth?

Of course Dostoevsky did not invent these objections. They are as old as rebellion. Furthermore, he knew that theodicy has always been incapable of an adequate response to these hostilities. He merely gave them the most powerful form in the history of antireligious writing. And this is why many readers think that the novel never manages to escape these pages, that the Christian Dostoevsky, in allowing such power to anti-Christian arguments, really produced not a Christian novel but an unconsciously atheistic one. The philosopher Lev Shestov, for instance, thought that Dostoevsky, for all his orthodoxy, was so corroded by doubt that when he came to imagine the doubter Ivan, he could not help giving him a vitality and appeal far beyond that of the saintly and bland Alyosha. Those of Shestov's mind think that even if the novel demonstrates that atheism is finally a murderous idea because it kills Fyodor, religion is so damaged by Ivan's onslaught that it cannot mount a proper reply.

Dostoevsky, however, very much wanted to reply to Ivan's attack. He worried that Father Zosima and Alyosha would not be what he called, in a letter to an editor, a "sufficient reply" to "the negative side" (i.e., the atheistical side) of his book. Well, can there be a reply to Ivan's arguments? Alyosha says what any Christian must, that Christ forgives all of us, that he suffered for us so that we may not suffer, that we do not know why the world is constructed the way it is. Depending on our beliefs, we will find this adequate or inadequate.

But the novel—and I think Dostoevsky intends this—enshrines, in its very form, a further argument. It is that Ivan's ideas cannot be refuted by other ideas. In debate, in "dialogism," there is no way of defeating or even of matching Ivan, and Alyosha does not even really try. At the end of Ivan's legend, he simply kisses his brother. The only way we can refute Ivan's ideas, the book seems to say, is by maintaining that *Christ is not an idea*. Socialism is an idea, because it is "reasonable"; atheism, too; but Christianity, so profoundly unreasonable—what Kierkegaard called "lunacy"—is not an idea. Yet painfully, the only realm in which Christ is not an idea, in which he is pure knowledge, is in heaven. On earth, we are all fallen, and we fall before ideas, we have only ideas, and Christ can always be kicked around the ideational playground.

But Christ is not an idea. This is surely the only way to explain the intellectually nonsensical behavior of Dimitri, who, though innocent, is willing to be guilty for all and before all; or of Father Zosima's advice that we should ask forgiveness "even from the birds"; or of Alyosha's final words, which close the book, about how resurrection does indeed exist: "Certainly we shall rise, certainly we shall see, and gladly, joyfully tell one another all that has been!" Such notions have really fallen off the cliff of ideas and into the realm of illogical, beautiful, desperate exhortation. Belief has smothered knowledge. And this exchange—of the unreason of Christianity for the reason of atheism—means finally that there can be no "dialogism" in this novel, either of the kind Bakhtin proposed or of the kind that Dostoevsky so dearly desired. There is neither a circulation of ideas nor an "answering" of atheism by Christianity. For the answer—the unreason of Christian love—no longer belongs to the realm of worldly ideas, and thus no longer belongs to the novel itself. It exists in paradise, and in that other, finally unnovelistic book, the New Testament.

Isaac Babel and the Dangers of Exaggeration

❧

I

Isaac Babel's writing was both short-legged and short-lived: his stories are truly short, and the best of them were produced in two quick firings, two claps of history, between 1923 and 1925, and between 1929 and 1934. This sense of compacted intensity is appropriate, because his prose is distinguished by its determination to render a sudden essence. He was himself obsessed with reduction, omission, the necessary diet of severe self-editing. His writing is startlingly discontinuous; in a typical Babel paragraph, each sentence seems to disavow its role in the ordinary convoy of meaning and narrative, and appears to want to begin the story anew. Here is the beginning of one of his finest, "My First Fee":

> To be in Tiflis in spring, to be twenty years old, and not to be loved—that is a misfortune. Such a misfortune befell me. I was working as a proofreader for the printing press of the Caucasus Military District. The Kura River bubbled beneath the windows of my attic. The sun in the morning, rising from behind the mountains, lit up the river's murky knots. I was renting a room in the attic from a newlywed Georgian couple. My landlord was a butcher at the Eastern Bazaar. In the room next door, the butcher and his wife, in the

grip of love, thrashed about like two large fish trapped in a jar. The tails of these crazed fish thumped against the partition, rocking the whole attic, which was blackened by the piercing sun . . .

Babel was a keen reader of Maupassant and Flaubert; but his hunger for the *mot juste* feels very different from Flaubert's. Valéry rightly complained that in Flaubert "there is always room for another detail." In Babel, we have the curious feeling that there is not enough room for another detail, that detail is clamoring to escape. The narrative advances, but, as it were, sideways. And there is no patience for explanation, rather a battle of propositions. The sentences have lost their connective tissue: we are told that the narrator was working as a proofreader, and then in the next moment we are asked to see the Kura River from the narrator's attic window. But only for a hovering second, for then we are introduced to the narrator's landlord.

Yet along with this high degree of interruption goes a jumpy kind of repetition: the word "misfortune" appears in the first sentence, and then again in the second; the Kura River appears once, and then again in the next sentence, as "the river's murky knots." The landlord and his wife are likened to a pair of thumping fish, and the next sentence repeats this simile, in order to develop it; and the sun in the morning, which shines over the river Kura, is also the "piercing sun" that, we are later told, has blackened the attic in which the narrator lives. This might as well be a definition of modernism: rhythmic discontinuity. Babel's prose constantly forces different temporalities together into one time signature. The habitual or eternal (the sun, the bubbling river) lies alongside the daily or traditional (the butcher at work in the Eastern Bazaar) and then alongside the immediate moment of the story (the young man's job, the landlord and his wife thumping like fish). But while Flaubert would observe the cosmic narratological hierarchy whereby the writer, when setting a scene, starts large and then narrows—eternal landscape followed by more recent town followed by immediate subject—Babel darts around in any order, shredding narrative etiquette and gathering all detail into the fist of an eternal present.

It is an art of great innovation, and also of some limitation. Singly experienced, Babel's stories are fizzing spots of time—some of the *Red Cavalry* stories are vignettes of only two pages. But the reader who reads all of the stories, going through them as if through one extended work, may weary at times of this lively accumulation of omissions, and may see not only the melodrama in this work but the high cost of Babel's vivid, grotesque, theatrical externality, which is the great lack of any inwardness in any of the characters. Babel's art may certainly be a decisively modern one, but its diminishment when compared to Chekhov or Tolstoy is in proportion to its modern resistance to ordinariness or patience—in language, activity, and thought. In this sense, whatever Babel's final relation to Soviet ideology, his art is devoted to revolution. One may at times miss the hierarchical lento of the ancien régime.

Babel's politics are a matter of contention. Babel famously rode as a correspondent with the Red Cavalry in 1920, in the war that broke out between the new Soviet republic and the new nation of Poland. He wrote four dispatches for the *Red Cavalryman*, the newspaper distributed to the fighters of the cavalry. Clearly his main occupation while with the cavalry was as a silent and crafty scout for the great stories he would write only a few years later. He was collecting, collecting—he was taking details prisoner. But it is dismaying, nonetheless, to encounter his four tinny pieces of propaganda.

Reading these pieces, one stumbles across unpleasant juxtapositions and abysses. For instance, the savage and brilliant story "Squadron Commander Trunov" tells of the last, demented hours of a wounded Soviet commander. Babel's stories frequently mixed real and fictitious names and events: Trunov existed, and was commander of the Thirty-fourth Cavalry Regiment. In the story, Trunov, bleeding from a gash in his head "like rain from a haystack," has taken some Polish prisoners, and wants to kill them forthwith. He plunges his saber into the gullet of one of them, and shoots another so that his brain "spatters" onto the hands of the narrator, who remonstrates fiercely with Trunov. Headquarters won't let you get away with this! says the narrator, to which Trunov replies: "At headquarters they'll chalk it up to the rotten life we live." Suddenly four bombers appear in the sky, and a little later Trunov is killed in the aerial bombardment. The story ends with the ironic lyricism characteristic of many of these stories: Trunov, the butcherer, is buried in the local town, "in a flower bed, in the public park, in the middle of town." A public park: Babel's story, a stanza written in dejection, effectively asks us to "look on my works, ye mighty, and despair!"

Yet one of Babel's propaganda pieces is a eulogy for this same Trunov, clangingly entitled "What We Need Is More Men Like Trunov!" and ending with "If there were more Trunovs among us, the masters of this world would be finished." One is grateful that Babel kept his art so separate from his official work, but the suggestion of duplicity, of utterly different private and public thought, opens an abyss. Babel's diary of his time with the cavalry, which was not published in his lifetime, suggests a revolutionary fervor tempered not so much by a clear-sightedness about the viciousness and plunder of revolution per se—as kindly Babel scholars tend to claim—as by an easier clear-sightedness about the viciousness and plunder of the brutal Cossack soldiers who were his effective colleagues-in-arms. Babel does indeed see that "this is not a Marxist Revolution, it is a Cossack uprising that wants to win all and lose nothing." He does indeed see that "we are destroying, moving forward like a whirlwind, like lava, hated by all, life is being shattered to pieces, I am at a huge, neverending service for the dead." But the necessity for revolution is not in doubt: "the dirt, the apathy, the hopelessness of Russian life are unbearable, the Revolution will do some good work here." Even in the *Red Cavalry* stories themselves, which constitute marvelously subtle, tragic, and often comic commentaries on the desecration of revolutionary activity, Babel hews to the belief that the masters—one is seen as "a pre-reform rat of a nobleman"—must be deposed, that the Catholic church is a slippery and Jesuitical organ of aristocratic power and superstitious oppression, that the peasants have been enslaved by the profit motive, and that revolution is and should be exportable: "Here, with the ropes of profit, the Jews had bound the Russian muzhiks to the Polish *Pans*, and the Czech settlers to the factory in Lodz."

I I

Isaac Babel was born in Odessa in 1894. Like Kipling, he was very precocious—he had already a sharp, instinctive talent for observation and narrative in his teenage years. Gorky, whom he revered, published his early stories in 1916. To judge from the autobiographical stories that Babel wrote in later years—they are his greatest pieces of work—he grew up with an inflamed fantasy of both Jewish sickliness and non-Jewish healthiness. Two of these stories, "My First Dovecote" and "First Love," concern the pogrom of 1905. In "First Love," the little Babel sees his father beg for help from a magnificent Cossack captain, seen in all his Tolstoyan grandeur in "striped trousers" and "lemon suede gloves." "Over there," says the father, "they're smashing everything I've worked for all my life, Captain." The Cossack finely replies, "I will see to it!" and does nothing at all. The contradictory vision displayed in this story, of both reverence for the physical power of the Cossack and a merciless awareness of how inimical to Jews that physical power could be, runs through all of Babel's *Red Cavalry* fiction. "Like all Jews, I was short in stature, weak, and plagued by headaches," the young narrator of "My First Dovecote" tells us.

"The Awakening," another of the later autobiographical stories, set in Babel's childhood Odessa, tells of the comic episode in which

Babel's father sends his young son to the local violin teacher to groom him to be a prodigy. Odessa, after all, had produced Heifetz, Zimbalist, Mischa Elman. "Our fathers, seeing they had no prospects of their own, set up a lottery for themselves. They built this lottery on the bones of their little children." But the little Babel is very bad at the violin—"Sounds scraped out of my violin like iron filings"—and he plays truant, running down to the harbor with a school friend. Alas, he cannot swim. "The hydrophobia of my ancestors, the Spanish rabbis and Frankfurt money changers, dragged me to the bottom." But a "local water god," a proofreader for the *Odessa News*, takes pity and tries to teach him. The proofreader, divining that the little boy yearns to be a writer, accuses him of lacking a feel for nature. A real writer, says the man, must know the names of trees. Though the story's comic frame concerns the discovery by Babel's father that his son has not been attending his violin lessons— there is shouting and tears, and fat Auntie Bobka, "quivering with sobs," restrains the father from nearly murdering his son—the heart of the story has to do with "awakening." The narrator awakens into healthy nature, and dies to the deadly, sickly forcing of traditional Jewish aspiration. "How late I learned the essential things in life! In my childhood, nailed to the Gemara, I led the life of a sage, and it was only later, when I was older, that I began to climb trees."

But the writer, of course, has always really chosen a "sickly" trade; Babel knows this as well as Thomas Mann does. And writing can become sickly insofar as it cooperates with, connives at, and even darkly lusts after abuses of so-called healthy power. "The Story of My Dovecote," in which a dove is crushed against the face of little Babel, was written after, and perhaps contains an echo of one of the *Red Cavalry* stories, "My First Goose," in which the narrator, a bespectacled writer, is billeted with a group of rough Cossacks who exclude him from their company. Only once the writer has brutally killed a goose ("its head cracking beneath my boot") do the Cossacks admit the addition, who has thus proved his mettle. Newly accepted, he reads Lenin's latest speech to them from *Pravda*, and that night, as he sleeps, his heart, "crimson with murder, screeched and bled." Again, one notes the ironic closing, whereby the narrator's guilt may refer not only to his earlier brutality toward the poor goose but more generally to the "murder" of the Cossacks, and even to the murder in Lenin's speech.

I I I

From Flaubert, Babel learned how to ration commentary; from Dostoevsky and Gorky he powerfully infused the idea that Russian history was a catalogue of violence and tragedy; from Gogol, he learned about grotesque portraiture; and from Tolstoy, he learned that detail should be always dynamic, always attached to activity.

Flaubert surely founded the calm control of war writing so crucial to the effects of Babel, Crane, and Hemingway in his descriptions of revolutionary bloodshed in *Sentimental Education*: "Frédéric felt something soft under his foot; it was the hand of a sergeant in a grey overcoat who was lying face down in the gutter." In that novel, when Roque fires into a crowd of prisoners and shoots someone, Flaubert writes: "There was a tremendous howl, then nothing. Something white remained on the edge of the grating." This is powerful: the withdrawal of obvious sympathy coaxes a proportionate craving for it on the reader's part, and forces us to imagine what is being left unsaid. Babel's fiction makes use of this method again and again: "There was something more Korostelyov had wanted to say, but he didn't manage to." Korostelyov has just been brutally shot by a local commissar. The danger of this style lies in its aestheticism. A style that, as it were, refuses to get emotionally involved may seem at times to act as if it denies its own subject matter, as if the subject is not there at all. There are times when Babel's style does indeed fall into aestheticism. In particular, he invokes sunset, moon, lightning, and the sky so regularly, but with such reliable vividness, that his visual eccentricity can seem formulaic, the equivalent of Chagall's flying troikas. "The blue tongue of the flame mingled with the June lightning." "Smoke from tobacco melted into the blueish lightning that flashed over the steppes." "The sunset was boiling in the skies, a sunset thick as jam . . ." "Green lightning bolts blazed over the cupolas." "The naked shine of the moon poured over the town with unquenchable strength." "The village street lay before us, and the dying sun in the sky, round and yellow as a pumpkin, breathed its last breath." "A timid star flashed in the orange battles of sunset."

But Babel's prose, despite its great sponsors, sounds like nobody else's (even in translation). Much of this has to do with the extraordinary discontinuities of his writing. And much of it has to do with a related quality: exaggeration, of which Babel was a master, and sometimes a servant. Take the story "The Awakening," for instance. The narrator, as we have seen, describes how the Jewish fathers bullied their sons into music. "They built this lottery on the bones of their little children." The sentence is flamingly alive—and obviously untrue. "The Awakening," in fact, abounds with sentences of the most impertinent exaggeration: "Zagursky [the local violin teacher] ran a factory that churned out child prodigies, a factory of Jewish dwarfs in lace collars and patent leather shoes." Once the boy has escaped to the harbor, "the heavy waves by the harbor wall separated me more and more from a home reeking of onions and Jewish fate." And later: "The hydrophobia of my ancestors, the Spanish rabbis and Frankfurt money changers, dragged me to the bottom."

These sentences have the Babel flair: they pounce on reality, and collapse epochs into themselves. In Babel, every narrative proposition is flautingly rendered. Mandelstam's prose has something of this emphasis too: in *The Noise of Time*, the poet's memoir, there appears a man who is bowed over by "an excess of Jewishness and Populism." But Babel is more extreme, reaching for wild and brilliant linkages. In "Guy de Maupassant," the narrator works for a hand-

some, wealthy, and well-built Jewish woman: "These women trans-
mute the money of their resourceful husbands into the lush pink fat
on their bellies, napes, and round shoulders." These sentences then
accrue an extra scandal from their context. For Babel is continually
asserting connections—male money becomes female fat; Jewish musical prowess rests on childish bones—where such connections are
not immediately apparent, and moreover in paragraphs where the
very idea of connection and continuity is constantly being interrupted and challenged. If his stories progress sideways, sliding from
unconnected sentence to sentence, then the very sentences vault forward within themselves at the same moment.

But it must be admitted that this can be the mode of melodrama
(Babel had read Dickens, and refers to him in one of the stories). It
is no great distance from violin lessons populated by Jewish "dwarfs"
to the story's final scene, in which the little boy has locked himself in
the bathroom while outside the women sob, the father tears his hair,
and "Auntie Bobka, quivering with sobs, was grinding her fat shoulder against the door." It is no great step from a home "reeking of
onions and Jewish fate" to the somewhat excessive and even vulgar
depiction, in "The Church in Novograd," one of the *Red Cavalry* stories, of the Catholic church. In that story, the narrator sits in the
kitchen of Eliza, the priest's housekeeper. "Her sponge cakes had the
aroma of crucifixion. Within them was the sap of slyness and the fra-
grant frenzy of the Vatican." Oh really? And lest we think that only
Catholic cakes have their own ethnic sap, we have Auntie Bobka in
the story "In the Basement": "Into that pie she put the heart of our
tribe, the heart that has withstood so many tribulations."

This is uncomfortably close to mere phrasemaking. In particular,
Babel's Odessa stories are streaked with melodrama and pantomime.
The Odessa gangsters who are forcefully rendered in some of these
tales speak only in exclamation points ("Get out of here you lout!
. . . You've clapped eyes on a slop bucket!"); but then so does Auntie
Bobka ("Her fat, kindly breasts bounced in all directions") and so

does Grandfather Levy-Itskhok ("His single tooth jiggled in his mouth"). In general, Babel's stories exhibit a very wide range of characters who themselves have a rather small range of attributes. Is it fair to say that essentially all his characters, even the Jews, are Cossacks of a kind? For he tends to arrest human beings in a moment of intense singleness, so that they quiver with essence; and more often than not, since this essence is necessarily strong, his characters are blocks of appetite. Unlike Chekhov, Babel has almost no interest in the weak—except in the weak writer, silently viewing all this mayhem, violence, and bloody theater from behind his mild spectacles.

However, the melodramatic in Babel's work, which can produce, over time, a monotonous excitability, cannot really be separated from what is great in his work. When we examine a bad sentence in Babel, we immediately sense its kinship with a good one. Take, for instance, "His single tooth jiggled in his mouth." Or, better, this line about a nurse: "The pince-nez on Judith's nose bounced, her breasts swelled out of her starched coat." What is untrue about these sentences is that they are rendering a specific action or event—the bouncing of pince-nez, the jiggling of a tooth—as habitual, eternal happenings. Yet this swift compacting also lends Babel's best prose its remarkable, almost atomic power to create instant energy. Here is a description of staff headquarters, from "At Saint Valentine's":

> I read the documents. The snoring of the orderlies behind me bespoke our never-ending homelessness. The clerks, sodden with sleeplessness, wrote orders to the division, ate pickles, and sneezed.

And here is a passage about the violin teacher, from "The Awakening":

> The door of the inner sanctum opened. Large-headed, freckled children came bustling out of Zagursky's chamber, their necks thin as flower stalks, a convulsive flush on their cheeks. Then the door closed, swallowing up the next dwarf. In the adjacent room Zagursky, with his red curls, bow tie, and thin legs, sang and

conducted in ecstasy. The founder of this freakish lottery filled the Moldavanka and the back alleys of the old bazaar with specters of pizzicato and cantilena.

And here is the beginning of "Gedali":

On the eve of the Sabbath I am always tormented by the dense sorrows of memory. In the past on these evenings, my grandfather's yellow beard caressed the volumes of Ibn Ezra. My old grandmother, in her lace bonnet, waved spells over the Sabbath candle with her gnarled fingers, and sobbed sweetly.

In each of these passages, every narrative proposition is seized as a picture. And this picture works by taking a momentary extremity of emotion and rendering it as habitual. The picture distends and arrests time. Thus, the clerks are seen as writing, eating pickles, and sneezing all at the same time, in one sentence. Zagursky is seen as *only* singing and conducting in ecstasy, whereas there were presumably many unecstatic days. And the narrator's old grandmother is seen as habitually sobbing sweetly over the Sabbath candle, whereas in likelihood there were also some dry-eyed Sabbaths. (That last passage shows how closely this style of writing resembles Old Country sentimentality.) In his diary, Babel often makes a note to himself to "remember the picture." This is clearly a painterly procedure, akin to the techniques of the vivid icons celebrated in his story "Pan Apolek." It is very powerful, in several different ways. It drops a single blot of color onto the page, a potent pigment of activity. It is ideally suited to very short stories, and less suited to the novel: if we are going to see Zagursky only once, we had better see him bow-tied and conducting in ecstasy.

An atmosphere at once modern and antique is created, which may be the true novelty we feel when reading Babel. He feels modern because detail is so interrupted and shaped and angled that it always seems to be the writer's stylistic choosing, and hence has the feel of something recollected, something filtered through memory (it is close to the technique of stream of consciousness); but it seems antique, almost fable-like, because when human beings are frozen in sharp, habitual activities, they are made eternal, made pieces of landscape and climate. Old grandmother, forever sobbing over the Sabbath candle, is necessarily at one with "the naked shine of the moon" and the many evocations of sunsets in Babel's work.

But at the same time, melodrama thrives on this singleness; melodrama is really just the drama of singleness, and Babel's is certainly a perilous art. And equally, painterliness—even Flaubert shows this—is the cousin of aestheticism. Babel's exuberant literary friezes or icons are obsessed with the rendering of dynamic essences: Zagursky in ecstasy, grandmother sobbing, Auntie Bobka bouncing, Trunov plunging his saber into the Pole's throat, and so on. In Babel, character tends to be instantly converted into function, and emotion into activity. Do you want to see a clerk? Then I will show you him eating pickles and sneezing and saturated in sleeplessness. My grandmother? Here she is, sobbing over the candle. But in such a world of activity and function, the only possessor of inwardness, the only vessel of vulnerability, the only carrier of sensitivity, is the writer himself—which represents the glorious, final, murderous triumph of style. Babel famously likened the writer to a man with spectacles on his nose and autumn in his heart. At times one wishes that he had hoarded that writerly autumn less jealously, and daubed his characters more generously with his complicating dapple.

Saltykov-Shchedrin's Subversion of Hypocrisy

❧

The hypocrite, among other things, may be a deformed ambassador of the truth. By so obviously misrepresenting the truth, he enables us to trace its smothered outlines. In fiction and drama, this traditional hypocrite acts rather like a reliably unreliable narrator. The reliably unreliable narrator is rarely truly unreliable, because his unreliability is manipulated by an author without whose reliable manipulation we would not be able to judge the narrator's unreliability. Similarly, the traditional hypocrite is always reliably hypocritical, which is why we so enjoy, indeed are so unthreatened by, the prospect of Polonius, Tartuffe, Parson Adams, Pecksniff, and others. Such characters are comic, and certify our rectitude, giving us the satisfaction that, whatever we have become, we have not become that kind of person. Though, in a curious, unintended way, such characters may turn *us* into hypocrites: the content and well-fed audiences watching Molière suggest that this has already happened.

We can see through the hypocrite because his zeal tends to be a perversion, almost a parody, of a visible moral code. He is nourished by the same food we consume; but, as it were, he eats far too much of it, and has become bullyingly large. Yet what would the hypocrite represent in a world starved of moral nutrition? A world in which no moral code exists, and in which the only one at hand—religion—has already been perverted, long before the hypocrite gets to it? What happens when the reliable hypocrite is no longer a reliable hypocrite? When the familiar hypocrite of the theatrical tradition is removed from the theater and put into an unreliable modern novel? Such a character becomes much more menacing than the traditional hypocrite, for there is no longer any truth for him reliably to misrepresent, and our reading of his motives becomes more difficult. Indeed, in a sense, he becomes opaque to us because he ceases to be that familiar and stable category, a "hypocrite," and he ceases to be a hypocrite precisely because he is not a liar: there is nothing for him to lie about. Accordingly, he would be more likely to be a tragic than a comic figure—or perhaps a tragicomic figure—and more likely to be a solipsist or fantasist than a liar. He has merged with his own horrid world.

In his extraordinary novel *The Golovlyov Family* (1875–80), Shchedrin (the nom de plume of M. E. Saltykov, sometimes known as Saltykov-Shchedrin) depicts just such a character and just such a world. The hypocrite is Porphiry Golovlyov, one of the sons of Arina Petrovna and Vladimir Mikhaylovich Golovlyov. This novel, called by D. S. Mirsky "certainly the gloomiest in all Russian literature," is set on the Golovlyovs' dismal estate, known as Golovlyovo. The Golovlyovs are minor landowners, a class Shchedrin satirized in many stories and sketches (and from which he himself came). The Golovlyov males are drunken, semieducated, grasping fantasists. Supported by the labor of their serfs, they squander a privilege of which they are unaware. As if color-blind without knowing it, they see only the world their vision falsely constructs.

Vladimir, the father, spends most of his time in his study drinking, imitating the songs of starlings, and writing bawdy verse. Golovlyovo is run by Vladimir's wife, the ferociously continent, parsimonious, and cruel Arina Petrovna. She has little but contempt for her three sons, Stepan, Porphiry, and Pavel. Of her middle son, Porphiry, known to his family as Little Judas or Bloodsucker, she has something like fear. Even when the child was a baby, "he liked to behave affectionately to his 'dear friend mamma,' to kiss her unobtrusively on the shoulder and sometimes to tell tales . . . But even in those early days Arina Petrovna felt as it were suspicious of her son's ingratiating ways. Even at that time the gaze that he fixed at her seemed to be enigmatic, and she could not decide what precisely was in it—venom or filial respect."

Golovlyovo is a house of death. One by one, the members of the family try to escape, and return there to die. Of course, they only come home because they are in desperate straits. Thus, having run through a family allowance, only forty but looking a decade older, Stepan comes back from Moscow, his eyes bulging and bloodshot, "inflamed by drink and rough weather . . . He looked around him morosely from under his brows; this was due not to any inward discontent, but rather to a vague fear that at any minute he might suddenly drop dead with hunger." Stepan hopes to squeeze a little more life out of the family estate, but the punitive Arina, who has her own survival to think of, rations her indulgence.

Stepan is already dying, in a sense. On the Golovlyov estate, where everyone is barely hanging on to existence, the best means of survival is a kind of shutting down of the moral system, as the body sleeps in very cold weather. Thus, the commonest emotion at Golovlyovo is the moral equivalent of boredom: a vacuous blindness. Stepan, for instance, is described thus: "He had not a single thought, not a single desire . . . He wanted nothing, nothing at all." His mother is no less sealed off. She allows him a diet that is just sufficient to keep him from starving; Stepan takes to the bottle. When his mother is told that Stepan is ailing, the words "did not reach her ears or make any impression upon her mind." For Arina has the Golovlyov disease: "She had lost all sight of the fact that next door to her, in the office, lived a man related to her by blood."

Likewise, Pavel, who locks himself away and drinks himself to death, is described as "one of those apathetic, strangely morose people who are incapable of any positive action . . . He was the most perfect instance of a man devoid of any characteristics at all." And near the end of the book, when Porphiry's niece, Anninka, also returns to die, she spends the time pacing up and down, "singing in an undertone and trying to tire herself out and, above all, not to think."

Golovlyovo is a place of evil in the sense that Augustine and Calvin understood evil: as nothingness, the absence of goodness. The religious emphasis is proper, for in this vacated world, the man who briefly prospers, Little Judas, is above all a brilliant manipulator of religious hypocrisy. He fills the abyss with a diabolic version of traditional religion. Once Stepan, Vladimir, and Pavel have died (the latter is "comforted" by the unctuous Porphiry, but has enough life in him to shout from his deathbed, "Go away, you bloodsucker!"). Porphiry comes alive, and takes control of the estate.

Porphiry is Shchedrin's great creation. His vivacity as a character proceeds, in part, from a paradox, which is that he is interesting in proportion to his banality. Traditionally, the great fictional hypocrites are generally interesting as liars are interesting. But Porphiry does not really lie to himself, for he has lost touch with the truth. He speaks the "truths" (as he sees them) that are all around him, and they are the most dismal, banal, lying platitudes. Shchedrin is explicit about this at one point in his novel. The hypocrites of French drama, he writes, are "conscious hypocrites, that is they know it themselves and are aware that other people know it too." Porphiry, he writes, "was a hypocrite of a purely Russian sort, that is, simply a man devoid of all moral standards, knowing no truth other than the copy-book precepts. He was pettifogging, deceitful, loquacious, boundlessly ignorant, and afraid of the devil. All these qualities are merely negative and can supply no stable material for real hypocrisy."

Porphiry grinds down his mother and his servants with endless banalities. His usual technique is to invoke God: "What would God say?" His sure idea of God's providence is used to justify his cruelty, his swindling, his meanness, and his theft. There is a vivid and comic scene as his brother Pavel is dying. Porphiry arrives in a coach-and-four; his mother immediately thinks to herself, "The Fox must have scented a carcass." Porphiry enters the house with his two sons, Volodenka and Petenka (Volodenka mimicking his father, "folding his hands, rolling his eyes and moving his lips"). Seeing his mother unhappy, Porphiry says to her: "You are despondent, I see! It's wrong, dear! Oh, it's very wrong! You should ask yourself, 'And what would God say to that?' Why, He would say, 'Here I arrange everything for the best in My wisdom, and she complains!' " He continues:

> As a brother—I am grieved. More than once, in fact, I may have wept. I am grieving over my brother, grieving deeply . . . I shed tears, but then I think: "And what about God? Doesn't God know better than we do?" One considers this and feels cheered. That's what everyone ought to do . . . Look at me. See how well I'm bearing up!

Still, Porphiry is afraid. He spends much of his time crossing himself, or praying before his icons. In true Golovlyov fashion, he prays not for anything positive, but to be saved from the devil. (It is a nice implicit joke that Porphiry is afraid of the devil, but is in fact the devil.) "He could go on praying and performing all the necessary movements, and at the same time be looking out of the window to see if anyone went to the cellar without permission, etc." He uses religious platitudes to protect himself from anything that would threaten his survival; religious hypocrisy is his moral camouflage.

One of the most horrifying events in the novel occurs when Porphiry's son Petenka comes home to beg for money. He has gambled away three thousand rubles belonging to his regiment, and if he cannot pay them back, he will be sent off to Siberia. When Petenka enters his father's study, Porphiry is kneeling, with uplifted arms.

Porphiry keeps him waiting for half an hour (Petenka rightly thinks that his father is keeping him there on purpose), and when Petenka finally explains that he has lost money, Porphiry replies, "amiably": "Well, return it!" When Petenka tells him that he doesn't have that kind of money, Porphiry warns him not to "mix me up in your dirty affairs. Let us go and have breakfast instead. We'll drink tea and sit quietly and perhaps talk of something, only, for Christ's sake, not this." Bitterly, Petenka says to his father: "I am the only son you have left." His father replies: "God took from Job all he had, my dear, and yet he did not complain, but only said, 'God has given, God has taken away—God's will be done.' So that's the way, my boy."

Hypocrisy is a familiar subject in Russian literature, and within it, religious hypocrisy has a special place. Chekhov makes fun of a priest in his story "In the Ravine," who pompously comforts a woman who has just lost her baby while pointing at her with "a fork with a pickled mushroom at the end of it." In "The Malefactor," a peasant standing before the examining magistrate yawns, and immediately makes the sign of the cross over his mouth.

When he began to write *The Golovlyov Family*, in the latter half of the 1870s, Shchedrin, who was Russia's greatest satirist, had already mocked religious hypocrisy in his *Fables*, a collection of Aesopian tales about feeble governors, greedy landowners, imbecilic bureaucrats, and cruel priests. In his fable "A Village Fire," a widow loses her only son to the flames, and the priest, like Porphiry, accuses her of grieving too much. "Why this plaint?" he asks her, "with kindly reproach." The priest tells her the story of Job, and reminds her that Job did not complain, "but still more loved the Lord who had created him." Later in the story, when the daughter of the village's landowner tells her mother of the widow's suffering, the landowner, like Porphiry, invokes destiny: "It's dreadful for her; but how worked up you are, Vera! . . . That will never do, my love. There's a Purpose in all things—we must always remember!"

At times *The Golovlyov Family* seems less a novel than a satirical onslaught. Its relentlessness has the exhaustiveness not so much of a search for the truth as the prosecution of a case. Indeed, Shchedrin would seem to enjoy shocking the reader by annulling the novel's traditional task, that of the patient exploration of motive in domestic settings. Instead, he gives us his sealed monsters, people whom we cannot explore since they are shut off from the moral world. Shchedrin knows how terrible, how—in the novelistic sense—*unconventional* it is to witness Stepan's homecoming, which is a cruel inversion of the parable of the prodigal son: "All understood that the man before them was an unloved son who had come to the place he hated, that he had come for good and that his only escape from it would be to be carried, feet foremost, to the churchyard. And all felt both sorry for him and uneasy." All except Stepan's mother, of course.

Shchedrin knows that it is a kind of affront both to decency and to the decency of the novel itself to present a family reunion in such inhuman terms, and his narration registers the offense. Usually Shchedrin breaks in to tell us what we should think about each character, acting as an omniscient satirist. In this novel, we do indeed see an older, more traditional kind of punitive satire availing itself of the greater tragicomic flexibilities of the novel form. For at other times Shchedrin writes as if from one of the characters' minds. Thus, when Stepan returns, a family conference is held between Arina, Pavel, and Porphiry on Stepan's fate. Arina tells Porphiry and Pavel that she has decided to grant Stepan a very mean allowance, on which he will be effectively living like a peasant, in one of the villages. Shchedrin comments: "Although Porphiry Vladimirich had refused to act as a judge, he was so struck by his mother's generosity that he felt it his duty to point out to her the dangerous consequences to which the proposed measure might lead." Since the reader can see that there is nothing "generous" about Arina, the novel's narration, at this point, is ironic, affecting to think of Arina as Porphiry might think of his mother. Yet, in a devilish twist, we know that Porphiry can never be trusted, and that Porphiry never thinks well of anyone. What does it mean to be told that Porphiry thought his mother generous? Is it possible that the moral sense has been so polluted in Porphiry that even though he hates his mother, he believes his own hypocritical lies, his own devious fawning and playacting, and *actually* believes his mother to be generous at this moment? Or, more simply, is it just that Porphiry truly thinks that Arina's terms are too good for Stepan, that, in effect, Porphiry hates his brother more than his mother? We do not know, but in either reading Shchedrin the omniscient satirist has left us alone for a moment, has become a novelist, and has decided not to finalize the ambiguity by breaking in and telling us how to think.

This technique brings us closer to the characters, letting us, if only for a minute, inhabit the wilderness of their souls. The method is especially effective when used to inhabit Porphiry, for we are made to share Porphiry's own self-deceptions. Here Shchedrin's narration is genuinely "unreliable," and unreliable about an already unreliable man. At one devastating moment in the novel, for example, Shchedrin writes, of Porphiry: "He had lost all connections with the outside world. He received no books, no newspapers, no letters. One of his sons, Volodenka, had committed suicide; to his other son, Petenka, he wrote very little, and only when he sent him money." The reader starts at this: the last time Volodenka was mentioned by Shchedrin, he was a little boy, mimicking his father. This is the first time we have heard anything about his committing suicide. But again, if we see the sentence as, in effect, issuing from Porphiry's mind, it is just the heartless way that Porphiry *would* think of his dead son—as an unimportant memory, hardly worth mentioning.

And yet the closer we come to Porphiry, the more unknowable he actually becomes. In this sense, Porphiry is a modernist prototype: the character who lacks an audience, the alienated actor. The hypocrite who does not know he is one, and can never really be told that he is one by anyone around him, is something of a revolutionary fictional character, for he has no "true" knowable self, no "stable ego," to use D. H. Lawrence's phrase. Around the turn of the twenti-eth century, Knut Hamsun, a novelist strongly influenced by Dosto-evsky and the Russian novel, would invent a new kind of character: the lunatic heroes of his novels *Hunger* and *Mysteries* go around telling falsely incriminating stories about themselves and acting badly when they have no obvious reason to. It is difficult to know when they are lying and not lying, and impossible to understand their motives. They too are unknowable; and they are also, in a sense, antihypocrites, so deeply in revolt against the pieties of Lutheranism that they have become parodically impious. They shout their self-invented sinfulness in the streets, though no one is really listening. The line from Dostoevsky, through Shchedrin, and on to Hamsun, is visible. *The Golovlyov Family*, that strange, raucous book whose characters aspire to the condition of nothingness, a book which is at times broad satire, at times Gothic horror, and at times a novel, becomes more modern the older it gets.

Anna Karenina *and Characterization*

❦

Everyone who reads Tolstoy feels that it is an experience different in kind, not just degree, from reading the other great novelists. But how, and why? Rather as one is supposed to approach an elephant not from the front but the side, the critic finds himself becoming, alongside Tolstoy's massive straightforwardness, a mere poser of angles. The transparency of Tolstoy's art—realism as a kind of neutral substrate, like air—makes it very difficult to account for, and more often than not one blusters in tautologies. Why are his characters so real? Because they are so individual. Why does his world feel so true? Because it is so real. And so on. Even Tolstoy himself was forced into paradox when once defending his writing. In a letter to his friend Nikolai Strakhov written in 1876, he argued that *Anna Karenina* was not a collection of ideas that could be abstracted from the book, but a network: "This network itself is not made up of ideas (or so I think), but of something else, and it is absolutely impossible to express the substance of this network directly in words: it can be done only indirectly, by using words to describe characters, acts, situations."

The novel's opening provides an example of Tolstoy's easy fullness. Stiva Oblonsky, vigorous and wellborn, simple, handsome, "cheerful and content," the possessor of a habitually kind smile, has been having an affair with the former governess of his children. Unfortunately, his wife, Dolly, has found out, and Stiva miserably recalls the recent evening when, returning from the theater and "holding a huge pear for his wife" (we are two pages into the novel and already Tolstoy's succulence of detail is bearing fruit), he found her not in the drawing room but in their bedroom, holding an incriminating letter.

But Stiva is incapable of depression, really. Like many of Tolstoy's men, he has a self-sufficiency which is almost solipsistic. As in Shakespeare, Tolstoy's characters feel real to us in part because they feel so real to themselves, take their own universes for granted. What can Stiva do about his wife's unhappiness? Life tells him to go on living, in obliviousness, and that is all. In effect, he forgets about it. Instead, he takes what is clearly a customary pleasure in the rituals of waking and dressing. He puts on his "grey dressing gown with the light-blue silk lining," and we see him "drawing a goodly amount of air into the broad box of his chest," going to the window "with the customary brisk step of his splayed feet, which so easily carried his full body . . ." A barber arrives, and with his "glossy, plump little hand" sets about "clearing a pink path between his long, curling side-whiskers." Then Stiva sits down to breakfast and opens "the still damp newspaper."

Tolstoy generally starts his characterization with the description of a body, and the body will tend to fix a character's essence. This essence is then repeatedly referred to in the novel. This is the method of "leitmotif" from which Thomas Mann and Proust both learned a good amount. Stiva's smile appears at the beginning of the novel and never, as it were, goes away. In the first thirty pages of the book he three times stops someone's hand by raising his (the barber, his secretary, and Levin)—isn't he really stopping the reader, as it were, raising his hand to us and, in effect, saying, "Watch me, I am full of commanding life"? Stiva's sister, Anna Karenina, also has "a quick step, which carried her rather full body with such strange lightness." And these essences are both physical and moral. It might be said that, morally speaking, both Stiva and Anna have too light a tread, are not grounded enough—unlike, say, Levin, Tolstoy's great hero and spokesman in the novel, who is described as "a strongly built, broad-shouldered man," and is first seen "pacing around" outside Stiva's office. Anna's husband, Alexei Karenin, is cold, dutiful, an unimaginative Petersburg bureaucrat, and far too grounded in the wrong way: he is first seen at the Petersburg station, by Vronsky, who is irritated by the way Karenin walks, "swinging his whole pelvis and his blunt feet." As Tolstoy repeats the appearance of these essences, so they take on a life of their own, begin to seem as if they are repeating of their own accord. And the characters respond to each other's essences. For instance, Vasenka Veslovsky, an unwanted houseguest, has an annoying habit of tucking his fat legs under him when he sits, and is defined by this one habit. Levin picks up on this motif, and complains that what he dislikes about Veslovsky is his habit of "tucking his legs under."

Stiva Oblonsky, like many of Tolstoy's characters, cannot help being himself, cannot help being his essence, and his essence is his body: simple, broad, sybaritic, and rather too light-footed. But such merry forcefulness is of course infectious, and Stiva is the kind of man who gives out a life-heat which others delight in being warmed by. His valet, Matvei, enjoys helping to dress his "pampered body," and a few pages later, when Stiva and Levin have lunch at the Anglia restaurant, the old Tartar waiter cannot help smiling with pleasure at Oblonsky's relish of the food. The reader is infected in the same way, and a curious transaction begins to occur—remember that the novel is only a few pages old—whereby we too yearn to be in the presence of a man so self-sufficient that he would probably barely notice us. With delight, we watch Oblonsky eat, "peeling the sloshy oysters from their pearly shells," we see the Tartar waiter, "his tails flying over his broad hips," and we see Levin sulking—Levin, the prig from the country, the self-competing moralist, who would rather be eating "white bread and cheese" and is offended by these "surroundings of bronze, mirrors, gas-lights, Tartars . . ."

It is the same throughout the novel. Tolstoy's details are superbly dynamic. Think of Alexei Karenin, in a fury with Anna, putting his portfolio under his arm and gripping it so tightly with his elbow "that his shoulder rose up"; or the merchant Ryabinin, wearing "high boots wrinkled at the ankles and straight on the calves." Or Levin, in the wonderful scene after his successful wooing of Kitty, waiting with ecstatic impatience in his hotel room for the hour when he can go and announce his intentions to Kitty's parents. Meanwhile, in the next bedroom of the hotel, "they were saying something about machines and cheating, and coughing morning coughs." Later in the book, when Kitty and Levin are married, he watches her combing her hair and sees "the narrow parting at the back of her round little head, which kept closing the moment she drew her comb forward." And there is Levin's housekeeper, Agafya Mikhailovna, who, "while carrying a jar of freshly pickled mushrooms to the cellar, slipped, fell, and dislocated her wrist." Or Dolly, sitting down to talk to the miserable Karenin and finding only the children's schoolroom private enough. So they sit down "at a table covered with oilcloth cut all over by penknives."

These details are surely a large aspect of the "network" which Tolstoy mentions in his letter. First, how vividly and exactly true his descriptions are: the "still damp newspaper," or the people next door coughing in the morning. But further, one notices that his details are almost always propelled by function, by life-movement—by work, in fact. Agafya is not carrying any pickled mushrooms, but ones "freshly pickled," ones she has recently pickled; the merchant's boots are wrinkled that way by movement, just as Kitty's narrow hair-parting opens and closes only when she touches it, and Karenin's arm goes up when he squeezes too tightly.

Something flows from this which makes Tolstoy feel very different from other modern realists. He is not interested in telling us what things look like to him, and he is not interested in telling us what they resemble. This is why he eschews simile and metaphor at these moments. Tolstoy's similes are often of the blandly universal kind: "He felt like a man does when he enters a shop and sees things that are too expensive for him," and so on. (Nabokov rightly noticed that at this kind of metaphor, Tolstoy is not very good.) When Flaubert writes of the long tail of steam flowing from a train's funnel as the train makes its passage through the countryside, and likens it to "a gigantic ostrich feather whose tip kept blowing away" (in *Sentimental Education*), it is very beautiful, but nevertheless a stylist is being a stylist. It is how Flaubert sees the world. Yet in Tolstoy, as in Chekhov, reality appears in his novels as it might appear not to a writer but to the characters.

When Flaubert describes the train, he is freezing it into pictorial arrest, and claiming it as his own. But reality in *Anna Karenina* is what the characters share, and reality is in the present, as the work of movement occurs in the present. Flaubert's train, as soon as it becomes style, becomes somewhat superfluous, and not least because metaphor, even the greatest metaphor, tends to insist on the accidental: we are meant to notice that X happens to resemble Y. Yet one of the powerful oddities we feel when reading Tolstoy is that, though everything is extraordinarily free—Tolstoy does as he pleases as a novelist, even inhabiting the thought and mental speech of Levin's dog, Laska, on several occasions—everything also feels curiously inevitable. This is partly because reality is not the novelist's toy in Tolstoy but his characters' necessary food. Proust, in an enigmatic paragraph on *Anna Karenina* and *War and Peace*, writes that each feature of these novels, though supposedly "observed" (i.e., stylized, "accidental," "literary"), is actually "the garment, the proof, the example of a law the novelist has identified, a rational or irrational law." Each gesture, each word, each action, says Proust, being only the signifying of a law, makes us feel that we are "moving inside a multitude of laws." Proust may well be gesturing, in part, to this sense of inevitability in Tolstoy, of physical detail as the product of the laws of dynamism: in the morning the newspaper will still be damp and people will cough morning coughs, and when people use their boots they will wrinkle, and oilcoth is always already scratched, and when you comb your hair a small hole opens and closes. The writer who uses metaphor is always describing the world hypothetically, as it might be; Tolstoy is simply describing the world as it is.

Tolstoy began writing *Anna Karenina* in 1873, though he told his wife in 1870 that he was planning a novel about a married woman disgraced by adultery. As in the case of *Madame Bovary*, an actual event occurred which perhaps propelled the novel. In January 1872 Anna Stepanovna Pirogov, the mistress of a neighboring landowner, threw herself under a train after being abandoned by her lover. Tolstoy went to look at the body at the station, and was deeply affected. There are familial similarities between the novels about fallen women that were written in the second half of the nineteenth century. Anna, like Emma Bovary, reads novels. Hardy's Tess, like Anna, is full-bosomed. Indeed, all three women are sensuous to the point of irresponsibility. Men cannot help being seduced by them, which of course is not thought to be the fault of men; Levin, after meeting Anna late in the novel, accuses himself of having yielded to her "cunning influence." Yet *Tess, Madame Bovary*, and *Anna Karenina*, while carrying the germs of male blame, produce their own antibodies, as it were, so that their doomed heroines are finally sympathized with rather than judged, written into rather than written off. There is a reason that the great age of novelistic character, the nineteenth century, was really the great age of female fictional character. These are heroines who are trying to escape society's imprisonment of them: it is because they seek to escape a world that merely characterizes them as types that these women become true characters.

Originally, Tolstoy planned a novel that would condemn Anna for her sin. In the early drafts, she is a fat and somewhat vulgar creature, and her cuckolded husband a saintly figure. Most of the novel's spaciousness, as we now know it, did not exist: Levin scything with the peasants, his marriage to Kitty (their fertile domesticity the wholesome "answer" to the sterile carnality of Anna and Vronsky), Kitty's family the Shcherbatskys (the old prince, Kitty's father, one of Tolstoy's finest small roles: it is hard not to smile with pleasure when recalling his term for one of the rooms at his club: "the clever room"). There was none of this, and instead a relentless concentration on the adulterous triangle. But, as Richard Pevear has written, as Tolstoy worked on his book, "he gradually enlarged the figure of Anna morally and diminished the figure of the husband; the sinner grew in beauty and spontaneity, while the saint turned more and more hypothetical."

Two objections to *Anna Karenina* are commonly made. One is that the great scything scenes—or, later, the chapters when Levin and others go hunting—are tedious or unnecessary. Turgenev and, later, James felt that the novel had no architecture; they are nowadays thirded by A. N. Wilson, in his intelligent biography of Tolstoy, in which he writes that "the extended Levin passages are not obviously justifiable in aesthetic terms . . . There is nothing artistic, nothing planned about these interludes." Now, it is all very well to view Tolstoy as a beast of instinct who can outrun the nervous zoologists of form, and it is true that Tolstoy is, in a sense, the great antiformalist. But he himself insisted that his novel had an invisible architecture. It seems worthwhile trying to find it.

Some of the novel's power—yet another of the qualities that make reading Tolstoy different in kind from reading other novelists —has to do with the way in which Tolstoy slows down the tempo of realism so that it no longer has the artificial pace of most realist novels, but rather has the more ample lento of life as we live it from day to day. Of course, the pages in which Levin scythes grass with the peasants are in themselves beautiful: "The tall grass softly twined around the wheels and the horse's legs, leaving its seeds on the wet spokes and hubs." Very touching is the little picture of one of the peasants, an old man working alongside Levin, who, upon finding mushrooms in the long grass, bends down each time and puts them in his pocket, muttering to himself, "Another treat for my old woman."

And these pages calm the habitual speed of novelistic realism. As Levin, amazed by how strenuous the work is, loses all sense of the day, so the novel loses its sense of the day. Vronsky falls from his horse, in the famous racing scene, on about page 200. We relive the race again, this time from Anna's perspective. Then, over the next eighty pages, Kitty goes to a German spa and meets the saintly Varenka; Sergei visits his brother, Levin, in the country; Levin scythes with the peasants, Dolly comes with her children to the country; and we see Alexei Karenin in pain and anger as he begins to live with the news that Anna finally gave him at the races: that she loves Vronsky, that "I listen to you and think about him. I love him, I am his mistress, I cannot stand you, I'm afraid of you, I hate you . . ." But over these hundred pages we do not once visit Vronsky, until around page 300. And what does Tolstoy now write? "Waking up late the day after the races, Vronsky put on his uniform jacket without shaving or bathing . . ." A hundred pages have elapsed for us, and yet, for Vronsky, barely an evening. And it has probably taken the average reader about an evening to read those hundred pages. The reader may be reading at the same speed at which Vronsky is living. It is difficult to think of a better example of "real time."

A more serious charge concerns Tolstoy's didacticism. Is it not the case that Levin is first bullied by Tolstoy into an identification with the peasants, and then, nearer the end of the book, toward a very Tolstoyan Christianity (three parts ethics to one part theology)? The book ends as Levin commits his life to "faith in God, in the good, as the sole purpose of man," to "that life of the soul which alone makes life worth living and alone is what we value." There is certainly something propagandistic about elements of the scything scenes. It is always hard not to laugh at Tolstoy when he writes of the peasants that "the long, laborious day had left no other trace in them than merriment."

But in fact, Levin's relations with the peasants are pictured with a sense of comic absurdity, for Levin, like most of the characters in the novel, is solipsistic. It is clear enough to the reader that Levin uses the peasants for his own moral hygiene. Later in the book, Tolstoy will make one of the finest episodes in the novel from the comedy of Levin's solipsism: his certainty, once he has won Kitty, that everyone else in the world shares his rapture. Returning to his hotel after his evening with his future wife, Levin falls into conversation with Yegor, the lackey on duty. Levin asks Yegor if, when he got married, he loved his wife. "Of course I loved her," says Yegor. "And Levin saw that Yegor was also in a rapturous state and intended to voice all his innermost feelings." A sly sentence, this, for does Levin think that Yegor is intending to voice all Yegor's innermost feelings, or does Levin assume that Yegor intends to voice all Levin's innermost feelings? We never really know, because a bell rings and Yegor leaves to answer it. The next morning, Levin decides that even the cabbies outside the hotel "evidently knew everything." Levin's self-involvement is delightful in these pages, but it complicates our earlier reading of his scything with the peasants, as Tolstoy surely means it to do.

Besides, the argument that Levin's sermonizing ratiocination forces our free sense of him, that it bruises his autonomy, assumes that he has such an autonomy, that Tolstoy "the artist" is spoiled by Tolstoy "the preacher." But Tolstoy is never really a pure enough artist for his characters to have the kind of purity which can be violated. His approach to character is always paradoxical: his characters are fixed as essences, and ever-changing as people. It is Levin's fixed essence that he will always have "a desire to be better, which never left him," though this does not mean we will always know how he will act. It is Karenin's essence that he is cold, despite the fact that, at one moving and unexpected moment in the novel, he sobs like a child and warmly forgives both Vronsky and Anna. In time, he returns to his essential coldness and refuses to grant Anna her divorce.

If Tolstoy's characters have a different kind of reality than do those of other novelists, it is because they are both inevitable and unpredictable, universal and private, and that while they are certainly their own individuals, we are always aware of who their maker is. Tolstoy has a premodern primitivism which puts me in mind of the famous Alfred Jewel, a ninth-century English object on which is written, in reference to King Alfred, "Alfred caused me to be made." There is a way in which, despite their autonomy, Tolstoy's characters all bear the stamp: "Tolstoy caused me to be made." Think of that very early scene when Levin and Stiva meet. Though we hardly know them, Levin and Stiva are already vivaciously established as characters and as essences. Tolstoy tells us that they have been friends for years and have loved each other. And then, in familiar mode, he breaks in and informs us that "in spite of that, as often happens between people who have chosen different ways, each of them, while rationally justifying the other's activity, despised it in his heart." In most other writers, this authorial meddling would be very dangerous: the characters have just been invented, and here is the author sticking his fat fingers into the web, telling us not only what to think about them but that there is a law which regulates how certain people feel about each other ("as often happens between people").

Yet the incursion—one of the first of many throughout the novel—does not destroy the individuality of Stiva and Levin, because their individuality lies precisely in the different and unpredictable ways they embody universal laws. Coleridge said that "as in Homer all the deities are in armour, even Venus," so "in Shakespeare all the characters are strong." By "strong" he means what he elsewhere says about Lady Macbeth, that she is, "like all in Shakespeare, a class individualized." John Bayley, in his great book on Tolstoy, tells us that in the early plans of *War and Peace*, Count Rostov appeared merely as Count Prostoy: *prostoy* means, in Russian, "honest, simple." Is this the artist or the preacher at work? Both, surely: it is not that Tolstoy begins with an idea (in the sense of an abstraction), but that he begins with a truth, a large truth about Rostov.

In *Anna Karenina*, too, the characters are heirs to universal emotions, as Hamlet is. When Levin feels that the whole world must be aware of his love for Kitty, he feels something individually true, and also generally true about the solipsism of infatuation. One could imagine Stiva feeling the same thing, or even Vronsky. When Anna and Vronsky argue, and he says "experimenced" by mistake, and she wants to laugh, many readers will acknowledge a characteristic subtlety of Tolstoyan detail. But it would be hard to say that this tells us anything strongly individual about either Anna or Vronsky; it is more that our pleasure, in recognizing such a detail, is in recognizing its broad human applicability. Yes, we say to ourselves, that is what happens in arguments. We might say then that Tolstoy's characters have feelings that are peculiar to themselves but not *that* peculiar. Paradoxically, they differ from each other while sharing this universality, something suggested by the fact that nearly all the men in *Anna Karenina* are described by Tolstoy as "handsome": Vronsky, Levin, Stiva, but also Levin's old beekeeper, and Dolly's driver, and even Veslovsky, the unwelcome visitor. All these men share a kind of law of manliness, and so, in this, resemble each other. Similarly, two different babies—Levin's and Anna's—are pictured in exactly the same way, as having fat little wrists that look as if cord has been tied around them. This is surely not a slip on Tolstoy's part; he is merely repeating the universal essence of babyhood.

In most novels, we see characters search for themselves, or lose themselves, or build themselves. In Tolstoy, the difficulty is in being anything other than oneself. It is what Tolstoy meant when, in late life, he said: "As I was at five, so I am now." This may be why he has such an interest in those moments when his characters find themselves forced to play roles, or when the natural sounds artificial, sounds unlike itself: to Nikolai Rostov on the field of Austerlitz, the crying of the wounded sounds feigned. It is always moving in *Anna Karenina* when we see a character struggling with the essence that is surging though him. Once Anna has truly left him, Karenin is so miserable that, very uncharacteristically, he thinks of speaking about his sadness to his office manager. But even caught in this uncharacteristic gully, Karenin has been more characteristic than he can know. For, Tolstoy tells us, he has prepared in advance, like the good bureaucrat he is, an opening line: "He had already prepared the phrase: 'You have heard of my grief?' " It is so comically stiff that we almost weep with laughter for poor Karenin. Of course, he says nothing.

Reading *Anna Karenina* again, one is struck by the self-absorption of the novel's characters. Vronsky, we are told, "was not in the habit of noticing details." Once he has declared his love to Anna, at the little station where the Petersburg train stops during the night, he gets back into his carriage, and "he now seemed still more proud and self-sufficient. He looked at people as if they were things." Alexei Karenin finds it impossible to imagine what it is like to be Anna. He tries for a second, and abandons the attempt: "To put himself in thought and feeling into another being was a mental act alien to Alexei Alexandrovich." Even Dolly and Kitty, the sympathetic mothers, fail to see that Anna is not merely "pathetic" in her isolation—Kitty's slightly condescending word to Dolly when, very late in the book, Anna visits them—but opium-sodden and close to suicide.

There is a powerful tension between the "sloshy" shared world of the novel—Tolstoy's fat notation of textures, substances, atmospheres—and the selfish interiority of many of the characters, who live in their own worlds. Accordingly, the most affecting incidents occur when the world breaks in upon these fantasists—when, for example, Vronsky first sees Alexei Karenin, meeting Anna at the Petersburg station, and thinks, "Ah, yes, the husband!" Tolstoy adds: "Only now did Vronsky understand clearly for the first time that the husband was a person connected with her."

The paradox of the world of *Anna Karenina* is that it is a highly shared world (families who know each other, and so on), shared by solipsists. Anna, whose face is repeatedly described as "sympathetic," is the only character who is not solipsistic; and yet her sensitivity is a sick liberty, for she has no actual world on which to practice her understanding. Deprived of society, she begins to wither—indeed, she is made solipsistic by a solipsistic society that refuses to see her properly. Vronsky's habit of not noticing details proves to be fatal for her. Nothing is finer in the book than its last hundred pages, in which Tolstoy shows the creeping disintegration of Vronsky and Anna's relationship. Again and again, Anna struggles with her essence, which is freedom, irrepressibility. Every day Vronsky goes out into society to claim his freedom. But she cannot do that. Society forbids it. Jealous and resentful, she reflects, "He has all the rights and I have none." Every day she promises to herself that she will not voice her resentment when Vronsky returns, and every day she plays truant with that promise, unable not to be herself. As she falls under the wheels of the train, she has, in a way, finally merged with her essence. For we are told that this woman with a light step "fell on her hands under the carriage, and with a light movement, as if preparing to get up again at once, sank to her knees." Light in step when we met her, she is now light unto death.

Italo Svevo's Unreliable Comedy

✦

Here is a characteristic piece of comedy from *The Book of Scottish Anecdote* (seventh edition, 1888). A gentleman upbraids his servant: Is it true, he asks him, that you have had the audacity to be spreading around the idea that your master is stingy? No, no, replies the servant, you won't find me doing that kind of thing: "I aye *keep my thoughts to mysel'*."

A great deal of comedy revolves around logical contradiction, in which means turn tail on ends, rather as if a scorpion were able to sting itself by accident. Comic contradiction tends to reproduce itself at several levels of possibility at once, and that is the case here. If we assume that this joke turns on the idea that the servant does indeed think his master stingy, we can find at least two comic contradictions. First, the servant, thinking that he is absolving himself of the crime of talking disrespectfully about his master, fails to realize that he is simultaneously convicting himself of the equal crime of thinking disrespectfully about his master. And second, by replying thus to his master, the servant is not keeping his thoughts to himself but unwittingly sharing them.

Misunderstandings between people are funny, invariably because, beyond the immediate farce of human impasse, they suggest the great vanity of the self, which is furred, like any vain beauty, in the minks of egoism. In that Scottish anecdote, two sealed egoisms talk past each other: the master, thinking of himself, asks the servant if he has been tarnishing his reputation; the servant, also thinking of himself, merely replies with information about his own private mental processes. If this is part of why the anecdote raises a smile, comedy would seem to be functioning here at its moral, corrective level, illuminating blindnesses and stupidities on both sides, scuffing the shine of vanity and entrapping the diabolical self. This is the rather severe, Bergsonian idea of comedy as cleanser.

But comedy forgives too, of course, and encodes a compassion within itself. If the spectacle of the vanity of the self makes us laugh, it makes us cry by the same token, because we are saddened by the great illusions of freedom that the self hoards. The Scottish anecdote is too small to generate pathos, but it holds in potential the comic-pathetic idea of a man condemning himself while he thinks he is actually freeing himself. *Don Quixote* may be the grandest treatment of the comic illusion of freedom; part 1 of Cervantes's novel ends with Quixote beautifully defending the mission of knight-errantry: "I can say that ever since I became a knight-errant I have been courageous, polite, generous, well-bred, magnanimous, courteous, gentle, patient and long-suffering." This is not a wholly outrageous self-characterization. But the pain of the passage is that in order to have been some of these things (and he has hardly been gentle), Don Quixote has not been himself: he has been mad. Imagining himself free, he is literally and figuratively imprisoned: as he declaims on his virtues, he is being taken, for his own protection, in a caged cart back to his village by a kindly priest and barber.

The great modern novel of the comic-pathetic illusion of freedom is *Confessions of Zeno* (to give it its familiar English title), by Italo Svevo, which first appeared in 1923. Svevo's novel belongs recognizably to the comic tradition of *Don Quixote* and *The Good Sol-*

dier Svejk, a comedy defined by Schopenhauer (a great influence on Svevo) as residing in the incongruity between our concepts and objective reality. Both Quixote and Zeno are fantasists, the former antique, religious, and chivalric, the latter modern, secular, and bourgeois. Quixote wants to serve the world, to set it to rights, and fails in this task; Zeno wants only to serve himself, and largely succeeds, though not by trying. Quixote wills, and fails magnificently; Zeno waits, and succeeds farcically.

Confessions of Zeno moves between these poles of comedy, between moral correction and tragic pathos; between the bracing spectacle of vanity and the sad prospect of an imprisoned self acting as if it were free. This prospect is made more acute by the way Svevo writes his novel: it is told in the first person, by Zeno Cosini, a Trieste businessman now in his late fifties, who has been asked by his psychoanalyst to make an account of his early life. Zeno is a hypochondriacal, neurotic, delightful, solipsistic, self-examining, and self-serving bourgeois, a true blossom of the *mal du siècle*. The novel we are reading is supposed to constitute those memories, in which the middle-aged Zeno recalls his student days; his lamentable and very funny attempts to give up smoking (which he considers the key to his insomnia, his fevers, his muscle pains); his father's death (in which the old man raises his hand and collapses at the very same moment, thus accidentally striking Zeno on the cheek as he dies); his farcical attempt to marry one of the many Malfenti sisters (Zeno marries, of course, the very one he at first found ugliest); and his adventures in business (Zeno is a terrible businessman who accidentally does very well).

Zeno's narration is as fantastic as his mind, and he is therefore a highly unreliable narrator, just as Quixote would be were he telling his own tale. In most novels, unreliable narrators tend to become a little predictable, because they have to be reliably unreliable: the narrator's unreliability is manipulated by the author. Indeed, without the writer's reliability we would not be able to "read" the narrator's unreliability. It is certainly true that after a few pages we learn to discount Zeno's claims for himself; we learn to believe almost the opposite of what he tells us. This offers us, in part, the comic prospect of the patient "resisting" our accurate diagnosis: we, the readers, become Zeno's analysts. So the more Zeno tells us he is strong, the more weak he seems. The more he tells us that he will give up smoking, or his mistress, the less likely we are to trust him. The more he fixates on an organic cause for his many illnesses, the more we take him to be an obvious example of a *malade imaginaire*.

Unreliable narration is almost entrepreneurially efficient: once the novelist has set up his stall, he can syndicate his technique in chapter after chapter. When Zeno tells us that he has mixed feelings about his aged colleague Olivi, he says: "He has always worked for me, and he still does; but I don't really like him, for I always think he has prevented my doing the work he does himself." Though the novel is only seventeen pages old, we are fairly sure that this is untrue, that Zeno could never competently do the work he blames Olivi for denying him. Likewise, when Zeno tells us about his courtship of his wife-to-be, and the insane manner he goes about asking three of the four Malfenti sisters, Ada, Augusta, and Alberta, to marry him, we are so primed by the unreliability of his narration that we have by now learned how to read him. The first sister he meets, Augusta, he finds ugly: unlike Zeno, we *know* in advance that this is the woman he will eventually marry, because we have divined the comic principle of Zeno's life, whereby the outcome is almost always the opposite of the ambition.

But Zeno would be easy to read were he merely reliably unreliable: he would be a hypocrite and a fool. (He is in fact a hypocrite, but only fitfully.) Svevo wonderfully modifies the technique of unreliable narration, in two ways, and it is this that deepens the novel's comedy. First, Zeno is really trying to be truthful about himself, and sometimes he succeeds. He does envisage his memoirs as confessions of a kind. His description of the chaos of his courtship contains this accurate self-observation: "For all my efforts I achieved the result of that marksman who hit the bullseye, but of the target next to his." He tells us, in this passage, of how he tries to woo Ada, whom he selects for her beauty and her seriousness. "And so I set out to win Ada, and persisted in trying to make her laugh at me, forgetting that what I had first chosen her for was her seriousness. I am rather fantastic, it is true, but to her I must have seemed positively fantastic."

Secondly, Zeno imagines that by writing his memoirs he has been detachedly analyzing, and thereby curing, himself. One of the great jokes of Svevo's novel is that Zeno thinks he is psychoanalyzing himself while busily resisting formal psychoanalysis. It is as if Augustine had written his confessions while palpably not believing in Christ. Near the end of the book, Zeno's analyst, who has supposedly read the pages we have just read, tells Zeno that he has suffered from the Oedipus complex. Not true, Zeno says. He respected his mother and loved his father. Besides, "the surest proof that I never had the disease is that I've not been cured of it." This absurd defense is consistent with the novel's mode of comedy, which is rigorously founded on the idea of logical contradiction and inversion: the idea that life is a disease cured only by death (and certainly not by psychoanalysis); the idea that Zeno can only give up smoking (temporarily) while not thinking of giving up smoking. Or, most movingly and funnily, the idea of going to one's doctor to get a certificate of mental health. When his father tells him that he thinks his son is mad, Zeno triumphantly informs him that, on the contrary, he has a certificate from the doctor attesting to his sanity. To which Zeno's father replies, in a sad voice and with tears in his eyes, "Ah, then you truly are mad!"

So Zeno's unreliable narration is not like, say, Humbert Humbert's. Humbert proposes his self-justification; Zeno his self-comprehension. Most unreliable narrators imagine themselves to be right when they are actually wrong. But very few imagine themselves, as Zeno does, to be analyzing their wrongness from a position they imagine to be right but which is actually wrong! Svevo bends confession back on itself and makes his readers equitable sleuths, hungry for a moral and psychic justice which is just out of reach.

The entire novel must be read in the light of this comic paradox, whereby Zeno thinks he is analyzing himself while at the same time being mistakenly certain that psychoanalysis lacks the means to analyze him. But given this paradox, what are his confessions for? Why has Zeno really written them? It begins to seem that they have been written as Zeno's description of his own imagined freedom. Yet we, the readers, can see that the man who wrote them is still imprisoned. Zeno thinks that if he confesses to once harboring a murderous impulse toward his brother-in-law, then he has absolved himself of the charge that he truly hates his brother-in-law. But we can see that he always hated his brother-in-law, from beginning to end. Similarly, everyone has always found funny—brilliantly funny—Zeno's struggles, at the beginning of the novel, to give up smoking. He confesses that as a young man he spent his days endlessly making resolutions to give up smoking; as a student he had to change his lodgings and have the walls of his room repapered at his own expense because he had covered them with the dates of his "last cigarettes." Last cigarettes have a taste all their own, he says. "The others have their importance because, in lighting them, you are proclaiming your freedom, while the future of strength and health remains, only moving off a bit." But what is moving is not just that Zeno, as we suspect, will never give up smoking but his earnest belief that giving it up would have anything to do with his physical and mental well-being, and anything at all to do with "freedom." Zeno continually assumes that he can control the terms of his freedom—which we can see are merely the terms of his imprisonment.

The man who wrote this marvelous and original book was born Ettore Schmitz, in Trieste, in 1861. His nom de plume, Italo Svevo, or Italus the Swabian, was adopted as a way of acknowledging his mixed heritage: Italian by language (Triestine dialect was spoken at home), Austrian by citizenship (Trieste was a city of the Austro-Hungarian Empire), and German (in fact, German Jewish) by ancestry. The family was large and prosperous: there were sixteen children, of whom eight survived. Whenever a new child was born, his businessman father, Francesco Schmitz, would exclaim, "Today my capital has been increased by a million!" But Francesco's capital was soon indeed figurative: he suffered a massive loss in 1880, and in that same year the dreamy and artistically ambitious Ettore was forced, for the family's sake, to take a job in the correspondence department of the Trieste branch of the Union Bank of Vienna. He stayed eighteen years, until rescued by his wife's family firm, manufacturers of anticorrosive marine paint.

In her delightful memoir of their life together, Svevo's wife, Livia Veneziani Svevo, recalls a man who sounds not unlike Zeno Cosini. Svevo was large-headed, deep-browed (he went bald early), dark, with kindly, protruding eyes. He was charming, insomniac, and neurotic, prey to psychosomatic twinges and spasms. During their courtship, so Livia says, Svevo anxiously warned her: "Remember that a single ill-chosen word would be the end of everything." Like Zeno, he was an incessant smoker, and spent his days in a cloud of "last cigarettes" and collapsing resolutions. Numerologically superstitious, he often decided to smoke his last cigarette at seven minutes past four, the time at which his mother had died. "Perhaps by smoking," Livia writes, "he tried to quieten the 'frogs,' which was what he called the insistent doubts that tormented him." Zeno is teased for his absent-mindedness by his competitor and future brother-in-law, Guido Speier; by his wife's account, Svevo was astoundingly absent-minded, quite capable of putting on two sets of cuff links and not noticing until the strange weight at his wrists alerted him. She tells a story in which her husband left the house with 150 lire to buy something needed at the Veneziani factory and returned hours later without the object, but with a box of sweets and 160 lire in his wallet.

Svevo's temperament has affinities with Chekhov's: a gentle voyeurism which perhaps masked an intense sensitivity to human and animal suffering; an unwillingness to act or think like an "intellectual," combined with an aversion to the high-flown, the poetic: "Why so many words for such few ideas?" was Svevo's view of poetry; a hostility to religion; and an eye for the subtly comic. He was devoted to *Witze*, to witty paradoxes and contradictions. When Joyce once told him reprovingly that he never used coarse language but only wrote it, Svevo was amused and commented: "It would appear then that his works are not ones that could be read in his own presence." *Confessions of Zeno* is full of such *Witze*, large and small: Zeno's mistress is pursuing a singing career despite her terrible voice; Zeno lectures Guido on playing the violin despite his own thin talents; there is the concept of the last cigarette and the certificate of sanity. The *Witz* can be found even in something as small as Zeno's description of his baldness (one of my favorite details): "A great part of my own head had been usurped by my forehead." The most celebrated *Witz* occurred as Svevo lay on his deathbed. Seeing his nephew smoking, he feebly asked for a cigarette, was refused, and then murmured, "Now that really would have been the last cigarette."

Svevo's hostility to the perceived lack of ideas in poetry is significant, because he is one of the most thoroughly philosophical of modern novelists. He could recite many passages of Schopenhauer from memory. Clearly the idea, central to *Confessions of Zeno*, of life as a sickness is indebted to Schopenhauer (to whom Freud in turn admitted his debts); but Svevo, I suspect, was also enthralled by the jaunty, grave, paradoxical wit of Schopenhauer, the philosopher who, for example, writes in *The World as Will and Representation* that walking is just a constantly prevented falling, just as the life of our body is a constantly prevented dying. Schopenhauer, who kept poodles, liked to say that he abused his dog with the epithet "man" only when it was especially badly behaved; Svevo, who loved cats and dogs, wrote animal fables all his life, the gist of which was that animals can never fathom the mysterious wickedness of humans.

Svevo's first two novels, *Una vita* and *Senilità*, are much more conventional than *Confessions of Zeno* (which was written twenty-five years after *Senilità*). Obviously "naturalistic" where *Zeno* is obviously modernist, they both concern men who get involved in unsuitable relationships with women. These heroes, Alfonso Nitti in *Una vita* and Emilio Brentano in *Senilità*, are ruined by their relationships in ways they do not really understand. They somewhat resemble Frédéric Moreau, the hero of *A Sentimental Education*, in their self-deluding capacity to dignify the helpless drift of their lives by thinking of themselves as purposeful and free. But Frédéric, who is essentially unintrospective, is somewhat empty; he is waiting to be filled by romance and history, and indeed by the romance of history. By contrast, Alfonso and Emilio fill themselves only with neurotic introspection. Like Zeno, they are obsessive self-brokers, continually doing smoky deals with their consciences, whereby they can convince themselves that they have done good when they have really done harm. Like Zeno, they have a nasty tendency to feel calm at precisely the moment they ought to be feeling concerned. In Svevo's first two novels, this tendency is not obviously comic; in *Zeno* it is as comic as it is pathetic. Near the end of *Senilità*, Emilio has to watch his sister die. He is largely oblivious to the fact that he has caused her decline, and in fact excuses himself from her deathbed to have a final meeting with his mistress at the quayside. At the water's edge, it is stormy, but "it seemed to Emilio that this turmoil reflected his own. This gave him an even greater sense of calm." He watches the fishermen, and reflects

that the inertia of his destiny was the cause of his misfortune. If, just once in his life, it had been his duty to untie or retie a rope; if the fate of a fishing boat, however small, had been entrusted to him, to his care, his energy; if he had been obliged to prevail over the howl-

ing of the wind and the sea with his own voice, he should be less
weak, less unhappy.

Emilio's strategy, of weakly wishing that destiny had made him
strong, is typical of the *senilità*, the early senility or moral feebleness,
that binds all of Svevo's heroes. In an excellent introduction to Beth
Archer Brombert's translation of *Senilità* (now given Svevo's first title, *Emilio's Carnival*), her husband Victor Brombert defines that imprisonment as "a special sensibility (some people are indeed born
old); or better still, a special kind of inertia, the inertia of the
dreamer, a modern version of acedia, or ironic ennui."

Una vita was published in 1892, and was wanly noticed; *Senilità*,
published in 1898, was born into oblivion. Trieste, a mixed and marginal city, was not considered by the Italian literary world a likely
mother of literary greatness; and Svevo's Italian, a curious, prosaic,
sometimes clumsy businessman's language, was faulted where it was
noticed at all. Trieste did not consider itself an artistic place either,
and Svevo, who was regarded by most locals as an industrialist rather
than a writer, reckoned that he gave away most of the copies of
Senilità (which, like all his books, he published at his own expense
anyway). Deeply hurt by his reception, by the impounding of his
deepest ambitions, Svevo essentially garaged his writing for twenty
years. "Write one must; what one needn't do is publish," he was fond
of saying. By 1902 he was writing that "the ridiculous, damnable
thing called literature has now been quite definitely cut out of my
life." He took up the violin (never playing very well, though possibly
better than Zeno), and said that it "saved him from literature."

Over these years, he assumed greater responsibility at the
Veneziani firm, overseeing the building of a factory in southeast
London, in Charlton. From 1903 until the outbreak of war, Svevo
spent a month or two every year in a rented house in Charlton—one
of those comic but actual dissymmetries that rival Schopenhauer in
Wimbledon and Kropotkin in Brighton. Typically, he made no at-

tempt to befriend writers or intellectuals in London—and besides, his English was poor—preferring the inky, subaltern routines of "mournful / Ever weeping" Charlton: the Sunday papers, library books, bottled beer, and a place in a local string quartet.

It was Svevo's poor English which brought him his friendship with Joyce, who had arrived in Trieste in 1904, as an English teacher for the Berlitz School. Joyce was working as a private tutor when Svevo contacted him in 1907. Joyce, who spoke Triestine dialect at home, was an unorthodox teacher of English; he once asked Svevo, as an English exercise, to write a review of the first chapters of *A Portrait of the Artist as a Young Man*. Svevo was initially secretive about his two ignored novels, but eventually admitted to having been a writer himself, and gave his teacher his books. Joyce, in a famous tale, returned from his reading of *Senilità* proclaiming Svevo a fine novelist, the equal in places of Anatole France, and claiming that he could recite by heart the novel's last pages.

Svevo and Joyce kept only a flickering friendship alive after Joyce's departure from Trieste at the outbreak of war. But he would call upon that friendship in 1923, after *Confessions of Zeno* had been published to the now familiar roaring silence. Svevo wrote to Joyce asking if he might be able to do something on behalf of *Zeno*. Joyce suggested, in France, Valéry Larbaud and Benjamin Crémieux, men of letters with an interest in Italian writing. Svevo duly sent copies to them, and Joyce busied himself in the kind of high-cultural bustle that he was now very good at. Thanks to Joyce, it was French literary culture that first took Svevo's greatest novel seriously ("Italy's Proust" was the warming if largely inaccurate refrain), followed by a blushing Italian literary world. Beryl de Zoete's translation into English appeared in 1930, and was the only standard version for seventy years, until the distinguished American translator William Weaver arrived with an excellent new rendering.

Weaver retitled the book *Zeno's Conscience*, returning some of the meaning to the Italian *La coscienza di Zeno*, which can mean both Zeno's consciousness and his conscience. Weaver says that the old compromise word, "confessions," not only confusingly flutters the laurels of Augustine and Rousseau but has an inappropriately Catholic resonance. On rereading Sevo's novel, I am not sure, however, that a religious resonance should be avoided. Because Svevo is well known to have disliked organized religion, and because his novel is framed by the procedures of psychoanalysis, *Confessions of Zeno* is generally only read in a secular light: here is the great comic document of modern stasis and neurotic introspection. Yet Svevo's antireligiousness, like that of Schopenhauer and Hamsun, is marked by what it has rejected. Svevo represents, in a way, the logical fusion of Augustine's religiously pessimistic view of life—"We must conclude that the whole human race is being punished," writes the miserable Augustine—and Schopenhauer's atheistically pessimistic view of life. Svevo's wife repeatedly described him as a melancholy man, sensitive to life's brevity and pain. He saw quite a lot of it: his brother Elio died in 1886, at the age of twenty-three, from nephritis; his sister Noemi died in childbirth; another sister, Ortensia, died of peritonitis; yet another sister, Natalia, gave birth to two deaf children; and in 1918, just before he started writing *Zeno*, his brother-in-law Alfonso died of heart disease. All these many misfortunes, writes Livia, "had helped to make Ettore pessimistic, almost resigned to the harshest blows of fate. He always expected the worst, and was prepared to meet suffering at any moment, almost as if in the deepest part of his being he had foreseen the appalling suffering the Second World War was to bring his beloved daughter." (Svevo's daughter lost all three of her sons during the course of the Second World War; Svevo's house was bombed.)

At one point in the novel, Zeno tries to impress Ada by letting her know how much he has grieved over his father's death. He goes on to suggest that if he had children he would try to make them love him less, so as to spare them suffering at his passing. Alberta wittily says, "The surest method would be to kill them"—an excellent Svevian *Witz*. Ada then says that she thinks it wrong to spend one's life only in preparation for death, to which Zeno forcefully replies: "I held my ground and asserted that death was the true organizer of life. I thought always of death, and therefore I had only one sorrow: the certainty of having to die."

Living only in preparation for death; but not wanting to die. What is this but an essentially religious vision, without the consolation of religion? Again and again, Svevo returns us first of all to the pure death-diligence of the ancients (and Zeno's name alone should do that), and then to the great medieval and Renaissance philosophers and writers. His novel reverberates with a grave wit, not unlike that of Sir Thomas Browne, who wrote that "the long habit of living indisposeth us for dying," and close in some ways to the seventeenth-century divine Jeremy Taylor, who tells us in *Holy Living* that balding is merely man's early preparation for death. Svevo would have loved that.

When Joyce returned to Trieste from Zurich in 1919, Svevo asked him about his experience of psychoanalysis. Joyce apparently replied: "Psychoanalysis? Well, if we need it, let us stick to confession." Svevo was apparently dumbfounded by Joyce's response. But perhaps he was stimulated by it, for the novel he would go on to write expresses a rather similar sentiment. Renato Poggioli once wrote that in *Zeno* Svevo psychoanalyzes psychoanalysis itself. But one might equally say that he forces it to confess itself. The idea of life as a disease, after all, is the logical conclusion of psychoanalysis's famous difficulty with how and when to end a patient's treatment; if the patient's sessions have to continue for years and years, for as long as life itself, then life is indeed a long sickness. This might be seen as the unwanted religious or metaphysical implication of psychoanalysis's resistance to religion, its determination to be a therapy rather than a faith. In that sense, *Zeno* does not merely psychoanalyze psychoanalysis but sees it as another religion, and hence merely a modern fraudulence.

Repeatedly Zeno finds himself exaggerating and parodying religious attitudes. He craves and defiles "innocence," a word that recurs throughout the book. He briefly manages to stop smoking for several hours, but "my mouth was cleansed and I felt an innocent taste such as a newborn infant must know, and a desire for a cigarette came over me." He longs to tell his father, who has just died, that he is "innocent," that it wasn't he who killed him. One night he feels "innocent" because he comes home earlier than normal from his mistress to his wife: "I felt very innocent in not having been unfaithful to the extent of staying away from home all night." He parodies the religious process of confession and expiation: he confesses to his wife that he had not been feeling love for his baby daughter, and instantly feels better: "I fell asleep again with a quiet conscience . . . in fact I was now completely free."

Read in this light, *Confessions of Zeno* is a darker book than it has sometimes seemed. P. N. Furbank, who has written so intelligently about Svevo, suggests that Joyce and Svevo "not only celebrated the bourgeois as hero, they cheerfully identified themselves with him." But Svevo, a writer in a businessman's suit for so many years, was in some ways not a cheerful bourgeois, and Zeno enacts a hypocritical parody of the bourgeois life, chiefly the hypocrisy of religious ailments and cleansings. Zeno's clearest fictional allies are the heroes of Knut Hamsun, who deliberately pervert religious categories of sin and punishment in an attempt to seize a control they can never possess. Hamsun is the wilder writer, for his demented characters actually invent the very sins which they feel they need to be punished for; they invent their corruption. Zeno's sins are real enough; it is his innocence that he invents, his innocence that is his fond fantasy. Hamsun, the atheist former Lutheran, is obsessed with sin; Svevo, the atheist Jew who converted to nominal Catholicism only in order to marry his wife, is consumed by confession.

Svevo had four brief years of fame as the great new Italian novelist, the creator of Zeno Cosini. He called this time "the miracle of

Lazarus." He died in 1928, after a car accident. On his deathbed, he was asked if he wanted to pray. "When you haven't prayed all your life, there's no point at the last minute." Gloriously and impressively, at the last moment of his life, Italo Svevo was not like Zeno Cosini at all.

Giovanni Verga's Comic Sympathy

❦

A Sicilian peasant is dying of malaria, and trembling on his bed "like leaves in November." His neighbors visit him, and while they stand around in his house "warming their hands at the fire," they fatalistically conclude that there's no hope, because "it's the kind of malaria that kills you quicker than a shot from a gun." As the man dies, he says to his son, Jeli: "When I'm dead, go to the man who owns the cows at Ragoleti, and get him to hand over the three *onze* and twelve sacks of grain owing to me from May up to the present." But Jeli corrects him: "No, it's only two and a quarter, because you left the cows over a month ago, and you mustn't steal from the hand that feeds you." "That's true!" agrees his father, and promptly dies.

This is a scene from "Jeli the Shepherd," a story by the Sicilian writer Giovanni Verga (1840–1922), who is not read much in English, and often only dutifully in Italy, where he has the cloudy venerability of the palpably canonical. In English, he is known, perhaps, for "Cavalleria rusticana," a tale which became a play and then an opera, about a young soldier who fights a duel with the man who stole the girl he had chosen, and is killed. But it is not one of his greatest stories, and can give the impression that Verga was merely a Daudet-like painter of authentic "scenes from Sicilian life."

This neglect of Verga is strange. D. H. Lawrence, who lived for a while in Sicily, discovered Verga's work with great excitement and translated him in the 1920s. He rightly called "Jeli the Shepherd" and another story, "Rosso Malpelo," two of the greatest ever written. At his best, Verga is quite the equal of Chekhov—his equal in the fiercely unsentimental depiction of ordinary rural life, in the coaxing of opaque inner lives, and most of all in his self-smothering ability to see life not as a writer might see it, but entirely from within the minds of his mostly uneducated characters. More than Chekhov indeed, who was always an intellectual, if an uncannily bashful one, Verga writes from within a community—that is, Sicilian peasants in villages, during the 1860s and 1870s. In English, his only obvious counterparts are Hardy and Lawrence, except that Verga is not interested in intellectuals or outsiders; his priests, for instance, are essentially indistinguishable from his peasants—they are as lean in spirit as everyone else in town; they are merely less poor.

In Italian, by contrast, Verga's influence has been immense: his fellow Sicilian Pirandello learned from him how to write stories that seem to emanate from his characters; Visconti based his film *La terra trema*, in which the parts are played not by actors but by Sicilian villagers, on Verga's novel *The House by the Medlar Tree* (*I Malavoglia*); Pavese's beautiful novel *The Moon and the Bonfire* has a Verga-like commitment to the patient comprehension of ordinary rural life; even Pasolini's film *The Gospel According to Saint Matthew*, which again uses nonactors, employs Verga's *verismo* to give the effect of Jesus ministering in a peasant region.

Yet all this makes Verga sound merely respectable, a necessary origin. He is much more exciting than that: I recall first reading "Jeli the Shepherd," led there by Lawrence's enthusiasm, and sitting stiff in my chair with concentrated delight. Here was something new to me, writing that was very direct and simple yet highly refined. One element of that refinement is that Verga is all detail. Because he presents these details without comment, they become enigmas for the reader, hard puzzles. For instance, the passage quoted above, about

Jeli's father, is breezily written, in Verga's usual rapid style of bitter comedy, but is actually dense. The dying man's friends seem to visit in order to console him, but it is characteristic of Verga to show them as only fatalistic, while greedily "warming their hands at the fire": in Verga's world of rural poverty, survival is the first and often the only motive; generosity is a toy. His humans are no different from animals in this respect, and indeed Verga has already described how Jeli's horses would cluster around the bonfire in winter and warm their tails.

And survival is what drives the morbid comedy of the final exchange between father and son. The father, thinking of the son, reminds him to collect a debt once he has died, and Jeli, utterly frustrating our expectations of either life or conventional fiction (we expect something like: "Shush, Father, all that will be taken care of"), sternly reminds him that the debt is smaller than he thought, "because you left the cows over a month ago, and you mustn't steal from the hand that feeds you." It is shocking that Jeli would rebuke his father at this moment, and it is of course comically absurd that a dying man would need advice about not stealing from the hand that feeds him when in a moment he will not need to be fed by anyone anyway. Yet Jeli is thinking of himself: *he* will need to be fed by one hand or another after his father has died; he is only a poor shepherd boy. And so his father, who surely know this, meekly agrees, says, "That's true!"—incidentally, a beautiful placing of the exclamation point, suggesting a final fervency before death, a fervency all the more affecting because it is about an apparent banality—and dies. These are the elements that make this scene, which lasts only fifty or so words, so moving. What seems to be a fleeting triviality is actually very important—this is both Verga's subject and his mode of writing: his banalities, like those of his characters, are never unimportant.

Verga's world is a cruel one. Sicily, at the end of the nineteenth century, was probably the poorest place in Europe. Verga's shepherds and fishermen are largely illiterate—in *The House by the Medlar*

Tree, a mother gets a letter from her son, who is away with the navy, and the writing looks to her "like a mess of fishhooks." These people are without much mercy for each other. And because the stories are narrated as if by a member of this community, the stories themselves at first glance seem to be without much mercy for their protagonists. Sometimes it seems that in this world humans are treated by the author in much the same way that those humans treat their animals, with only a rough sympathy and a tender cruelty. In *The House by the Medlar Tree*, 'Ntoni, a young man, leaves his small village to earn his fortune in the city. He fails, and returns empty-handed, and is so ashamed that he cannot go out for eight days. When he does, how do the villagers respond? "As soon as they saw him," writes Verga, "they all laughed in his face." This is presented without comment, not merely as a fact of life but almost as if it were good and right.

The end of "Jeli the Shepherd" is even more bitter. Jeli is told by a boy who looks after the sheep with him what the reader already knows: that Jeli's wife is having an affair with a gentleman, Don Alfonso. (Jeli and Don Alfonso, despite their difference in rank, were childhood friends.) But the boy does not break this news to Jeli gently; in fact, it seems that he has been envious of Jeli, thinks that Jeli has been putting on airs, and thus suddenly, during an argument "over certain bits of cheese that were missing," he blurts out: "Now that Don Alfonso has taken your wife, you treat him like a brother-in-law, and you walk around with your nose in the air like a crowned prince, with those horns on your head." In his envy, the boy turns the usual symbol for the cuckold—the horns—into a crown! But Jeli, who is a simple soul, cannot believe the news. Not because he thinks his wife is above suspicion, but because he doesn't really know what a cuckold is, and as Verga beautifully and simply remarks: "It was difficult for him to grasp anything that was unusual."

But of course, readers crave sympathetic identification with characters, and Verga knows this. Indeed, he knows that the more brutally he deprives us of sympathy, the more we long to apply it. In

fact, Verga knowingly uses the cruelty of his Sicilian world to provoke the reader's sympathy. He planned a series of five novels, of
which *The House by the Medlar Tree* was the first, with the general
title *I vinti*, or The Defeated. We are supposed to feel sorry for poor
Jeli when the boy tells him about his wife, or for poor 'Ntoni when
the villagers laugh at his misfortune, and Verga surreptitiously
prompts us to feel this way, by inserting into his narration his usual
epithets, "poor wretch" or "poor fellow." Thus when the neighbors
come to visit Jeli's father on his sickbed, Verga writes: "All the poor
wretch could do by way of reply was to yelp like a puppy taking suck
from its mother." This again carries a sense of rough, hasty sympathy,
as if the community were pausing for a moment to confer feeling before fatalistically closing the book on the particular case.

Verga's use of this narration-as-if-by-the-community is extraordinarily subtle, because readers, faced with such pitiless judgment,
tend to work against the narration, against the community, in order
to extract the pathos we require. Thus Verga's fiction is peculiar because his characters are not free—they are all *i vinti*, and the narrator
knows it—but his readers are free to resist such determinism, and are
indeed slyly encouraged to do so by Verga's very narration. This is
the inverse of what usually happens when a novelist appears to write
with the weight of the community behind him. Roland Barthes
called the traditional style of omniscient narration the "reference
code," meaning those moments when a writer appeals to something
consensual that everyone knows. Tolstoy uses it with great simplicity
and force, for instance. In *The Death of Ivan Ilyich*, he describes a
group of men who are discussing the recent news of Ivan's death.
Tolstoy remarks that "as is usual in such cases," each man was thinking that he was glad that it was Ivan Ilyich who was dead and not
him. In such an instance, we are encouraged to agree with Tolstoy
about this universal fact of life.

But Verga uses the "reference code" to effect almost the opposite,
almost disagreement. To begin with, unlike Tolstoy, he never leaves

the voice of his community, so that every judgment about the characters, and every truism, comes not from the writer Giovanni Verga (as, say, there are moments when it's clear that the writer Leo Tolstoy is addressing us) but from a little village a few miles from Catania: a limited community, limited in intelligence, and often limited in kindness. And secondly, the truths and universal facts we are asked to agree with are so cruel, and so brutally stated, that the reader is forced to rise up against them. For example, in *The House by the Medlar Tree*, a fisherman, Bastianazzo, dies at sea. Verga writes of Bastianazzo's family that "all the others began crying again, and the children, seeing the grown-ups cry, began to cry too, although their papa had been dead for three days." Though this novel does not formally have a narrator—it is formally third-person omniscient—we have to imagine the book as if narrated by a rather cruel fishwife; and it is clear, when we examine that strange sentence, that the fishwife is implying that Bastianazzo's children are being a bit soft for crying. That word "although" is the key: after all, runs the narrator's implication, they've already had three whole days to get over it! The reader, who naturally thinks three days is not very long for children's grief, resists Verga's cruelty of implication, and sympathizes with the children, against, as it were, the writer.

This way of storytelling is also a marvelous vessel for comedy, because it allows a whole community unwittingly to reveal its foolishness and superstition. In the same novel, Verga is describing the local sexton, who is not a popular figure because "he was always ringing the Angelus bell when he had nothing else to do, and for the Mass he bought the kind of wine the crucified Christ drank on the cross, which was a real sacrilege." Again, we are made to feel that it is not Verga who is writing this novel, but an old gossip from the village. And a foolish one, too, both censorious and witless at the same time, one who thinks that "the kind of wine the crucified Christ drank on the cross" is available in the local shop.

Giovanni Verga was a patrician, and he didn't always write like this. He was born in Catania, in 1840, into a landowning family. At school, a patriotic teacher inspired him to write fiery and romantic works, and his early novels, so-called *romanzi giovanili*, were popular and sentimental, influenced by the most vivid storytellers of the day, Dumas, Hugo, Scott, Sue, Feuillet. One scholar, Giovanni Cecchetti, has described one of these novels, *Una peccatrice* (1866), as "repetitious and overextended, and it seems to have been written in a state of sexual delirium." These were stories of ambitious young gentlemen who fall in love with glamorous ladies; there are duels, suicides, ecstatic letters, and many feverish deaths. By the late 1860s Verga was well established in Florence, and famous. Verga's earlier work continued to be popular well into the twentieth century, and more popular than his later fiction about Sicilian peasants.

But despite his fashionability, Verga began to return frequently to Sicily during the 1870s. His sister died in 1878, and he spent two years in his native town. Out of this time came his stories of rural life, *Vita dei campi* (*Life in the Fields*, 1880), which contained "Jeli the Shepherd" and "Rosso Malpelo," and a year later his great novel, *The House by the Medlar Tree*, called *I Malavoglia* because it traces the terrible downfall of one family, the Malavoglia, through three generations. It would be hard, without knowledge, to find Verga the author of both the early and the later work; they are like different seasons of existence. It is correspondingly difficult to know why and how Verga developed into the writer who has lasted: it is as if Flaubert had first written like Dumas before going on to produce *A Simple Heart*. Scholars mention the influence of Verga's fellow Sicilian Luigi Capuana, who was excitedly exploring folk stories and the oral tradition. Verga may well have read Flaubert, indeed; certainly he read Zola (whom he later met), and began to fashion his own kind of naturalism, which was known as *verismo*.

Verga did not think that fiction had to be "scientific" or present sociological case studies, but he did come to believe that fiction's duty was to comb life with the finest teeth, and that the writer should abscond from his fiction, in aid of "objectivity." In one of the stories in *Vita dei campi*, "Gramigna's Mistress," he writes a kind of manifesto: "At the present day we are renewing the artistic process . . . using a different method, more precise and more intimate. We gladly sacrifice the narrative's climax and its psychological effect . . ." Verga hoped that "the hand of the artist will remain completely invisible," and that when this happens, "the work of art will seem to have created itself, to have grown spontaneously and come to fruition as though it were a part of nature."

The subject of this new kind of fiction was rural life in Sicily; the mode of narration was as if the story were told by a peasant. This meant that everything had to be seen as if through the eyes of one of the protagonists. Thus there is very little of that nineteenth-century familiarity, nature description, in Verga's work. The landscape is taken for granted, or written about in homely similes. At almost the same time, Chekhov was becoming a master at this: in one story, a bittern crying sounds as if a cow has been locked up in a shed all night, and is lowing; an accordion heard in a poor village is brilliantly described by Chekhov as "an expensive-sounding accordion." Like Chekhov's, Verga's similes are plausibly "unliterary" while never being flat or ordinary. In *The House by the Medlar Tree*, the sea in turbulence is described thus: "The boat leaped over the waves like a mullet in love . . . [W]hen the weather was bad or the nor'wester blew, all day long the corks danced on the water as though somebody were playing the violin for them." Verga also studs his fiction with proverbial sayings, sometimes spoken by his characters and sometimes woven invisibly into the narration, as part of the "reference code": "Some people carry their conscience on their backs, so they can't see it." "Saint Joseph shaved himself first and then the others." (This might be taken as an epitaph for the whole ideology of survival in Verga's world.) "Uncle Crocifisso was in just the right mood to discuss that business, which never seemed to end, because, as they say, 'long things turn into snakes.'" "Marriages and bishops are made in heaven."

Heeding every illogicality and non sequitur of his characters, with such sensitivity and care, produces a world of great vitality and sad comedy, whose limits are always apparent to the reader. Often the effects are breathtaking—there is no other word for it. There is a moment when Jeli, who is of course illiterate, gets a friend to write the name of his sweetheart on a piece a paper, which he carries around like an amulet. Jeli reflects on this great mystery of writing: "Anyone who knows how to write is like a person who stores his words in a steel safe, and who could carry them around in his pocket, and even send them wherever he wants." There are very few writers in the whole of literature (Shakespeare is obviously one; Bottom comes to mind) who can write as humanely as that. Elsewhere one encounters a man "so happy that he could scarcely fit into his shirt." Or a marvelous scene in *The House by the Medlar Tree* when a crowd is discussing the news of the battle of Lissa, at which Italy was defeated by Austria:

> "It's all a lot of talk, just to sell newspapers."
> "But everybody says we've lost!"
> "Lost what?" said Uncle Crocifisso, cupping his hand behind his ear.
> "A battle."
> "Who lost it?"
> "I, you, in short, everybody, Italy," the pharmacist said.
> "I haven't lost a thing!" Uncle Crocifisso answered, shrugging.

But the Malavoglia family have lost something: Luca, a son and grandson, who was on one of the defeated ships; and in a typical modulation, Verga follows this scene of piazza comedy with a melancholy report of how the family wait to hear the news, hear nothing for weeks, and finally, fearing the worst, travel to Catania to make further inquiries. At the port, they are tartly treated. A navy official runs through a book of the dead, finds Luca's name, and simply says: "It's been more than forty days . . . It happened at Lissa. Didn't you know yet?"

Writing from within the community also meant finding a new,

loose kind of Italian that can seem scrappy and unfinished precisely because it is not "literary." But Verga does not use Sicilian dialect; instead he rearranges standard Italian, shuffles the syntax, imports proverbs and similes, so that it might plausibly have been used by his characters were they speaking standard Italian. Visconti's film *La terra trema* vandalizes Verga's subtle technique by employing a voice-over which tells us, in standard Italian, that Sicilians use dialect. This voice-over then proceeds to lecture us about the radical political dimensions of the material, turning the pessimistic, rather unideological Verga into a proto-Marxist. We are told that the wholesalers cheat and exploit the fishermen: "The old men," goes the voice, "accept the situation: 'The poor always pay.' But the young men have their eyes wide open." This destroys in one stroke Verga's subtle evasion of just this kind of omniscient authority.

Nowhere is Verga's narrative power better evidenced than in the heartbreaking tale "Rosso Malpelo." It is one of those stories which, once encountered, you want to read out loud to someone. It concerns the short, miserable life of Rosso Malpelo, a troubled boy, a red-haired little monster who works in a Sicilian sand mine. The boy is known as Malpelo, which means "evil-haired," because of the popular idea that red hair is from the devil, and spells trouble. The story is told as if narrated by one of Malpelo's coworkers, all of whom fear and despise poor Malpelo. That is to say, the story is told without any apparent sympathy. In fact, it overflows with surreptitious sympathy; it represents Verga's greatest achievement at the generation of comic pathos out of comic cruelty.

This very grim story begins with a non sequitur, whereby the community, as it were, tells us what it thinks of Malpelo. This is the opening line: "He was called Malpelo because he had red hair, and he had red hair because he was a mischievous rascal who promised to turn out a real knave." He had red hair *because* he was evil: in a sense the entire story turns on this non sequitur, since the story is premised, in some extraordinary way, on *not* knowing Malpelo, on not even attempting to understand him. As far as the story is concerned, to know Malpelo is to blame him, and that is the end of it: Verga writes that the miners beat Malpelo "even when he was not to blame, on the grounds that if Malpelo was not responsible, he was quite capable of having done it." And Malpelo accepts this regime of the non sequitur. When he is beaten for a crime he did not commit, he never denies it, but merely shrugs and says: "What's the use? I'm *malpelo*."

Certainly Malpelo is nasty. He is an abused abuser. His father died in the mine, smothered by sand, and his mother shrinks from her son. The narrator adds that "his own mother had never known him to embrace her, so that she had never done the same to him either," a terrifying line, given out with all of Verga's usual brusque simplicity. But this is also the very principle of the story's narration, which effectively insists on the unembraceability of Malpelo, so that the reader desires to embrace him instead. It is as if the narrator were saying: "Since Malpelo has never embraced us, we won't embrace him. He's not knowable or lovable. He's just bad, and that's the story we'll tell." The only thing Malpelo understands is force. He beats the poor mule who works underground, muttering as he does so: "That'll kill you off more quickly." In some way, Malpelo wants to be dead, and wants everyone else to be dead, too. When a new boy arrives at the mine, Malpelo takes him under his wing and begins to tutor him in the ways of cruelty. He tells him: "The mule gets beaten because it can't fight back, and if it could, it would trample us under its feet and steal the food out of our mouths." When the mule eventually dies, Malpelo comments: "It would have been better for him if he'd never been born at all."

The new boy at the mine is cruelly nicknamed "The Frog," because he once fell off some scaffolding and dislocated his leg: "When he was carrying his basket of sand on his back, the poor wretch would hop along as if he was dancing the tarantella, and all the mineworkers laughed at him and called him The Frog." As elsewhere in his work, Verga here flourishes a cruelty, told entirely from within the terms and values of the mine community, but prompts us to defy the cruel laughter of the men—and therefore the laughter of Verga's own narration—with that epithet "poor wretch." And Verga means us to do likewise with Malpelo. Malpelo is a poor wretch too, even if no one will acknowledge it. The most blatant example occurs when Verga writes about how Rosso lovingly looked after the shoes of his dead father: "He carefully hung the shoes on the same nail where he kept his pallet, and on Sundays he would take them down, polish them and try them on. Then he would place them on the floor, one beside the other, and stare at them for hours on end with his elbows on his knees and his chin resting in the palms of his hands, and it was anybody's guess what ideas were running through that calculating little head of his." Of course, we are being prompted by the story to resist this cruelty; we strongly suspect that although Rosso may be a monster, he is looking at those shoes and simply grieving for his father.

In the story's most awful series of scenes, The Frog, whose health is poor, is taken ill. Malpelo thinks The Frog a sissy, and boasts of his own strength. He tries to force some health into The Frog by hitting him, but he hits him so hard that The Frog begins to cough blood. Malpelo is alarmed: "He swore that he could not have done him any great harm by hitting him as he did, and just to prove it he beat himself severely about the chest and the back with a large stone."

But The Frog is seriously ill, and is taken to his bed, where he wheezes for breath and begins to wither away. Malpelo visits the boy, and sits staring at him "with those huge eyes of his bulging out of his forehead, as though he was going to paint his portrait" (what a sublime simile). Malpelo is bewildered by the boy's failing health, and thinks he is being self-indulgent. He can't understand why The Frog's mother is weeping so much, and asks The Frog why his mother is making such a fuss "when for two months he had been earning less than it cost to feed him." After all, Malpelo's mother has never once embraced *him*. "But The Frog paid no attention to him, and simply seemed intent on lying there in bed."

I remember first reading that last sentence, and then slowly, almost frightenedly returning to it, and reading it once again: "But The Frog paid no attention to him, and simply seemed intent on lying there in bed." This makes it sound as if The Frog is choosing to luxuriate in bed, as if he had a choice, when in fact he is dying, chained to his bed, in effect. The sentence is presented as third-person narration by Verga, but must represent the thought of Malpelo, to whom The Frog's bedriddenness seems a perplexing luxury ("seemed intent on lying there in bed"). And indeed in this horribly bleak story, death *is* a kind of luxury, since it is a relief from work, from life. The Frog dies, and a little later Malpelo gets lost in one of the labyrinthine mine shafts that stretch under the volcano, and is "never heard of again."

It would have been better for him if he'd never been born at all.

Joseph Roth's Empire of Signs

※

I

With Joseph Roth, you begin—and end—with the prose. The great delight of this Austrian novelist, who wrote in the 1920s and 1930s, lies in his strange, nimble, curling sentences, which are always skewing into the most unexpected metaphors. It is rare to find luminous powers of realism and narrative clarity so finely combined with a high poetic temperature. Joseph Brodsky said that there is a poem on every page of Roth, and certainly Roth's almost nervous fondness for metaphor recalls the image-blessed, image-sick prose of another poet, Osip Mandelstam, sooner than that of any novelist.

Like Mandelstam's, Roth's details and images are often not primarily visual, in the usual Flaubertian sense. He isn't especially interested in describing the exact color or shade of a man's mustache and then likening it, say, to rolled filaments of copper (though he is perfectly capable of writing this way). Instead, he comes at his images from behind, or sideways, and then climbs toward something at once magical and a little abstract. In *The Emperor's Tomb* (1938), he pictures a businessman talking about his prospects in the Austro-Hungarian Empire during the First World War: "As he spoke he stroked both sides of his mutton-chop whiskers as if he wished to caress simultaneously both halves of the monarchy [i.e., Austria and Hungary]."

This level of magical abstraction can be found in all of Roth's novels, from the earliest, *The Spider's Web* (1923), to his last published work, *The Tale of the 1002nd Night* (1939). *The Spider's Web* is a generally rather crude and flat book, but Roth's next novel, *Hotel Savoy* (1924), suggests the power of the more mature writer. It tells the story of Gabriel Dan, who has spent three years in a Siberian POW camp and who has ended up in an unnamed Eastern European town as a resident of the enormous Hotel Savoy, which is full of the refugees of war—Poles, Germans, Russians, Serbians, and Croats. This early book already shows a deep command of simile and metaphor. "My room—one of the cheapest—is on the sixth floor, number 703. I like the number—I am superstitious about them—for the zero in the middle is like a lady flanked by two gentlemen, one older and one younger." Dickens, and more acutely Gogol, may have influenced Roth, but probably the strongest impression was made by Viennese journalism, in particular the practice and perfection of the *feuilleton*, or short literary article. *Feuilletons* were brief sketches, sometimes arguments but often exquisite descriptive snatches. Karl Kraus was an earlier master of the form; in the 1920s, when Roth started writing them, Alfred Polgar was the most celebrated exponent. Walter Benjamin called Polgar "the German master of the small form." In 1935, writing in honor of Polgar's sixtieth birthday, Roth said that he considered himself Polgar's pupil: "He polishes the ordinary until it becomes extraordinary . . . I have learned this *verbal carefulness* from him."

The brevity of the *feuilleton* put every sentence under pressure, packing it with twice the usual energy. Polgar, in one of his pieces, describes a man's cane in very Rothian style: "A small walking-stick made out of rhinoceros hide danced between his fingers. It was a woolly light-yellow in colour and looked like a pole of thickened honey." These articles—Benjamin's essays are stylistic cousins—often proceed in a pretty shuffle, as if each sentence were a new beginning. The writing is essentially aphoristic, even when not obviously so, because each sentence attains the status of aphorism. Kraus described the aphorism as both half the truth and one and a half times the truth, and this might also stand as a description of metaphor, certainly of metaphor as it appears in Roth's work, where the similes are both magically untrue and magically more than true.

Roth, in effect, novelized the techniques of the *feuilleton*, producing fictions that behave as if they are always about to end, and which therefore always include one more superb phrase before the deferred closure. His books are highly patterned, but each sentence is a discrete explosion. There is, for example, the disagreeable Lord von Winternigg in Roth's greatest novel, *The Radetzky March* (1932), who rides through the garrison town in his barouche: "Small, ancient and pitiful, a little yellow oldster with a tiny wizened face in a huge yellow blanket . . . he drove through the brimming summer like a wretched bit of winter." Or, from the same novel, this passing scene-setter: "It was getting dark. The evening fell vehemently into the street." Or again, from the same novel, the description of the peasant Onufrij, and his effort to write his name: "The beads of sweat grew on his low brow like transparent crystal boils . . . These boils ran, ran down like tears wept by Onufrij's brain." And from *The Emperor's Tomb*: "All little stations in all little provincial towns looked alike throughout the old Austro-Hungarian Empire. Small and painted yellow, they were like cats lying in the snow in winter and in the sun in summer." Or: "The lonely lantern which stood before it reminded one of an orphan vainly trying to smile through its tears." From *Flight Without End* (1927): "It was an icy night, so cold that at first I thought even a shout must freeze the instant it was uttered, and so never reach the person called." Or: "The lady's smoothly shaved legs lay side by side like two similarly clad sisters, both in silk sheaths." Or: The waiters "moved about like gardeners; when they poured coffee and milk into the cups, it was as if they were watering white flower-beds. Trees and kiosks stood on the kerbs, almost as if the trees were selling newspapers." From *Right and Left* (1929): "In the gloaming, only the silver birches in the little wood opposite would shimmer, standing amongst the other trees like slips of days among ancient nights."

Joseph Roth was born in 1894 on the rim of the Hapsburg empire in Brody, Austrian Galicia, which is now part of Ukraine. Until David Bronsen established the facts in his German-language biography (an English translation is in progress), the record of Roth's life was an evocative smudge, a rumor worthy of the shadowy border town in which he was born—a town about which, in different versions, he writes repeatedly in his fiction.

Brody had a sizable Jewish population, but it appears that in later life Roth would conceal his Jewishness, claiming that his father, a businessman from Galicia called Nachum, had been an Austrian government official, and even, on one occasion, a Polish count. Such fantasies may have had their origin in Viennese anti-Semitism, or more likely in Roth's conservative romanticism, and his almost naïve love of the Austro-Hungarian military. It was no doubt easier to invent a fictitious father once the real one had disappeared: while Joseph was still a boy, Nachum went mad and was locked away in a German asylum. As readers are bound to notice, Roth's fiction is painfully concerned with the relationship of son and father, with absent or useless fathers and damaged, aimless sons. The rawest treatment of this theme is in *Zipper and His Father* (1928), the portrait of a young man, Arnold Zipper, who is spiritually ruined by his service on the front during the First World War, and by his father's thoughtless support for that war.

The Radetzky March is Roth's deepest consideration of fathers and sons. The novel's formal beauty flows from its dynastic current, which irrigates the very structure of the book. We begin with Captain Joseph Trotta, who inadvertently saved the young Emperor Franz Joseph's life at the battle of Solferino in 1859. Thanks to this,

the captain is ennobled and the doomed, quixotic Trotta line established, each generation less heroic, but more absurdly quixotic, than
its predecessor. Baron Trotta's son, Franz, is only a dutiful district
captain in a garrison town in Austrian Silesia; but Franz's son, Lieutenant Carl Joseph Trotta, who is the novel's real protagonist, is
more spectacularly unhappy—first in the cavalry, from which he dis-
charges himself, and then in the infantry, where he dies a foolish
death during the First World War.

Hanging like a golden cloud over Lieutenant Trotta's head is the
reputation of his grandfather, "the hero of Solferino." Young Trotta
can never match this heroism, not least because it was accidental;
part of his affliction is precisely that he strives to emulate a quality
that was, originally, not the product of striving. Roth beautifully expands this into a larger celebration and critique of the Austro-
Hungarian Empire: Lieutenant Trotta comes to represent an entire
generation of enfeebled young men, living off the recessive heroism
of an earlier imperial age and unable to achieve by force of will what
was once achieved by instinct. What remains changeless, however, is
the Emperor Franz Joseph himself, who ascended to the throne in
1848 and reigned until his death in 1916. The emperor is the om-
nipresent yet absent father of all the empire's inhabitants; in a sense,
he is both father and grandfather to Lieutenant Trotta, because his
long reign has spanned the generations. The emperor, of course, is
the true hero of Solferino, under whose heroic reputation Trotta
lives and fails. Whenever Trotta sees, in a café, the standard portrait
of the emperor "in the sparkling white uniform," it merges in his
memory with an old family portrait of his grandfather. The Trotta
and Hapsburg dynasties are one, a conflation which, characteristically, Roth both idealizes and mocks.

History marked Joseph Roth's life at least twice, viciously. First
came the assassination of the emperor's nephew Franz Ferdinand
in Sarajevo in June 1914. This, followed by Franz Joseph's death
in 1916, started the unraveling of the Austro-Hungarian Empire.

In at least half of Roth's thirteen novels comes the inevitable, saber-like sentence, or a version of it, cutting the narrative in two: "One Sunday, a hot summer's day, the Crown Prince was shot in Sarajevo." Then there was the Anschluss. The news of the German occupation in 1938 precipitated a collapse of morale in Roth, who was exiled in Paris at the time, and drinking heavily. He died fourteen months later, in May 1939. Nevertheless, he was able to make the Anschluss the dramatic epilogue of *The Emperor's Tomb*, which is a kind of sequel to *The Radetzky March*, extending the story of the Trotta family (via a cousin of Lieutenant Carl Joseph) from 1914 to 1938.

So Roth lived through light and then twilight and then darkness, seeing his beloved empire mutate into a neglected and unmonarchical Austria and finally disappear into Hitler's pouch. The empire was already on the verge of dissolution when Roth became a student at the University of Vienna in the summer of 1914. He joined up in 1916 and a year later was sent to the Galician front. He returned from the war with tales of capture by the Russians and a forced march across Siberia, a history he awards Franz Tunda in *Flight Without End*, and Gabriel Dan in *Hotel Savoy*. But he probably never saw combat, serving instead in the army's press office. During the next ten years, living on and off in Berlin, he wrote the novels which would make him unpopular with the Nazis: in particular *Flight Without End*, which tells the story of a man who returns from the war and grows steadily more disenchanted with the confident rise of German "culture"; and *Right and Left*, which logs the growth of fascism in Germany during the 1920s.

Roth fled to Paris in 1933, a year after *The Radetzky March* had made him celebrated. There he marinated himself in drink and in the impossibility of his romantic nostalgia. His solution to the advance of the Nazis seems to have been a proposal to restore the Hapsburg monarchy. He "renounced" his Jewishness in 1935, calling himself a Catholic. He died in 1939, apparently attended, at his deathbed, by a priest, a rabbi, and a representative of the league for the restoration of the Hapsburgs.

II

For the citizens of the Austro-Hungarian Empire, especially those who, like Stefan Zweig and Joseph Roth, were of a nostalgic and idealizing cast, Sarajevo was momentous not because it precipitated the First World War, but because the First World War precipitated the collapse of the adored Hapsburg empire, the impossible archipelago of different countries and races that, like a child's cartographic fantasy, stretched northward from Vienna to take in Prague, eastward to include Moravia, Silesia, and some of what is now Poland, and southward from Vienna to include Croatia and Bosnia-Herzegovina, which it annexed in 1908. The Austro-Hungarian Empire was, of course, the nineteenth-century incarnation of the earlier Holy Roman Empire; it was the pampered child of more than five hundred years of historical privilege, looked after since 1848 by its spiritual father and commander in chief, the Emperor Franz Joseph, who ruled until his death in 1916. Two years later, the empire had disappeared, and the Hapsburg dynasty faded out of history into historiography, and out of succession into the little monthly coups of the society gossip pages.

Roth is the great elegist of that empire; Robert Musil its great analyst; Kafka its dark allegorist. Roth's most characteristic novels are portraits of men who, either infatuated with the empire or merely unthinkingly dependent on it, are disappointed by it in some way or another, and who subsequently lose their way, or fall into aimlessness and finally despair. Generally, this hero will have left the embrace of the Austrian army, which stands in for the empire, either because the First World War has just ended or because he has been discharged in cloudy circumstances (like Baron Taittinger in *The Tale of the 1002nd Night*). In the course of the novel, this hero may travel either to the rim of empire (the border districts) or to the center (to Vienna). In the border towns, among Cossacks and Jews, the hero may fight in the Great War, may die (as Lieutenant Trotta does in 1916, in *The Radetzky March*), or may be captured by the Russians and sent to Siberia (as Trotta's cousin is in *The Emperor's Tomb*, and Franz Tunda is in *Flight Without End*). If he survives, he must return to hollow postwar Vienna, like poor, aimless Arnold Zipper in *Zipper and His Father*, or like Andreas Pum, the protagonist of *Rebellion*, Roth's third novel.

Roth's novels delight in, insist on, the uniformity of the empire and its livery in all its varied lands; they enact a kind of fictive imperialism of their own, imposing the same conditions on different characters in different books. In Roth's novels, Sunday lunch in the empire is always noodle soup, brisket of beef, and cherry dumplings. In spring, the laburnums flower and the new sunlight makes the silverware in the Vienna coffeehouses sparkle. The governmental officers are mustachioed and upright, like waxworks. In the border districts, there is always a Hotel Bristol, where the hero puts up for a while, and a tavern where Russians pay their entire savings to cross into the empire. The larks trill, the frogs croak, and everywhere can be seen the portrait of the beloved emperor, and everywhere can be heard bands playing evocative martial tunes, first and foremost "The Radetzky March."

But even at their most nostalgic, his novels also exaggerate and mock the presence of the empire in its citizens' lives. If Roth loved the empire because it imposed an imperial uniformity on so many different peoples, it is also seen in his books as a kind of tyranny, almost a totalitarianism, so that Roth and Kafka have more in common than might at first seem to be the case. His novels so insist on the empire that they end up gesturing toward the impossibility of realizing it. Roth's elegy suggests to the reader not simply that the empire is dead and gone but that it could never, in reality, have equaled the absurd dreams Roth cherished of it. Roth, one feels, was elegiac for the empire even when the empire existed, because it was not alive enough for his idea of it. Thus his novels, which were all, of course, written after the collapse of the empire, are elegies twice over: in a sense, they are elegies for an *original* feeling of elegy.

So it is that Roth's greatest novels squeeze, simultaneously, comedy and romanticism from their depiction of the Austro-Hungarian Empire. The romanticism *is* comedy, because the unwieldy human diversity of the empire is both magnificent and absurd. In *The Emperor's Tomb*, published in 1938, Roth has his hero, Franz Ferdinand Trotta, describe the extraordinary human resources of the empire:

> The brilliant variety of the Imperial Capital and Residence [i.e., Vienna] was quite visibly fed . . . by the tragic love which the Crown Lands bore to Austria: tragic, because forever unrequited. The gypsies of the Puszta, the Huzulen of Subcarpathia, the Jewish coachmen of Galicia, my own kin the Slovene chestnut roasters of Sipolje, the Swabian tobacco growers from the Bacska, the horse breeders of the Steppes, the Osman Sibersna, the people of Bosnia and Herzegovina, the horse traders from the Hanakel in Moravia, the weavers from the Erzgebirge, the millers and coal dealers of Podolia: all these were the open-handed providers of Austria; and the poorer they were, the more generous. So much trouble and so much pain so freely offered up as though it were a matter of course and in the natural order of things, so as to ensure that the centre of the Monarchy should be universally acclaimed as the home of grace, happiness and genius.

This is Roth, in high nostalgia, in 1938, after the Nazis had occupied Austria. But there is something terribly unstable about the passage ("and the poorer they were, the more generous") and this seems intentional, as if it should be difficult for the reader to tell if Roth is entirely in earnest: what empire could possibly be such a utopia? Roth relishes the strange, crooked proper names (the Osman Sibersna, the coal dealers of Podolia), which he rolls on the tongue like a lyric poet listing the proper names of flowers (saxifrage, amaranths, myrtles). The nouns become almost abstract, lift out of reference and hover in the unaccountable, where they cannot be verified or really known: where is Podolia?

When Roth is at his most extravagant, his very extravagance is a form of sad irony. This is supremely true of *The Radetzky March*, which is full of magnificently romantic, despairing prose. At one marvelous moment, for instance, Lieutenant Trotta takes his mistress to Vienna to see the annual Corpus Christi procession, in which the different regiments of the vast empire parade before the Viennese:

> The light-blue breeches of the infantry were radiant. Like the serious embodiment of ballistic science, the coffee-brown artillerists marched past. The blood-red fezzes on the heads of the azure Bosnians burned in the sun like tiny bonfires lit by Islam in honour of His Apostolic Majesty [i.e., the emperor]. In black lacquered carriages sat the gold-decked Knights of the Golden Fleece and the black-clad red-cheeked municipal councillors . . . And the lieutenant's heart stood still yet pounded fiercely—a challenge to medical science. Over the slow strains of the anthem, the cheers fluttered like small white flags amid huge banners painted with coats of arms.

"The blood-red fezzes on the heads of the azure Bosnians burned in the sun like tiny bonfires lit by Islam in honour of His Apostolic Majesty." One reads this glorious passage as Roth intends us to, in the spirit one feels Roth wrote it in, which is childish wonderment. This is a dream, in which even metaphor is co-opted by the empire, and red hats become oblatory fires for Franz Joseph. This combination of the childishly romantic and the surreally ironic or comic, of realism and excess, innocence and sophistication, gives Roth's writing a paradoxical air. It is at once modern and old-fashioned. His gifted translator, Michael Hofmann, has noted how many different textures can be found in a Roth novel: "the caricatures of Grosz, the semi-abstract gorgeousness of Klimt, and the freewheeling, home-made, modern inventions of Paul Klee." To which I would only add the streaming, ruddy fullness of Ilya Repin, the Repin of those famous large canvases of soldiers eating and laughing. Which means, in novelistic terms (more or less): Tolstoy (and perhaps also Babel). Here, for example, in a rich, streaming passage, Roth celebrates the horsemanship of the Cossacks, who are found on the edges of the empire:

> In the vast plain between the two border forests, the Austrian and the Russian, the sotnias of the borderland Cossacks, uniformed winds in military formations, raced around on the mercuric ponies of their homeland steppes, swinging their lances over their tall fur caps like lightning streaks on long wooden poles—coquettish lightning with dainty pennons. On the soft, springy, swampy ground, the clatter of hooves could barely be heard . . . It was as if the Cossacks were soaring over the meadows . . . With their strong yellow horse teeth, the saddled Cossacks, in mid-gallop, lifted their red-and-blue handkerchiefs from the ground, their bodies, suddenly felled, ducked under the horses' bellies, while the legs in the reflective boots still squeezed the animals' flanks. Other riders flung their lances high into the air, and the weapons whirled and obediently dropped back into the horsemen's raised fists—they returned like living falcons into their masters' hands. Still other riders, with torsoes crouching horizontal along the horses' backs, human mouths fraternally pressing against animal mouths, leaped through wondrously small rounds of iron hoops that could have girded a small keg.

In such passages, there is no greater modern writer than Joseph Roth (Babel, whom he resembles, lacks his scope), none more appealing in his capacity to combine the novelistic and the poetic, to blend lusty, undamaged realism with sparkling powers of metaphor and simile.

III

If there is something a little sickly in Roth's love of the empire, Roth's characteristic hero is a little sickly too—sick with love for empire but also made sick *by* empire. And Thomas Mann, a considerable influence on Roth, had shown that a fictional hero who has been made sick by the epoch he lives in—like Hans Castorp in *The Magic Mountain*—can be used by the novelist to offer a critique of the sickness of that epoch.

This is the case with *Rebellion*, written in 1924, when the thirty-year-old Roth still considered himself something of a leftist. The story is fabular. Andreas Pum has come back from the war without a leg. He is a simple, loyal subject of the empire who unquestioningly believes that the government will provide him with a pension and a small job for life. Things go well for him at first. The authorities do indeed issue Andreas with a permit to play a barrel organ, and Andreas spends his days churning out sentimental songs and patriotic marches for appreciative crowds. He finds a kindly war widow to marry. But a chance incident inverts his life: he becomes involved in a scuffle with a wealthy industrialist and assaults a policeman who intervenes. His organ permit is taken away, and he is imprisoned.

Andreas's time inside is only six weeks, but they are fateful weeks. During this period, he ages terribly and turns into a silent rebel, mentally siding with those malcontents, Communists, angry war veterans, and other agitators he had always previously despised and disdainfully called "heathens." On his release, Andreas feels that life has become a prison. The old empire he had always believed in has steamrolled over him. One of the novel's recurring symbols is the lavish official summons that Andreas receives, with its imperial eagle stamped on it; Andreas has become nothing but the prey of the empire. *Rebellion* ends mordantly: Andreas can only find work as a lavatory attendant at one of the Vienna cafés now run by his successful friend Willi, and Roth tells us that Andreas has "decided that he

would like to be a revolutionary," like the firebrands he reads about
"in the newspapers that the café supplied him with." But at the café
lavatory all his newspapers are "generally a couple of days old by that
stage, and the news he got was no longer news when he chopped the
newspaper into rectangles and hung them on nails in tidy packages.
Willi was constantly telling him to economize on expensive toilet tissue." In other words, the gentlemen of the empire wipe their asses
on such revolutionaries, and by extension on such mental revolutionaries as Andreas.

Andreas is more rebellious than Lieutenant Trotta in *The Radetzky March*, or Arnold Zipper in *Zipper and His Father*, or Baron Taittinger in *The Tale of the 1002nd Night*, who are all curiously indifferent
to their aimlessness, but no less defeated than them. Roth's heroes
are victims of the Hapsburg empire, contaminated by what they so
love, which is the paternal security and presence of the empire.
Baron Taittinger, who is discharged from the army for dishonorable
conduct, drifts without purpose and then kills himself. "I think he
lost his way in life," a colleague memorializes. "A man can lose his
way!" A friend describes Arnold Zipper as having fallen into "indif-
ference, melancholy, indecision, weakness, and lack of critical faculty," and blames this collapse on Arnold's father, and his father's
entire generation: "All our fathers are responsible for our bad luck.
Our fathers belong to the generation that made the war."

But really, it is the empire that is being blamed, and the great
father-of-all, Franz Joseph. In *Hotel Savoy*, Gabriel Dan notices that
all the other hotel residents, who, like him, are refugees of the empire, blame the hotel for their misfortune and stasis: "Every piece of
bad luck came to them through this hotel and they believed that
Savoy was the name of their misfortune." Like the Austrian army, the
Hotel Savoy is one of Roth's microcosms of the empire. It is the empire that is really "the name of their misfortune."

But why does the empire so disappoint its citizens? Partly because, like Roth's, their love of it is desperate and uncontainable.
And partly because, as Roth's novels so delicately suggest, the em-

pire is not quite a reality, is not itself quite containable. Not only love for it but comprehension of it will always exceed the reality. Robert Musil writes about this in *The Man Without Qualities* when he praises the empire as a place that allowed its citizens "inner space," partly because it did not really exist. The empire, writes Musil, is "only just, as it were, acquiescing in its own existence. In it one was negatively free, constantly aware of the inadequate grounds for one's own existence."

Roth seems to have cherished the "inadequate grounds" of the existence of the empire. His novels delight in the fact that the empire was functionally inefficient—the Austrian army, for instance, was famously feeble—but efficient at glamour; in other words, he loved the rhetoric of empire, and loved that the empire was first and foremost a rhetoric. There is a constant sense in his fiction that such a fantastic assemblage of different peoples could only really be magical, fictional—as if it could only really exist *for* the novel (those blood-red fezzes). Roth enjoys the empire as a fictional form, as something analogous to the novel itself. For Roth, and for his heroes, the empire is too magical for life, but not too magical for the novel.

And his novels, correspondingly, are not just about the empire; they enact it symbolically, using an empire of signs to create the closed world of his novels, and to insist on its dreamlike inescapability. Roth's imagery pulls its comedy and its magic from this insistence. There is the man already encountered, in *The Emperor's Tomb*, who is seen rubbing both sides of his whiskers, "as if he wished to caress simultaneously both halves of the monarchy." In *The Radetzky March*, Roth makes sympathetic fun of Trotta's father, the dutiful district captain, when he describes how thin and gaunt he has become. The district captain resembles "one of the exotic birds at the Schönbrunn Zoo—creatures that constitute Nature's attempt to replicate the Hapsburg physiognomy within the animal kingdom." And in *Zipper and His Father*, the regulars sit in a Vienna café as if it were "a besieged garrison in a castle."

Roth uses this unreal world, in which everything interlocks for the glory of the empire, both to elegize a lost time of uniformity and security and, more interestingly, to so exaggerate the uniformity of the empire that a kind of disappointment and mockery of it must result. For how can such imperial intrusion—in which the very birds in the zoo have taken on the Hapsburg physiognomy, and even a café is like a garrison—not verge on the totalitarian or tyrannous, as Andreas Pum discovers? For instance, one of Roth's finest achievements in *The Radetzky March* is the evocation of the slow, eternal repetitions of routine in the empire. There is a marvelous description of Sunday lunch as Trotta recalls it, with the local town band playing "The Radetzky March" outside the dining room windows, and the Trotta family consuming brisket of beef and cherry dumplings, a meal which never varies, on any Sunday of the year. But the book is also a devastating portrait of the inertia of the habitual, and of the oppression of uniformity, and all the best comedy in the novel flows from this apprehension. After all, that café in Vienna may well resemble a "garrison" to its deluded patrons but it is into just such a coffeehouse that a man will stride, as at the end of *The Emperor's Tomb*, to announce that the city has been occupied by the Germans. Roth's characters are made the more vulnerable to history by their refusal of it. Above all, they are people who are acted on; the empire is their fate and the source of their infantilization, inasmuch as they have handed over their volition to the great present-absent father, Franz Joseph. The army is the imperial institution which manages this childhood. Lieutenant Trotta, gazing up in cafés at the portrait of the supreme commander in chief, is the most pathetic example. When Baron Taittinger, in *The Tale of the 1002nd Night*, is discharged from the cavalry, he is at a loss, and Roth has a lovely phrase about how Taittinger must act as if he were a newly recruited civilian. In Roth's fiction, to be discharged from the army is like being "sent down" from the empire.

These ironies and comedies enliven and complicate Roth's conservatism. Roth sees that Lieutenant Trotta in *The Radetzky March* thinks he is conserving his patrimony by honoring his grandfather's name and joining the army. But Roth lets us also see that Trotta is letting that patrimony congeal by not extending it. Roth describes Gabriel Dan as having "fallen prey" to the Hotel Savoy, and elsewhere in that book a character remarks: "A man lays his head on a block—it is a Jewish destiny." Seen in this light, and despite Roth's difficult relations with his own Jewishness, all of his self-defeating heroes, even the gentiles, are ultimately Jewish.

Because the empire is everything to Roth's characters, they tend to convert everything, even metaphysics, into the terms of the empire; they make a religion of the Hapsburgs. This is constantly hinted at in *Rebellion*: "Then he remembered he didn't have his permit anymore. All at once he felt he was alive, but without any authority to live. He was nothing anymore!" So reflects Andreas when his organ-grinder's permit is taken away. It is the empire that gives him authority to exist, that tells him what to do and promises to look after him. In Roth's novels, marching orders are more than merely figurative. They are everything. But at some critical moment in a life, they will not be enough.

The empire is a religion in Roth's novels, the God that failed, and it fails its citizens rather as God may fail His more desperate believers, by being indescribable, by being *too much*. This religion produces both devotion and a secular rebellion against that religion. Roth's wish fulfillment sows the seeds of its own disappointment, and this frustration is shared with his embattled fictional heroes, who are epic heroes in a mere age of the novel, junior Don Quixotes, all, as it were, going at life with inappropriate weaponry. It might be said that Roth's novels are war novels without any real war in them. Again one thinks of Kafka, and not just because in *Rebellion* Andreas is promised in prison that a shadowy "Director" will help him to gain an early release. Kafka once famously said that "there is infinite hope, but not for us." In Roth's sad comic world, there is an infinite empire, but not for us.

Bohumil Hrabal's Comic World

What is funny and forlorn in the following sentence? "A fortune-teller once read my cards and said that if it wasn't for a tiny black cloud hanging over me I could do great things and not only for my country but for all mankind."

Instantly a person opens before us like a quick wound: probably a man (that slight vibration of a swagger), grandiose in aspiration but glued to a petty destiny, eccentric and possibly mad, a talker, rowdy with anecdote. There is a comedy, and a sadness, in the prospect of an ambition so large ("for all mankind") that it must always be frustrated, and comedy, too, in the rather easy and even proud way that this character accepts his frustration: is he not a little pleased with the "tiny black cloud" that impedes his destiny?—at least it is the mark of something. So this character may be grandiose in his ambition, but also in his fatalism. And isn't that phrase "tiny black cloud" done with great finesse? It hints at a man whose sense of himself has so swelled that he now sees himself geographically, like a darkened area experiencing a bout of low pressure on a weather map of Europe. "Tiny," above all: a marvelous word, because it suggests that this man, while possibly proud of his handicap, might also disdain it, or believe that he could just brush it away whenever he wanted and get on with the business of doing great things.

Such are the goods packed in a typical comic sentence by the great Czech novelist Bohumil Hrabal, who died in 1997. The character relieving himself of this little confession is a garrulous cobbler who admits to being "an admirer of the European Renaissance" and is the narrator of *Dancing Lessons for the Advanced in Age*. But many of Hrabal's comic heroes are equally talkative. There is Hanta, the narrator of *Too Loud a Solitude*, who has been compacting waste for thirty-five years, and educating himself on the sly using the great books he rescues from the trash. He wanted to grow up to be a millionaire, he tells us, so that he could buy "phosphorescent hands for all the city clocks" in Prague. Now he reads his rescued Kant and Novalis, and dreams of going on holiday to Greece, where he would like to visit Stagira, "the birthplace of Aristotle, I'd run around the track at Olympia, run in my underwear." Hanta doesn't take baths because he suspects them of spreading disease, "but sometimes, when a yearning for the Greek ideal of beauty comes over me, I'll wash one of my feet or maybe even my neck."

And there is Ditie, the picaresque hero of *I Served the King of England*, a waiter in a Prague hotel who once served the Emperor of Ethiopia and worked with a headwaiter who once served the king of England. Ditie is usually wrong about everything—he marries a German athlete just as the Nazis are invading Czechoslovakia—but sometimes he says something wise or prescient, and whenever he is complimented for this, he replies, "modestly": "I served the Emperor of Ethiopia." And there is Milos Hrma, the young, timid railway signalman in Hrabal's most famous novel, *Closely Observed Trains*. When he discovers that the stationmaster may become an inspector of State Railways, he is excited, and reverently asks: "An inspector, like that . . . that's the same rank on the railways as a major in the Army, isn't it?" Yes, it is, says the stationmaster. "Ah, and then," Hrma cries, "instead of the three small stars you'll have just one, but bordered with the inspector's field!"

Hrabal's obvious model for these buffeted heroes is the Czech soldier Svejk, Jaroslav Hasek's comic simpleton who finds himself entangled in the First World War. Svejk is a kind of Sancho Panza, living on into an age that is no longer epic, not even comic. Hrabal deeply admired *The Good Soldier Svejk*, and in *Total Fears*, a selection of letters written to an American scholar of Czech literature, he praises the way Hasek's novel is "written as though he tossed it off with his left hand, after a hangover, it's pure joy in writing." Svejk resembles many of Hrabal's heroes, a "little man" who seems to wander cheerfully into large historical events. As Svejk effectively talks himself into being arrested by a secret policeman and is later sent to the front, so Hrabal's absurd waiter, Ditie, who has become rich, is outraged to hear that the Communists have arrested all the millionaires in the country but have somehow overlooked him. Since he has always wanted nothing more than to be a millionaire, he goes to the police, bank statements in hand, to argue that he should be immediately taken in. (He is, though not without some effort on his part.) Svejk's apparent idiocy hides an intelligence bent on thwarting the authorities, with whom he only seems to comply; similarly, Hanta, the man who rescues books from the compacting machine in *Too Loud a Solitude*, is not only a uselessly learned autodidact but a little rebel against a large book-censoring regime.

Like Hasek, Hrabal kept his ear close to the pub table. He sat for hours in his favorite Prague establishment, the Golden Tiger, listening to beer-fed stories foam. Those who knew him recall a man who liked to pass himself off as a beer drinker rather than a writer, content to sit silently and gather—the community's generous beggar. Ondrej Danajek wrote a eulogy for Hrabal in 1997, and remembers "a very spiritual artist and free-thinker with the ways and looks of a labourer. You were as likely to find him (maybe smiling shyly) in the already slightly drunk crowd at a Third Division football game as overhear him commenting on the game quoting Immanuel Kant or another of his philosophical gods."

Hrabal, who was born in 1914 in Moravia, started writing poems under the influence of French surrealism. The poems quickly squared their shoulders and became paragraphs: prose poems, epiphanic jottings, broken anecdotes. The *Prague Revue* (no. 5) has printed a number of these early poems, written in the 1940s, and many of them are touched with a characteristic Hrabalian oddity: "In the little pub overhanging the river, in a corner by the window, I was reading. You were weeping, I too was weeping and the tubby landlady was weeping."

In the early 1950s he was a member of an underground literary group run by the poet Jiri Kolar. His poems had now become stories, but he did not submit them for publication. Instead, he read them aloud to the group's members (who included the novelist Josef Skvorecky). The tale is told—it is rather like those "symbolic" stories about rulers that were collected by Tacitus and Plutarch—that one day Hrabal overheard Kolar, who was selling dolls at the time, being asked: "Kolar, do you have another death?" The question referred, apparently, to a marionette of the Grim Reaper, popular in Prague, but to Hrabal's ears it suggested a new way of writing whereby heterogeneous elements could be forced against each other, in a natural, comic manner, arising out of ordinary human business rather than the obviously surreal.

Hrabal began to experiment with an unlimited, flowing style, almost a form of stream of consciousness (he admired Joyce, Céline, and Beckett) in which characters associate and soliloquize madly. He called it *pabeni*, to which the closest approximation, according to Skvorecky, is "palavering." This palavering is really anecdote without end. The lovely truancy with which Hrabal's work vibrates has to do with its hospitality to an abundance of stories. Often one senses that Hrabal has taken a brief comic tale heard in the pub and exaggerated its comic essence. The narrator of *Dancing Lessons* tells us, just in passing, of a man who hangs himself on the cross marking his mother's grave, at which the local priest becomes very angry because he has to reconsecrate the whole churchyard. Hanta, in *Too Loud a*

Solitude, is accosted by a man who puts a knife to his throat, starts reciting a poem celebrating the beauties of the countryside at Ricany, then apologizes, "saying he hadn't found any other way of getting people to listen to his verse." In *I Served the King of England*, a general arrives at the hotel where Ditie works. He is very greedy, but has a curious habit. After each sip of champagne and each capture of an oyster, he shudders with disgust and denounces what he has just consumed: "Ah, I can't drink this swill!" This reminds one of Chekhov (Hrabal loved both Chekhov and Babel), who stole stories from the newspapers, and who kept a notebook full of whetted enigmas, such as this one: "A private room in a restaurant. A rich man, tying his napkin round his neck, touching the sturgeon with his fork: 'At least I'll have a snack before I die'—and he has been saying this for a long time, daily."

Chekhov is more gloomily scrupulous than Hrabal, who likes to heat his caught enigmas, his snatches of story and strange facts, so that they begin to emit a magical vapor. He is quite capable of a Chekhovian realism (Hanta recalls a village market at which a woman was standing selling only "two bay leaves"), but, always watchful for the splendid or sublime in a story—what he called "the pearl on the bottom" of a tale—he more usually allows his garrulous narrators to run on, prolonging and stretching their stories. A peerless example occurs in *I Served the King of England*, which was written in the early 1970s, though not published until 1983. Ditie has been telling us about the different traveling salesmen who stayed at the Golden Prague Hotel. One of them represents a famous tailoring firm from Pardubice, and he has brought with him a revolutionary fitting technique. It involves putting pieces of parchment on the body of the client and writing the measurements on them. Back at the workshop, the strips are taken and sewn together on a kind of tailor's dummy with a rubber bladder inside that is gradually pumped up until the parchment strips are filled out; they are then covered with glue so that they harden in the shape of the client's torso. When the bladder is removed, the torso floats up to the ceiling, permanently inflated, and a cord with a name and address is tied to it. The client's mannequin "is up there among several hundred colourful torsos, until he dies."

Ditie, predictably, is enthralled by this absurd and wonderfully pointless innovation, and longs to order a new dinner jacket from this prestigious firm, "so that I and my mannequin could float near the ceiling of a company that was certainly the only one of its kind in the world, since no one but a Czech could have come up with an idea like that." He spends his savings and is fitted with a suit. He travels to Pardubice to pick it up, and this "little man" (Ditie is, in fact, very short, and wears double-soled shoes) is overwhelmed by the social grandeur of the firm's torsos:

> It was a magnificent sight. Up near the ceiling hung the torsos of generals and regimental commanders and famous actors. Hans Albers himself had his suits made here, so he was up there too . . . A thin thread bearing a name tag dangled down from every torso, and the tags danced gaily in the breeze, like fish on a line. The boss pointed at a tag with my name and address on it, so I pulled it down. It looked so small, my torso. I almost wept to see a major-general's torso beside mine, and Mr Beranek the hotelkeeper's, but when I thought of the company I was in I laughed and felt better.

Hrabal may have heard from someone about a real company's mad scheme, but he takes the story and passes it through the madness of his escapist hero, and in doing so glazes it with a further strangeness. There is a magic in Hrabal's determination to visualize this anecdote, to color its enigmas, so that we are not just given the suggestion of the company's method but invited to picture a room full of dangling torsos. Hrabal is sometimes called a cinematic writer, probably because a successful film was made of *Closely Observed Trains*. But this visual quality, oddly enough, poses a problem for cinema, since it invites film simply to mimic it. Yet a curious element of scenes like this one is that, although they are pictorial, they retain a kind of hypothetical status, which is the status of dream. Isn't this scene, in some sense, Ditie's dream, despite the fact that it is undeniably happening? Hrabal's descriptions often have a paradoxical visibility and invisibility about them. They are vaporous. The invitation, we feel, is not simply for the reader to see these hanging torsos but to imagine someone imagining them, which is a little different.

In some respects, Hrabal is an early magical realist, and superficially he resembles some of those contemporary writers who are fond of abundant stories, exotic coloration, jokes and puns, and farcical escapism: Rushdie, Grass, Pynchon in his most recent novel, David Foster Wallace, and others. In novels by those writers, we have lately encountered terrorist groups with silly names, a genetically engineered mouse, two clocks having a conversation with each other, a giant cheese, a baby who plays air guitar in his crib, and so on. But this is more like hysterical realism than magical realism: it borrows from the real while evading it. These novels are profligate with what might be called inhuman stories: "inhuman" not because they could never happen, but because they are not really about human beings. By contrast, Hrabal's magical stories are comic and human—they are really desires embodied. And as such they are, paradoxically, not as parasitical on the real as some magical realism. They inhabit a utopian province, the realm of laughter and tears. How funny and sad it is to imagine Ditie impressed by the celebrity of the dangling torsos, and how fine that Ditie is seen to be as impressed by the presence of the torso of Mr. Beranek, the hotelkeeper, as he is by those of the major generals and actors.

Hrabal was never a strongly ideological or allegorical writer. Nevertheless, his first book of stories, *Lark on a String*, was withdrawn a week before it was due to be published, in 1959. It appeared four years later, as *Pearl on the Bottom*. According to Skvorecky, this book "launched its author on a meteoric career that elevated him to peaks of popularity no other Czech writer had enjoyed before him." *Dancing Lessons* appeared in 1964, *Closely Observed Trains* a year later. The film's success made Hrabal untouchable. Yet he could still be unprintable: once the Soviet tanks rolled in, Hrabal, who was always a prolific author (his collected works run to many volumes, and only a handful of these writings have been translated into English), was silenced again. Skvorecky left Czechoslovakia for Toronto, where he would publish Hrabal and others in émigré editions.

Hrabal began work on *I Served the King of England* during this period of prohibition, in the early 1970s. It was circulating in samizdat form by 1975, and Hrabal is said to have been especially keen for it to be formally published. Karl Srp, writing in the *Prague Revue*, has given a gripping (and often comically Hrabalian) account of how he and his colleagues in the jazz section of the Czech Musicians' Union semilegally published the novel in 1983, in the form of a "private" edition for its members. "Boys," said Hrabal, "publish just one copy and I can go ahead and die." They printed five thousand copies and distributed a leaflet telling people that they could come and collect the novel at the jazz section's offices. Hrabal's drinking friends were turning up, Srp writes, with beer coasters on which was written: "Give him one copy of *I Served the King of England*—B. Hrabal." Karl Srp and other members of the jazz section were imprisoned in 1986. Party members, having found boxes of the novel, sold them to each other as Christmas presents. Srp and his friends were released in 1988. "Shortly afterwards," as Skvorecky nicely cracks, "Communism went bust."

I Served the King of England is a joyful, picaresque story which begins with Baron Münchhausen–like adventures and ends in tears and solitude, a modulation typical of Hrabal's greatest work. Ditie, the book's narrator, is a cloud always chasing the sun of experience—a scudding, flighty, mobile simpleton who naïvely pursues one world-historical event after another. Awarded a medal with a fine blue sash by the Emperor of Ethiopia for his exemplary service, he takes out the sash every so often and puts it on, just to remind himself and others of what a personage he is. In fact, he is a fool, though he learns a fool's wisdom. When he marries the Nazi athlete, he is ostracized by his friends, and later imprisoned for collaboration. Released, he becomes a millionaire, and runs a successful hotel. "But the guests who came now were sad, or if they were gay it was not the kind of gaiety I was used to, but a forced gaiety." (The kind of humor later baptized by Kundera as "laughable laughter," the forced laughter of those pure and in power, "the angels.") It is 1948. Hrabal shows subtlety in allowing this little shard of political critique to be wielded by such an unreliable and fantastical man.

Having forced the new Communist authorities to arrest him as a bona fide millionaire and confiscate his property, Ditie is eventually released and ends his days mending roads in a remote village, sharing his cottage with a horse, a dog, and a goat. The novel has suddenly thinned out, as if Hrabal had been walking through a train and finally come to the last carriage, with almost no one in it. The ending is beautifully bereft. Sitting in the pub, Ditie asks each of the villagers where they would like to be buried. They are wordless. Ditie himself nominates a graveyard at the top of the local hill, and a grave straddling its crest, his body balanced like a boat, so that his remains would trickle down each side of the hill, one part into the streams of Bohemia, and the other part over the border into the Danube. In a rising aria, mixing both absurd aspiration and genuine solemnity, Ditie explains: "I wanted to be a world citizen after death, with one half of me going down the Vltava into the Labe and on into the North Sea, and the other half via the Danube into the Black Sea and eventually into the Atlantic Ocean."

As with the narrator of *Dancing Lessons* and his "tiny black cloud," Ditie has expanded into the realms of geography. He has fulfilled, ridiculously, the Czechoslovak dream of being both a nation itself and something more than a nation: he is a posthumous citizen of the world at large. The depth of this desire, and its comic thwart-

ing, are Hrabal's abiding themes. At one point Ditie refers to the uncle of a colleague, an old bandmaster who wrote a number of polkas
and waltzes for his military band in the time of the Hapsburg empire. Since this music is still played, says Ditie, the uncle always puts
on his old Hapsburg uniform when he goes out to chop wood. This
is not so far, in impulse, from Hanta, the narrator of *Too Loud a Solitude*, who longs to run around the track at Olympia in his long
johns, fulfilling his dream of the Greek ideal of athleticism.

What is moving about all these characters is the enormity of the
gulf between their aspiration and the limited means by which they
often satisfy it: Ditie is, in a way, content to wear his Ethiopian
medal and to dream of being a "world citizen" in death. When
Hanta feels like being "Greek," he washes a leg or an arm and reads a
bit of Aristotle. And then, in a marvelous twist of the dialectic, the
limited means of satisfaction come to seem equivalent in size to the
original aspiration, come to seem a big enough fulfillment, and then
become the source of a new kind of swagger for these characters:
the old man chopping wood in his Austro-Hungarian uniform is not
really defeated. Grandiose in ambition, grandiose in fatalism.

Hrabal's comedy, then, is complexly paradoxical. Holding in balance limitless desire and limited satisfaction, it is both rebellious and
fatalistic, restless and wise. Politically, it is not a dependably radical
humor: Hrabal described himself as one taught by Hasek to be "a
man of the Party of Moderate Progress, that is my modus vivendi in
this Central Europe of mine." His heroes want to be everything, but
they are hardly aware of the size of those wants, and settle for less
without knowing that they are doing so.

It is a comedy of blockage, of displacement, entrapment, cancel-
lation. Hardly surprising, then, that Hrabal sometimes said that he
rooted his comedy in one of his favorite findings, a dry cleaner's
receipt, which read: "Some stains can be removed only by the destruction of the material itself." In *Total Fears*, Hrabal glancingly
commends Freud's writing about comedy and jokes, and calls it

"typically Central European, and especially typical of Prague." Freud, it may be remembered, distinguishes humor from comedy and the joke. He is concerned with "broken humor"—"the humor that smiles through tears." This kind of humorous pleasure, he says, arises from the prevention of an emotion. A sympathy that the reader has prepared is blocked by a comic occurrence, and transferred onto a matter of secondary importance. In Ditie's case, the solemnity we feel as he contemplates death is comically blocked by his instructions for burial. This is blocked humor about blocked people. Hrabal, in Freud's terms, is a great humorist.

And a great writer. His finest book, *Too Loud a Solitude*, enacts an even more acute modulation, from early buoyancy to late despair. Hrabal, who himself worked for a while as a trash compactor, creates, in Hanta, his subtlest "idiot." Hanta may also represent the closest Hrabal came to a self-portrait. (Hrabal, like Hanta, rescued books from the compacting machine and built a library of them in the garage of his country cottage outside Prague.) Hanta's wide reading allows Hrabal to use all the mental resources of his hero, however insanely, and the result is a free-flowing prose of extraordinary flexibility, a prose with many interiors within interiors, like some of the Dutch masters—or perhaps many false bottoms. That would be the proper, unsolemn, Hrabalian image.

Hanta is put out of work, effectively, by the arrival, on the outskirts of Prague, of a much larger, industrial-scale trash compactor. He visits it, and does not like what he sees. It is clear that this machine does not simply compact trash, with the occasional discarded book, as his small press does, but is swallowing thousands of books. The books are lined up on lorries. It is a giant metal censor, and the harbinger of a sinister new era. But although Skvorecky describes this novel as Hrabal's "poetic condemnation of the banning of books," this is too heavy a reading. For how nimbly Hrabal describes a comic crescent around obvious political allegory. What is Hanta's response to this huge machine? He returns to his one-man press and tries to increase his output by 50 percent, so as to keep his job. As usual in Hrabal, political critique is slyly neutralized by the unreliability, indeed in this case the madness, of the narrator.

Hanta's increased production little avails him. He is sacked, and wanders through Prague, stopping every so often to drink a beer. He sits in the park and watches naked children playing, noticing the stripes across their midriffs from the elastic in their pants. This sets in train a succession of observations and allusions, in a passage of stunning vivacity which runs on a thousand feet, a passage which alone and without any context at all should secure Hrabal's prestige in world literature:

> Hasidic Jews in Galicia used to wear belts of loud, vivid stripes to cut the body in two, to separate the more acceptable part, which included the heart, lungs, liver and head, from the part with the intestines and sexual organs, which was barely tolerated. Catholic priests raised the line of demarcation, making the clerical collar a visible sign of the primacy of the head, where God in Person dips His fingers. As I watched the children playing naked and saw the stripes across their midriffs, I thought of nuns, who sliced head from face with one cruel stripe, stuffing it into the armour of the starched coif like Formula One drivers. Those naked children splashing away in the water didn't know a thing about sex, yet their sexual organs, as Lao-tze taught me, were serenely perfect. And when I considered the stripes of the priests and nuns and Hasidic Jews, I thought of the human body as an hourglass—what is down is up and what is up is down—a pair of locked triangles, Solomon's seal, the symmetry between the book of his youth, the Song of Songs, and the *vanitas vanitatum* of his maturity in the Book of Ecclesiastes.

This torrent of speculation is true and wise and lofty and simultaneously madly comic (those nuns dressed in starched coifs like Formula One drivers). It is also the thought of a man in despair, the fruit of Hanta's thirty-five years of compacting trash and rescuing great books—a thief of ideas, his very mind a compacted bale of allusion. All this is aquiver in this short, flying passage.

On February 3, 1997, Bohumil Hrabal, sick and in despair, haunted by what he called his own "loud solitude" and obsessed with the idea of "jumping from the fifth floor, from my apartment where every room hurts," fell from the fifth floor of a hospital while he was trying to feed the pigeons. Some stains can only be removed by the destruction of the material itself. But if what is up is down, then what is down is up.

J. F. Powers and the Priests

⚜

Does anyone, really, like priests? Anticlericalism seems a healthy human instinct, our peasantry of spirit asserting itself. I grew up among priests; they were stationed throughout my family, as uncles and cousins. A certain kind of Church of England rectory became as familiar to me as my bedroom: the heavy woods and meager ornaments of the main rooms, faintly warmed either by the woolly heat of an electric fire or by the unpleasant residue of the last supplicants to occupy it—those needy parishioners with apparently nothing else to do. Sometimes, as cheap stays against the cold, plastic sheeting had been pinned to the windows, so that the garden beyond seemed submarine. One dreaded having to use the bathroom, down the frigid corridors, invariably to be faced with green medicinal soap attached by an ingrown magnet to its stingy holder. And then there were the priests: the pedants or the saints, the zealots or the retirees, the trendy or the tired. Their long cassocks appeared to be hiding things. To a child it seemed, impossibly, that these men, dressed from neck to shoes in black, the tough vestments always a little shiny, were entirely clothed in shoe leather. They hung their heads with loud modesty. One of them had a fondness for the verb "titivate"; another always introduced each of his self-pleasing observations with a pompous "Apropos of nothing . . ."

This is also the world, though Catholic, of the American writer J. F. Powers, a novelist who wrote supremely well about the postwar midwestern Catholic church between the late 1940s and late 1980s. Powers, who was born in Jacksonville, Illinois, in 1917, and who died in 1999, is now barely visible at the end of that stretched telescope, "the writer's writer." He wrote sparely and sparingly, and produced only two novels—one of which, *Morte D'Urban*, won the National Book Award in 1963—and three collections of short stories, which were praised by Evelyn Waugh, Flannery O'Connor, and Philip Roth. He disappeared into a rather cloudy posterity while still alive; that is to say, he lived to see all his works go out of print. Actual posterity, in the form of reprints of all his writing by The New York Review of Books, has been kinder (*Morte D'Urban*, and a second novel called *Wheat That Springeth Green*, along with *The Stories of J. F. Powers*), though it seems sadly likely that the combination of Powers's refined style, ironic pessimism, and chosen subject—priests and more priests—will eventually deal his work a second death.

Though Powers has inevitably been claimed by his fellow communicants as a "Catholic writer," his world is the opposite of an advertisement for the church. By and large, his priestly heroes are ferociously unappealing, and in such a way that one wonders if Powers really liked or approved of most Catholic priests. They are not glamorously errant, like the priests of Greene and Mauriac, whose sins make them interesting, and possibly better shepherds. They are petty disappointments. Greene's priests are too worldly, but also ultimately too religious, to be conventional believers; Powers's men of the cloth are too conventional to be really religious. What piety and spiritual alertness they ever had has long softened amid the gluey fixtures and routines of daily parish life. Freed of all their old seminary ideals, they have become courtiers of compromise.

Greene is enjoyed by Catholics in part, one suspects, because his pessimism is not threatening. He tells us, in effect, that the religious life is more complicated than we imagined, which ultimately consoles us. But Powers is very threatening, and ought not to be easily enjoyed by Catholics, because the cumulative suggestion of his work is that the religious life, at least for priests, has become practically unattainable. Hardly ever, in over a thousand pages of fiction, do we see one of Powers's priests reflect spiritually on a spiritual matter. It is not simply that, on the principle of the Koran's never mentioning camels, these men do not speak of what surrounds them. It is that they are slaves to what Kierkegaard attacked as "Christendom"—the business of priestly activity rather than the practice of Christian witness, love of the world rather than imitation of Christ.

Powers was himself a true priest of his craft: devout, retiring, and unworldly, qualities rarely found in his subjects. He was a conscientious objector in the Second World War and served thirteen months in prison. His writing, he felt, was God-given. "I am in the alphabet God uses when I do my best work . . . I think God has given me talent," he said in 1988. "I have thanked God for it, usually every day in my prayers." A delicate stylist, he husbanded that talent: the nice hazard of a single phrase, or even a word, could consume days of effort. In his excellent introduction to the collected stories, Denis Donoghue writes that the Irish short story writer Sean O'Faolain would joke about how Powers "spent the morning putting in a comma and the afternoon wondering whether or not he should replace it with a semicolon." It is a firm, rich, American prose, at once a literary style and a way of talking, in which the dominant tone, belying the effort that went into its making, is a kind of heightened relaxedness. A characteristic passage, from the story "The Presence of Grace," has a priest sitting unwillingly with some drowsy parishioners after lunch:

> There was a lull during which Velma loaded her cigarette case and Father Fabre surveyed the room—the bookcase with no books in it,

only plants and bric-a-brac, and the overstuffed furniture rising like
bread beneath the slipcovers, which rivaled nature in the tropics for
color and variety of growing things, and the upright piano with the
mandolin and two photographs on top: one would be the late Mr.
Mathers and somewhere in the other, a group picture of graduating
nurses, would be the girl he had married, now stout, being now
what she had always been becoming. Mrs. Mathers was openly nap-
ping now. The room was filled with breathing, hers and Mr. Pint's in
unison, and the sun fell upon them all and upon the trembling ferns.

For many years Powers taught at St. John's University in Col-
legeville, Minnesota, a Benedictine foundation, where he shared the
daily religious observances. He has that devotion to the church
which often expresses itself in a kind of smothered anger, in disgust
at the failures of the church. Because he is a comic writer, this anger
is bandaged in smiles, and sometimes difficult to make out. But his
work really offers a hard critique of the church in its useless postwar
prime.

In his history of religion and philosophy in Germany, Heine
writes that Martin Luther failed to see that the idea of Christianity,
in its "annihilation of sensuality," demands the impossible of human
nature. But the Catholic church, says Heine, did acknowledge this,
and appropriately worked out a contract between God and the devil,
spirit and matter. Powers's priests are such contractualists. These are
not men who would bother to throw an inkpot at the devil; they
might hand him a pen and a dotted line. In one of Powers's stories,
"Zeal," a bishop tires of listening to a zealous priest who has been
idealistically telling parishioners that they should not tip waiters,
since the activity infringes the dignity of those who serve. In response, the bishop thinks to himself that "people should do what
they could do, little though it might be, and shouldn't be asked to
attempt what was obviously beyond them."

Father Urban, the hero of *Morte D'Urban*, and Powers's most engaging character, is a roving ambassador of Minnesota's churches

who wants "simply to pump a little life into the parish, without being pretentious about it." He busies himself in addressing the Great
Plains Commercial Club, drives around in a borrowed English
sports car, and builds a golf course at his order's retreat house. Vain,
ambitious, slippery, he is greased in secularism and slyly avoids theological controversy—"He could meet somebody on the other side tomorrow." In Powers's second novel, *Wheat That Springeth Green*
(1988), Father Joe Hackett—he is indeed a hack—begins his seminary life determined to be saintly, but quickly squanders the impulse
in parish life: "The truth was *he* hadn't sacrificed his spiritual life—it
had been done for him, by his appointment to Holy Faith."

These priests tend to shrink from the more pious worshippers.
Father Burner, in "Prince of Darkness," "liked his parishioners to be
retiring, dumb, or frightened." Some of the funniest scenes in this
very funny body of work involve priests fleeing from, or more subtly
evading, their most passionate solicitors. "A backslider he could han-
dle, it was the old story, but a red-hot believer, especially a talkative
one, could be a devilish nuisance. This kind might be driven away
only by prayer and fasting, and he was not adept at either." Often
they are cynical. Of the bishop in *Morte D'Urban*, Powers writes:
"Great Plains, after all, was a rural diocese, and so the Bishop made a
point of being for everything rural—hence the prayers all summer
long for whatever it was he was told that the farmers wanted in the
way of weather."

They are spiritually incurious, philistine—Father Burner thinks
Studs Lonigan "the best thing since the Bible"—and their daily bread
is merely the spoiled grain of bureaucratic trivialities: whether they
will get their free railway passes, the guttering and the heating, the
fund-raising for new buildings, the Men's Club, the Altar and Rosary
Society, whether attendance percentages are up or down. These are
men who, against Jesus's exhortation in the Gospels, give all of their
thought to the morrow. They are full of ambition—but only the ambition to go from curate to pastor, from "mouse to rat, as the saying

went . . ." An archdeacon is seen reading *Forbes*. In another of the
stories, a former bishop is praised because "he did know real estate."
The church is a corporation, "second only to Standard Oil" in its efficiency, and is to be managed as such.

Powers, in this jiggly satirical mode, can sound, for better or
worse, like Sinclair Lewis. At times perhaps, as more regularly in
Lewis, the ironies are too broad: Father Burner thinks to himself,
"Yes, if he had to, he would die for the Faith," while driving to a café
for a hamburger. (Though the moral stutter of that "if he had to" is
finely judged.) But Powers suggests a deeper criticism of the church.
The priesthood was originally imagined as a retreat from the world,
as monkishness; and for all the obvious worldliness of Powers's
priests, there is something still rather unworldly about them. Indeed, one might say that they have also been corrupted by their unworldliness. The parochialism and claustrophobia of their minds and
conversation, for all the sour prosperity of their businesslike approach, has a naïveté, a complacency, a closedness. It is shop-talking
with nothing to sell. They may not be worldly enough, in fact. Their
worldliness may be that they are too easy inside their *own* little
world.

Powers captures this closedness with fine artistry—and of course,
if he did not, his fiction would have only sociological value. Here are
the rectories, womenless but for their bitter housekeepers, their awful food ("hashed brown potatoes, scorched green beans, ground
meat of some kind . . . sliced canned peaches and cardboard
Fig Newtons"), their wordlessly loyal janitors, their mean, self-
absorbed, dry pastors, and the fresh curates sent to assist them, still
idealistic and pious from the seminary but suddenly standing on the
precipice of utility. His writing has a Chekhovian concreteness of detail, whereby each detail is not static—not jelled in its own little
pride of chosenness—but dynamic, mobile, a wheel of story. Reading Powers, one is often reminded of Chekhov's "The Bishop," in
which is briefly told the anecdote of the short priest and his enor-

mously tall son, a theological student, who one day lost his temper with the cook and called her "thou ass of Jehudiel," which caused the student's father to go very quiet—"ashamed that he could remember no such ass in the Bible." Chekhov stole from Ivan Bunin the real anecdote of a deacon who ate all the caviar at a funeral, and made it the opening of his story "In the Ravine."

Powers's details are like that: exploding anecdotes. Joe Hackett, in *Wheat That Springeth Green*, tips a little extra in a restaurant "in case the waitress was a Catholic, or a non-Catholic . . ." But parsimony is more common in Powers's priests. In "The Presence of Grace," we make the acquaintance of a memorably mean pastor, "a graying dormouse" who speaks to his curate only in savagely arrested phrases. Presumably to save money, he blows out, at the end of the last Mass, all the prayer candles lit by parishioners. " 'Fire hazard,' he'd said, caught in the act." In "One of Them," an equally stingy priest is said to have kept the Christmas ham in the trunk of his car, bringing it out only for meals. Of yet another unpleasant priest, a proud and chilly monsignor, in "The Forks," Powers writes that he "could not conduct a civil conversation." The monsignor delivers an arid little lecture on the history and significance of handshaking rather than shake the hand of his new curate, and is seen, with devastating irony, entering a doorway thus: "He held the screen door open momentarily, as if remembering something or reluctant to enter before himself—such was his humility . . ."

These rectories are chambers of denial, and we see how, trapped inside them, priests might overcompensate with a cynicism of permissible worldliness. But it is only a faux worldliness, limited in danger, since it substitutes for the real worldliness, the carnality that cannot be. A slick businesslike manliness, a virility about attendance percentages and fund-raising, a gluttony in food and drink and tobacco, an antisocial selfishness, a stupefied obeisance to television sports—Powers's characters submit to these allowed lapses as flights from the unreality of their domestic habitats, and as escapes into a merely sanctioned secularism. They are shallow sinners, as they are shallow believers.

The carnality that cannot be is sex, of course—not just the desire or the act but the realm of normality to which sex is the introduction: family life, free relations with other women (Powers's priests keep their study doors open when females are visiting), a life with one's body which is inevitable rather than forced. Sex is at the heart of sin because it is the central desire; and if, as Kierkegaard said, sin is at the heart of Christianity, then so must sex be. And sex is also limitless, because it is the most natural desire. Alcohol, gluttony, cynicism—these are controllable sins, even if only notionally, because they are not entirely natural, not universal. The priest can have these little moral hernias, but he cannot allow the enormous collapse into sexual desire. Jesus wished us to police the mind itself. Thus, strangely, the church praised by Heine for its compromise between spirit and matter in fact demands the impossible of its priests, demands an "annihilation of sensuality."

One has to infer some of this from Powers's work. For his priests are curiously hulled—bereft of sexual desire, so that all their small sins and failures seem ruins around this dark absence. The reader is struck by the fact that Powers's priests are never seen discussing sex, are never depicted thinking about sex or desiring other humans. One would like to suppose that this was Powers's way of gesturing toward the unspeakable, the truly impermissible, in these men's lives. But "the absence of the imagination had / Itself to be imagined," as Wallace Stevens has it. Instead, Powers never addresses this lack at all, and this silence comes to seem not deliberately expressive but a peculiar omission on Powers's own part, one that marks out one of his occasional weaknesses as a writer—an unwillingness, at times, to freely enter the consciousnesses of his characters.

After all, insofar as we are not allowed to see what these men truly desire—and it is inconceivable that they would not desire sexually—we do not partake of their damaged wholeness. There is

an externality—brilliant, vivid, marvelously rendered—to these characters and their trials, but sometimes a corresponding lack of interiority. Very occasionally we see priests resist sexual temptation, but
the temptations are put in their way; their minds are never seen as
themselves generating temptation, as happens every day in life. Father Urban, for instance, is challenged by a woman who undresses in
front of him, and Powers winningly writes that he takes his eyes off
her, and keeps them off. "It was like tearing up telephone directories,
the hardest part was getting started." He is like Father Burner, who,
hearing high heels outside, turns "firmly away from the window."
There is a pathos in this determination, and the writing has force because it is so glancing. But we are never admitted to the pain this
determination causes these men. We are only at the lintels of their
minds.

It might be argued that Powers rarely shows his characters enjoying spiritual lives, either, and that we are to understand *this* silence as
indicative of a painful lack. But Powers does write every so often of
the almost forgotten attempt to pray. He does write, for instance,
about the regret Father Hackett experiences when he sees that his
spiritual life has been compromised. But we never read of Father
Hackett's regret about the loss of a past sexual life. Yet *Wheat That
Springeth Green* begins by narrating the teenage years of Joe Hackett.
Powers writes of Joe's sexual adventures, tells us that the boy caught
VD, and then leaps over several years to the seminary. From this moment through the next 280 pages, in which we see Father Hackett indulge in a range of vices, sex is never again mentioned by Powers,
not even as an external temptation. It drops out of Joe's mind, and
out of the novel, and the VD begins to seem like a rather clumsy way
of effecting this silence. Of course, Father Hackett is the duller fictional character for it.

Powers's reticence about the matter of the spiritual life does become something of a problem in his two novels. The heroes of those
books lack sufficient consciousness in part because the novels are pi-

caresque in motion, character revealing itself in the journey of action. The relentless emphasis on worldly parish activity, or on petty vices, at the expense of any discussion of spiritual aspiration, becomes, after a while, a little stultifying. Especially in Powers's second novel, we feel we should not have to share, quite so entirely, the barrenness of these men's lives. The problem with writing about priests as if they were business managers is that, inevitably, one is really reading about business managers. Powers is often praised for depicting priests as if they were no different from other men. But in itself this can't be a virtue, only a lesson. Implicit in this praise, I think, is the suggestion that the secularism of priests may be more interesting than the secularism of nonpriests. But actually, the secularism of priests might be somewhat less interesting than other men's secularism—first, because it is more limited, and second, because it may be presented as interesting only because it is the secularism of people who are not usually secular.

These problems afflict the novels only, and acutely only the second. The stories—and many short-story-like scenes in the novels—blaze, because Powers is not compelled to stretch his hero's interiority over hundreds of pages. (He resembles Eudora Welty and V. S. Pritchett in this talent for the short visit, and comparative weakness at the long engagement.) Like many writers of short stories, he is a master of the portrait, of character as a bright blot of essence. Since his stories present only a quick swipe of life, we do not attempt to construct wholeness from particles, and do not feel its lack. Instead, we revel in the vitality of his people, leased only briefly to their fictional worlds.

Powers's prose is consistently superb—rare but not thinned by mandarinism, richly metaphorical but never unbudgeted in its wealth, each sentence a pondered finality. The slightest phrases bloom: "a few twigs folded in death"; a priest "caught in the old amber of his inadequacy"; the same priest, seen lying on his bed trying to get his trousers on, "his legs heaving up like howitzers." A disagreeable pastor is seen, from above, by a nun who dislikes him: "Father massaged his bald head to rouse himself. He wrinkled the mottled scalp between his hands and it seemed to make a nasty face at her."

Like some, but by no means all, stylists—like Joyce, not Nabokov—Powers is a stylist of conversation; dialogue is style by other means. From Chekhov and Joyce, perhaps also from Pritchett (who praised his stories), he learned how to observe the brief non sequiturs by which people express themselves, and to see that these bursts of illogic represent little riots of freedom, and thus actually of trapped logic, in otherwise orderly souls. In these stories, the parishioners who so bother their priests are invariably little bursting egotists, humble people for whom the pastor is a mobile confessional into which an almost punitive expansiveness can be spilled. Mrs. Klein, recently widowed, comes to see Father Eudex, in "The Forks," and, without invitation, comments: "It's a German name, Father. Klein was German descent . . . It ain't what you think, Father . . . Some think it's a Jew name. But they stole it from Klein." Gradually it becomes clear that Mrs. Klein has come to ask her priest for advice about how to invest her new inheritance. She becomes angry when Father Eudex suggests that she might give her money away. "But I got to say this—you ain't much of a priest. And Klein said if I got a problem, see the priest—huh! You ain't much of a priest!"

Powers is at his most comic when catching, as if by luck, this brackish overflow of people's souls. Father Urban, when asked by a stranger where he comes from, replies that for many years he traveled out of Chicago, at which the man suddenly bursts out: "Chicago! Don't tell me you haven't got a problem there!" Mrs. Stoner, a miserable housekeeper, in "The Valiant Woman," keeps a list of new Catholic converts. She is sitting with the pastor after a meal. "And Henry Ford's grandson, Father. I got him down." A second elapses, and then Mrs. Stoner remarks, for no apparent reason: "I see where Henry Ford's making steering wheels out of soybeans, Father." (The obsequious placement of that final "Father" is wonderful.) Or—my favorite—a fat man churning ice cream: " 'By Dad!' he breathed, a little god invoking himself."

Just as Powers alights gently on these little storms of egotism, so he slantingly illuminates the sad cruxes in which his priests find themselves—a fat, lonely curate, long passed over for promotion, is encouraged to think that the bishop wants to discuss a new job with him, and imagines how he'll look when he receives the news: "reliable, casual, cool, an iceberg, only the tip of his true worth showing"; he has, of course, merely been transferred ("Prince of Darkness"). A bishop is excited about building a new cathedral until one day, visiting the site, he notices that the arches are not built with keystones. Feeling that he is himself of diminishing importance in his diocese, not enough of a keystone, he broods on this architectural lack, and his interest in the cathedral withers ("Keystone"). A pastor does not feel powerful enough to speak firmly to the housekeeper who lords it over him ("The Valiant Woman").

The best of these stories are surely among the finest written by an American. Powers shows again what comic realism can do: how it attends to the human exception, how it scathes our pretensions and blesses our weaknesses. Modern comedy, the comedy of forgiveness, is incurably secular. For despite Powers's Christian faith, and despite the severity of his disappointment with the Catholic church, his writing, in its humane irony, tends toward an unwitting inversion of Christianity, whereby his characters are not punished but already forgiven for sins they do not repent of, and the dry ground of their souls is moistened by the author's gentle laughter.

Hysterical Realism

❧

I

A genre is hardening. It is becoming possible to describe the contemporary "big, ambitious novel." Familial resemblances are asserting themselves, and a parent can be named: Dickens. Such recent novels as Rushdie's *The Ground Beneath Her Feet*, Pynchon's *Mason & Dixon*, DeLillo's *Underworld*, David Foster Wallace's *Infinite Jest*, and Zadie Smith's *White Teeth* overlap rather as the pages of an atlas expire into each other at their edges.

The big contemporary novel is a perpetual-motion machine that appears to have been embarrassed into velocity. It seems to want to abolish stillness, as if ashamed of silence. Stories and substories sprout on every page, and these novels continually flourish their glamorous congestion. Inseparable from this culture of permanent storytelling is the pursuit of vitality at all costs. Indeed, vitality is storytelling, as far as these books are concerned. A parody would go like this. If a character is introduced in London (call him Toby Awknotuby, i.e., "To be or not to be"—ha!), then we will be swiftly told that Toby has a twin in Delhi (called Boyt: an anagram of Toby, of course) who, like Toby, has the same very curious genital deformation, and that their mother belongs to a religious cult based, oddly enough, in the Orkney Islands, and that their father (who was born at the exact second that the bomb was dropped on Hiroshima) has been a Hell's Angel for the last thirteen years (but a very curious Hell's Angels group, devoted only to the fanatical study of very late Wordsworth), and that their mad left-wing aunt, Delilah, was curiously struck dumb when Mrs. Thatcher was elected prime minister in 1979, and has not spoken a single word since.

Is this a caricature, really? Recent novels by Rushdie, Pynchon, DeLillo, Wallace, and others have featured a great rock musician who, when born, began immediately to play air guitar in his crib (Rushdie); a talking dog, a mechanical duck, a giant octagonal cheese, and two clocks having a conversation (Pynchon); a nun called Sister Edgar who is obsessed with germs and who may be a reincarnation of J. Edgar Hoover, and a conceptual artist who is painting retired B-52 bombers in the New Mexican desert (DeLillo); a terrorist group devoted to the liberation of Quebec called the Wheelchair Assassins, and a film so compelling that anyone who sees it dies (Wallace). And Zadie Smith's novel features, among other things: a terrorist Islamic group based in North London with a silly acronym (KEVIN), an animal rights group called FATE, a Jewish scientist who is genetically engineering a mouse, a woman born during an earthquake in Kingston, Jamaica, in 1907, a group of Jehovah's Witnesses who think that the world is ending on December 31, 1992, and twins, one in Bangladesh and one in London, who both break their noses at about the same time.

This is not magical realism but what might be called hysterical realism. Storytelling has become a kind of grammar in these novels; it is how they structure and drive themselves on. The conventions of realism are not being abolished but, on the contrary, exhausted, overworked. Appropriately, then, one's objections should be made not at the level of verisimilitude but at the level of morality: this style of writing is not to be faulted because it lacks reality—the usual charge—but because it seems evasive of reality while borrowing from realism itself. It is not a cock-up but a cover-up.

One is reminded of Kierkegaard's remark that travel is the way to

avoid despair. For these books share a bonhomous, punning, traveling serenity of spirit. (This is less true of *Infinite Jest* than of the
other books; and Wallace's subsequent work represents a deepening
of what can seem like puerility in his authorial voice.) Their mode of
narration seems to be almost incompatible with tragedy or anguish.
Underworld, the darkest of these books, nevertheless, in its calm profusion of characters and plots, its flawless carpet of fine prose on
page after page, carries within it a soothing sense that it might never
have to end, that another thousand or two thousand pages might
easily be added. There are many enemies, seen and unseen, in *Underworld*, but silence is not one of them.

And that optimism is shared by readers, apparently. Again and
again, books like these are praised for being brilliant cabinets of
wonders. Such diversity! So many stories! So many weird and funky
characters! Bright lights are taken as evidence of habitation. The
mere existence of a giant cheese or a cloned mouse or three different
earthquakes in a novel is seen as meaningful or wonderful, evidence
of great imaginative powers. And this is because too often these features are mistaken for *scenes*, as if they constituted the movement or
workings or pressure of the novel, rather than taken for what they
are—props of the imagination, meaning's toys. The existence of vitality is mistaken for the drama of vitality.

What are these busy stories and substories evading? One of the
awkwardnesses evaded is precisely an awkwardness about the possibility of novelistic storytelling. This in turn has to do with an awkwardness about character and the representation of character in
fiction, since human beings generate stories. It might be said that
these recent novels are full of *inhuman stories*, whereby that phrase is
precisely an oxymoron, an impossibility, a wanting-it-both-ways. By
and large, these are not stories that could never happen (as, say, a
thriller or a magical realist novel often contains things that could
never happen); rather, they clothe people who could never actually
endure the stories that happen to them. They are not stories in

which people defy the laws of physics (obviously, one could be born in an earthquake); they are stories which defy the laws of persuasion. This is what Aristotle means when he says that in storytelling "a convincing impossibility" (a man levitating, say) is always preferable to "an unconvincing possibility" (say, the possibility that a fundamentalist group in London would continue to call itself KEVIN). And what above all makes these stories unconvincing is their very profusion, their relatedness. One cult is convincing; three are not. Cervantes has a famous story about two talking dogs, but it is only a few pages long and feels more like a fable than an exercise in verisimilitude (he called it, precisely, "an exemplary story").

Novels, after all, turn out to be delicate structures, in which one story judges the viability, the actuality, of another. Yet it is the relatedness of these stories which their writers seem to cherish, and propose as an absolute value. Each of these novels is excessively centripetal. The different stories all intertwine, and double and triple on themselves. Characters are forever seeing connections and links and hidden plots, and paranoid parallels. (There is something essentially paranoid about the idea that everything connects with everything else.) These novelists proceed like street planners of old in South London: they can never name one street Ruskin Street without linking a whole block and filling it with Carlyle Street, and Turner Street, and Morris Street, and so on. There is an obsession in these novels with connecting characters with each other, as information is connected in the World Wide Web.

For instance, near the end of *White Teeth*, one of the characters, Irie Jones, has sex with one twin, called Millat, but then rushes round to see the other twin, called Magid, to have sex with him. She becomes pregnant; she will never know which twin impregnated her. But it is really Smith's hot plot which has had its way with her. In *Underworld*, everything and everyone is connected in some way to paranoia and to the nuclear threat. *The Ground Beneath Her Feet* suggests that a deep structure of myth, both Greek and Indian, binds all the characters together. *White Teeth* ends with a clashing finale in which all the novel's characters—most of whom are now dispersed between various cults and fanatical religious groups—head toward the press conference which the scientist Marcus Chalfen is delivering in London, to announce the successful engineering of his mouse.

Alas, since the characters in these novels are not really alive, not fully human, their connectedness can only be insisted on; indeed, the reader begins to think that it is being insisted on precisely because they do not really exist. After all, hell *is* other people, actually; real humans disaggregate more often than congregate. So these novels find themselves in the paradoxical position of enforcing connections which are finally merely conceptual rather than human. The forms of these novels *tell* us that we are all connected—by the bomb (DeLillo), or by myth (Rushdie), or by our natural multiracial multiplicity (Smith); but it is a formal lesson rather than an actual enactment.

An excess of storytelling has become the contemporary way of shrouding, in majesty, a lack; it is the Sun King principle. That lack is the human. Of course, there has been since modernism a crisis in how to create human character on the page. Since modernism, many of the greatest writers have been offering critique and parody of the idea of character, in the absence of convincing ways to return to an innocent representation of character. Certainly the people who inhabit the big, ambitious contemporary novels have a showy liveliness, a theatricality, that almost succeeds in hiding the fact they are without life. This is much less true of Zadie Smith than of Rushdie; Smith's principal characters move in and out of human depth. Sometimes they seem to provoke her sympathy, at other times they are only externally comic.

But watch what she does with one of the many bit parts in her large, inventive book. Smith is describing the founder of KEVIN, the fundamentalist Islamic group based in North London. She tells us that he was born Monty Clyde Benjamin in Barbados in 1960, "the son of two poverty-stricken barefoot Presbyterian dypsomani-acs," and converted to Islam at the age of fourteen. At eighteen, he fled Barbados for Riyadh, where he studied the Koran at Al-Imam Muhammad ibn Saud Islamic University. He was five years there, but he became disillusioned with the teaching and returned to England in 1984. In Birmingham, he

> locked himself in his aunt's garage and spent five more years in there, with only the Qur'an and the fascicles of Endless Bliss for company. He took his food in through the cat-flap, deposited his shit and piss in a Coronation biscuit tin and passed it back out the same way, and did a thorough routine of press-ups and sit-ups to prevent muscular atrophy. The *Selly Oak Reporter* wrote regular by-lines on him during this period, nicknaming him "The Guru in the Garage" (in view of the large Birmingham Muslim population, this was thought preferable to the press-desk favoured suggestion, "The Loony in the Lock-Up"), and had their fun interviewing his be-mused aunt, one Carlene Benjamin, a devoted member of the Church of Jesus Christ of Latter-Day Saints.

Clearly Smith does not lack for powers of invention. The problem is there is too much of it. The passage might stand, microcosmically, for her novel's larger dilemma of storytelling: on its own, almost any of these details (except perhaps the detail about passing the shit and piss through the cat-flap) might be persuasive. Together, they van-dalize each other: the Presbyterian dypsomaniacs and the Mormon aunt make impossible the reality of the fanatical Muslim. As realism, it is incredible; as satire, it is cartoonish; as cartoon, it is too realistic; and anyway, we are not led toward the consciousness of a truly de-voted religionist. It is all shiny externality, a caricature.

II

It might be argued that literature has only rarely represented character. Even the greatest novelists, like Dostoevsky and Tolstoy, resort to stock caricature, didactic speaking over characters, repetitive leitmotifs, and so on. The truly unhostaged, the Chekhovs, are rare. *Buddenbrooks*, a first novel written by a writer only a year older than Zadie Smith when she wrote hers, makes plentiful use of the leitmotif as a way of affixing signatures to different characters. (Yet how those tagged characters live!) Less great but very distinguished writers indulge in the kind of unreal, symbolic vitality now found in the contemporary novel—for instance, the autodidact in Sartre's *Nausea*, who is somewhat unbelievably working his way alphabetically through an entire library, or Grand, the writer in *The Plague*, who writes the first line of his novel over and over again.

Dickens, of course, is the great master of the leitmotif (and Dostoevsky read and admired Dickens). Many of Dickens's characters are, as Forster rightly put it, flat but vibrating very fast. They are souls seen only through thick, gnarled casings. Their vitality is a histrionic one. Dickens has been the overwhelming influence on postwar fiction, especially postwar British fiction. There is hardly a writer who has not been touched by him: Angus Wilson and Muriel Spark, Martin Amis's robust comic gargoyles, Rushdie's outsize characters, the intensely theatrical Angela Carter, the Naipaul of *Mr. Biswas*, V. S. Pritchett, and now Zadie Smith. In America, Bellow's genius for grotesquerie and for vivid external description owes something to Dickens; and what was *Underworld* but an old-fashioned Dickensian novel like *Bleak House*, with an ambition to describe all of society on its different levels?

One obvious reason for the popularity of Dickens among contemporary novelists is that his way of creating and propelling theatrically alive characters offers an easy model for writers unable to, or unwilling to, create characters who are fully human. Dickens's world seems to be populated by vital simplicities. Dickens shows a novelist how to get a character launched, if not how to keep him afloat, and this glittering liveliness is simply easier to copy, easier to figure out, than the recessed and deferred complexities of, say, Henry James's character-making. (And I say this not merely as the apparently untouchable critic but also guiltily, as a first novelist whose own characters owe more than a little to the hard edges of Dickensian caricature.) Dickens makes caricature respectable for an age in which, for various reasons, it has become hard to create character. Dickens licenses the cartoonish, coats it in the surreal, or even the Kafkaesque (the Circumlocution Office). Indeed, to be fair to contemporary novelists, Dickens shows that a large part of characterization *is* the management of caricature.

Yet in Dickens there is always an immediate access to strong feeling, which tears the puppetry of his people, breaks their casings, and lets us enter them. Mr. Micawber may be a caricature, a simple, univocal essence, but he feels, and he makes us feel. One recalls that very passionate and simple sentence in which David Copperfield tells us: "Mr. Micawber was waiting for me within the gate, and we went up to his room, and cried very much."

It is difficult to find a single moment like that in all the many thousands of pages of the big, ambitious, contemporary books. It has become customary to read 700-page novels, to spend hours within a fictional world without experiencing anything really affecting or beautiful. Which is why one never wants to reread a book like *The Ground Beneath Her Feet*, while *Madame Bovary* is faded by our re-pressings. But that is partly because some of the more impressive novelistic minds of our age do not think that language and the representation of consciousness are the novelist's quarries anymore. Information has become the new character. It is this, and the use made of Dickens, that connects DeLillo and the reportorial Tom Wolfe, despite the literary distinction of the former and the cinematic vulgarity of the latter.

So it suffices to make do with lively caricatures, whose deeper justification arises—if it ever arises—from their immersion in a web of connections. Zadie Smith has said, in an interview, that her concern is with "ideas and themes that I can tie together—problem-solving from other places and worlds." It is not the writer's job, she says, "to tell us how somebody felt about something, it's to tell us how the world works." Citing David Foster Wallace and Dave Eggers, she comments: "These are guys who know a great deal about the world. They understand macro-microeconomics, the way the Internet works, math, philosophy, but . . . they're still people who know something about the street, about family, love, sex, whatever. That is an incredibly fruitful combination. If you can get the balance right. And I don't think any of us have quite yet, but hopefully one of us will."

III

This is gently, modestly put. Smith may not actually believe what she says; she seems to me a writer who is quite interested in telling us "how somebody felt about something"—it is one of her many strengths. And to give Smith her considerable due, she may be more likely to "get the balance right" than any of her contemporaries, in part just because she sees that a balance is needed, and in part because she is very talented and still very young. At her best, she approaches her characters and makes them human; she is much more interested in this, and more naturally gifted at it, than Rushdie is, for example. To begin with, her minor Dickensian caricatures and grotesques, the petty filaments of *White Teeth*, often glow. Here, for instance, is a school headmaster, a small character who flares and dies within a few pages. But Smith captures his physical essence surely: "The headmaster of Glenard Oak was in a continual state of implosion. His hairline had gone out and stayed out like a determined tide, his eye sockets were deep, his lips had been sucked backwards into his mouth, he had no body to speak of, or rather he folded what he had into a small, twisted package, sealing it with a pair of crossed arms and crossed legs." This conjures a recognizable type, and indeed a recognizable English type, always in the process of withdrawing or disappearing— as Smith's highly Dickensian image suggests, always mailing himself out of the room. The headmaster is like Miss Dartle in *David Copperfield*: "She brings everything to a grindstone and sharpens it, as she has sharpened her own face and figure . . . [S]he is all edge."

Smith, as Rushdie has said, is "astonishingly assured." About her, one is tempted to apply Orwell's remark, that Dickens had rotten architecture but great gargoyles. The architecture is the essential silliness of her lunge for multiplicities—her cults and cloned mice and Jamaican earthquakes. Formally, her book lacks moral seriousness. But her details are often instantly convincing, both funny and moving. They justify themselves. She tells the story, really, of two families, the Joneses and the Iqbals. Archie Jones is married to a Jamaican woman, Clara Bowden, and is the father of Irie. He fought in the war, as a teenager, alongside Samad Iqbal, a Bengali Muslim from Bangladesh. The two men have been friends for thirty years, and now live near each other in North London. This is a bustling, desolate area, full of gaudy Indian restaurants and yeasty pubs and unclean laundromats. Smith bouncily captures its atmosphere. Any street in this region will include, "without exception,"

> one defunct sandwich bar still advertising breakfast
> one locksmith uninterested in marketing frills (KEYS CUT HERE)
> and one permanently shut unisex hair salon, the proud bearer of
>   some unspeakable pun (*Upper Cuts* or *Fringe Benefits* or *Hair Today, Gone Tomorrow*).

Samad's wife, Alsana, is an engaging creation. She earns a living sewing black plastic garments at home, that are bound "for a shop called Domination in Soho." (One of the many good jokes in this comic book.) Samad is a waiter at a restaurant in central London, an intelligent man, frustrated by his foolish occupation, and a moral man, frustrated by the lax country he lives in. He spends much of the novel in a fury—he is, precisely, a caricature more than a character—about England and English secularism. He is determined that his twin sons, Millat and Magid, will grow up in the ways of the Koran. But Millat, at least initially, has joined a tough street gang who speak "a strange mix of Jamaican patois, Bengali, Gujurati and English," and hangs out on streets populated by "Becks, B-boys, Indie kids, wide-boys, ravers, rude-boys, Acidheads, Sharons, Tracies, Kevs, Nation Brothers, Raggas and Pakis." (This is what Smith means by bringing us the information. But this crocodile of youths has a time bomb inside it; Colin MacInnes brought us the information about the London of the 1950s in *Absolute Beginners*, and where is that novel? At an absolute end.) Millat's brother, Magid, is a scientific rationalist, and apparently no more interested in Islam than his brother. But his father decides to send Magid, the better student, back to Bangladesh for a safely religious education. The plan backfires, of course.

When Smith is writing well, she seems capable of almost anything. She more than justifies the excitement she has provoked. For example, at several moments she proves herself very skilled at interior monologue, and brilliant, in several passages, at free indirect style:

> "Oh Archie, you *are* funny," said Maureen sadly, for she had always fancied Archie a *bit* but never more than a bit because of this strange way he had about him, always talking to Pakistanis and Caribbeans like he didn't even notice and now he'd gone and married one and hadn't even thought it worth mentioning what colour she was until the office dinner when she turned up black as anything and Maureen almost choked on her prawn cocktail.

That is a fabulous bit of writing, the narrative running on as if in the jumbled and prejudiced head of Maureen; how deftly that vicious little "even" is placed in the sentence. Can't one immediately hear Maureen's voice, with its silly emphasis as it greedily alights on the stressed "even"?

One of the novel's best chapters is a gently satirical portrait of the Chalfen family, middle-class North London intellectuals of impeccable smugness with whom Millat, Magid, and Irie become involved. (One of the Chalfen sons, Joshua, attends Glenard Oak school with the Jones and Iqbal children.) There is Marcus Chalfen, busy with his genetic experiments, and his wife, Joyce, who writes about gardening. She lives the politically unexamined life of the liberal who is sure that she is right about everything. Even her gardening books encode her *bien pensant pensées* about the importance of hybridity. Smith invents a long passage from one of them: "In the garden, as in the social and political arena, change should be the only constant . . . It is said cross-pollinating plants also tends to produce more and better-quality seeds."

But this same Joyce cannot help exclaiming, when Millat and Irie first appear in her house, about the delightful novelty of having "brown strangers" in the house. By mocking the Chalfens, even gently, Smith works against the form of her own novel, and seems to guard against a Rushdie-like piety about the desirability of hybridity, an important novelistic negative capability which she then, alas, deforms by inserting a little Rushdie-like lecture of her own into the very same chapter: "This has been the century of strangers, brown, yellow and white. This has been the century of the great immigrant experiment." One attributes this kind of lapse to immaturity. Far more powerful than such announcements on the authorial Tannoy is a lovely moment when Marcus Chalfen puts his arms around his adored wife (the two are devoted, if a little complacently, to each other) "like a gambler collecting his chips in circled arms," whereupon the fifteen-year-old Irie, whose parents are much less communicative, thinks "of her own parents, whose touches were now virtual, existing only in the absences where both sets of fingers had previously been: the remote control, the biscuit tin, the light switches."

But Smith is a frustrating writer, for she has a natural comic gift and yet is willing to let passages of her book descend into cartoon-ishness and a kind of itchy, restless extremism. Here, for instance, is her description of O'Connell's, a bar and café where Archie and Samad have been regulars for many years. Comically, it is run by a family of Iraqis, "the many members of which share a bad skin con-dition," but it has kept its Irish name, and various Irish accou-trements. It is where, we are told, Archie and Samad have talked about everything, including women:

> Hypothetical women. If a woman walked past the yolk-stained win-dow of O'Connell's (a woman had never been known to venture inside) they would smile and speculate — depending on Samad's religious sensibilities that evening — on matters as far-reaching as whether one would kick her out of bed in a hurry, to the relative merits of stockings or tights, and then on, inevitably, to the great de-bate: small breasts (that stand up) vs big breasts (that flop to the sides). But there was never any question of real women, real flesh and blood and wet and sticky women. Not until now. And so the unprecedented events of the past few months called for an earlier O'Connell's summit than usual. Samad had finally phoned Archie and confessed the whole terrible mess: he had cheated, he was cheat-ing . . . Archie had been silent for a bit, and then said, "Bloody hell. Four o'clock it is, then. Bloody hell." He was like that, Archie. Calm in a crisis.
>
> But come 4:15 and still no sign of him, a desperate Samad had chewed every fingernail he possessed to the cuticle and collapsed on the counter, nose squished up against the hot glass where the bat-tered burgers were kept, eye to eye with a postcard showing the eight different local charms of County Antrim.
>
> Mickey, chef, waiter and proprietor, who prided himself on knowing each customer's name and knowing when each customer

was out of sorts, prised Samad's face off the hot glass with an egg slice.

This kind of writing is closer to the low "comic" style of a farceur like Tom Sharpe than it ought to be. It has a pertness, but it squanders itself in a mixture of banality and crudity. And unlike many passages in the book, it cannot shelter behind the excuse that it is being written from within the mind of a particular character. This is Smith as narrator, as writer. Yet nothing we know about Samad (and nothing we later learn, incidentally) convinces us that Smith is telling the truth when she asks us to imagine this hotheaded Muslim talking about women's breasts; the topic seems, instead, to have been chosen by Smith from the catalogue of clichés marked "Things Men Talk About in Bars." And then there is the extremism of the language—Samad is not just anxious but has bitten his fingernails down to the cuticles, and has to be "prised" off the counter "with an egg slice." It seems only a step from here to exploding condoms and the like. The language is oddly thick-fingered—from a writer capable of such delicacy—and stubs itself into the vernacular: that juvenile verb, "squished," for instance. It comports bewilderingly with sentences and passages elsewhere that are precise and sculpted.

In general, the first half of *White Teeth* is strikingly better written than the second, which seems hasty, the prose and wild plots bucking along in loosened harnesses. Just as the quality of the writing varies, sometimes from page to page, so Smith seems unable to decide exactly the depth of her commitment to the revelation of character. Samad offers a good example. Overall, he must be accounted a caricature, complete with Indian malapropisms and Indian (or Bengali) "temperament," for he has, really, only the one dimension, his angry defense of Islam. Yet every so often Smith's prose opens out, into little holidays from caricature, apertures through which we see Samad tenderly, and see his frustrations, such as the restaurant he works in: "From six in the evening until three in the morning; and then every day was spent asleep, until daylight was as rare as a decent tip. For what's the point, Samad would think, pushing aside two mints and a receipt to find fifteen pence, what is the point of tipping a man the same amount you would throw in a fountain to chase a wish."

This is breathtaking, and peers into a depth of yearning: it is very fine to link the tip to money thrown into a well, and link both to Samad's large desires; and those "two mints," roughly pushed aside! One wonders if Smith knows how good it is. For it is bewildering when, thirty pages later, she seems to leave Samad's interior and watch him from the outside, satirically (and rather crudely). She is describing Samad's and Archie's war experiences, and the moment they first met. The tone wavers drastically around the mock heroic. Archie has been staring at Samad, and Samad, all of nineteen, mala-propistically demands: "My friend, what is it you find so darned mysterious about me that it has you in such constant revelries? . . . Is it that you are doing some research into wireless operators or are you just in a passion over my arse?" We seem to be in the world of Tom Sharpe again.

Forty pages later, Smith has a funny passage about Samad trying and failing to resist the temptation of masturbation. Samad be-comes, for a while, an enthusiastic masturbator, on the arrangement (with Allah) that if he masturbates, he must fast, as recompense: "This in turn . . . led to the kind of masturbation that even a fifteen-year-old boy living in the Shetlands might find excessive. His only comfort was that he, like Roosevelt, had made a New Deal: he was going to beat but he wasn't going to *eat*." As in the passage about O'Connell's, the question is one of voice. Again, Smith is not writ-ing from inside Samad's head here; the sophomoric comparison to a boy in the Shetlands is hers. The reference to the New Deal is utterly misplaced, and merely demonstrates the temptation that this style of writing cannot resist, of bringing in any kind of allusion. Equally, take that phrase "he was going to beat but he wasn't going to *eat*."

"Beat" is not Samad's word; he would never use it. It is Smith's, and in using it she not only speaks over her character, she reduces him, obliterates him.

And so it goes on, in a curious exchange of sympathy and distance, affiliation and divorce, brilliance and cartoonishness, astonishing maturity and ordinary puerility. *White Teeth* is a big book, and does not deal in fractions: when it excites, and when it frustrates, it "o'erflows the measure." Indeed, its size tests itself, for one reason it disappoints has partly to do with the fact that it becomes clear that over the length of the book Smith's stories will develop, and develop wildly, but her characters will not. Yes, Smith's characters change — they change opinions, and change countries. Millat, once an urban rapper, becomes a fundamentalist terrorist; Joshua Chalfen, once a rationalist and loyal son of his scientist father, becomes an animal rights freak. Yet whenever these people change their minds, there is always a kind of awkwardness in the text, a hiatus, and the change itself is always rapidly asserted, usually within a paragraph or two. It is as if the novel were deciding at these moments whether to cast depths on its shallows, and deciding against.

Which way will the ambitious contemporary novel go? Will it dare a picture of life, or just shout a spectacle? *White Teeth* contains both kinds of writing. Near the end, an instructive squabble occurs between these two literary modes. The scene is the conference room where Marcus Chalfen is delivering the news about the mouse. All of the book's major characters are present. Irie Jones is pregnant, and looks from Millat to Magid and cannot decide which twin is the father of her child. But she stops worrying, because Smith breaks in, excitedly, to tell us that "Irie's child can never be mapped exactly nor spoken of with any certainty. Some secrets are permanent. In a vision, Irie has seen a time, a time not far from now, when roots won't matter anymore because they can't because they mustn't because they're too long and they're too tortuous and they're just buried too damn deep. She looks forward to it."

But it is Smith who made Irie, most improbably, have sex with both brothers, and it is Smith who decided that Irie, most improbably, has stopped caring who is the father. It is quite clear that a general message about the need to escape roots is more important than Irie's reality, what she might actually think. A character has been sacrificed for what Smith called, in that interview, "ideas and themes that I can tie together—problem-solving from other places and worlds." This is problem-solving, all right. But at what cost? As Irie disappears under the themes and ideas, the reader perhaps thinks wistfully of Mr. Micawber and David Copperfield, so uncovered by theme and idea, weeping together in an upstairs room.

Jonathan Franzen and the "Social Novel"

❧

I

If anyone still had a longing for the great American "social novel," the events of September 11, 2001, may have corrected it, through the reminder of an asymmetry of their own: that whatever the novel gets up to, the "culture" can always get up to something bigger. Ashes defeat garlands. If topicality, relevance, reportage, social comment, preachy presentism, and sidewalk smarts—in short, the contemporary American novel in its big triumphalist form—are the novel's chosen sport, the novel will sooner or later be outrun by its own racing material. The novel may well be, as Stendhal wrote, a mirror carried down the middle of a road; but the poor Stendhalian mirror would explode with reflections were it now being walked around Manhattan. For example, a passage at the end of Jonathan Franzen's novel *The Corrections*, about the end of the American century, now seems sadly archival:

> It seemed to Enid that current events in general were more muted
> or insipid nowadays than they'd been in her youth. She had memo-
> ries of the 1930s, she'd seen firsthand what could happen to a coun-
> try when the world economy took its gloves off . . . But disasters of

this magnitude no longer seemed to befall the United States. Safety features had been put in place, like the squares of rubber that every modern playground was paved with, to soften impacts.

Despite the falter of this passage, Jonathan Franzen would probably agree that the novel should not go chasing after the bait of social information. Five years ago he wrote an essay, published by *Harper's*, in which he declared the social novel no longer possible. The piece was so intelligent and affecting—it had the charm and directness typical of all his work—and above all so long, that few noticed its incoherence. He began by admitting to a recent depression, a depression about the social novel, a "despair about the possibility of connecting the personal and the social." No challenging novel since *Catch-22*, he wrote, had really affected the culture. As a young writer he had believed that "putting a novel's characters in a dynamic social setting enriched the story that was being told." The novel, he used to believe, should bring "social news, social instruction," it should "Address the Culture and Bring News to the Mainstream," and it had "a responsibility to dramatize important issues of the day."

And Franzen's first novel, *The Twenty-Seventh City*, was such a book. But it came and went, fairly quietly, and Franzen was left pondering "the failure of my culturally engaged novel to engage with the culture I'd intended to provoke; what I got instead was sixty reviews in a vacuum." There was a book tour, a photo spread in *Vogue*, a large advance, but this was merely "the consolation of no longer mattering to the culture." His second novel also dribbled into the celebrity-sand. There were good reviews, "decent sales, and the deafening silence of irrelevance." The social novel, it seemed, had no utility. The novel had lost its centrality, its cultural power; modern technologies such as television "do a better job of social instruction." And how to create something permanent whose subject—modern culture—is itself ephemeral? Franzen rightly asked the acute question, perhaps the most tormenting among contemporary novelists, of how to write a novel both of its time and properly resistant to it: "How can you achieve topical 'relevance' without drawing on an up-to-the-minute vocabulary of icons and attitudes and thereby, far from challenging the hegemony of overnight obsolescence, confirming and furthering it?"

By the end of his essay, Franzen had decided that there was "something wrong with the whole model of the novel of social engagement," and had admitted to a "conviction that bringing 'meaningful news' is no longer so much a defining function of the novel as an accidental product." The solution, it seemed, was aesthetic. "Expecting a novel to bear the weight of our whole disturbed society—to help solve our contemporary problems—seems to me a peculiarly American delusion. To write sentences of such authenticity that refuge can be taken in them: isn't this enough? Isn't it a lot?"

Franzen's aesthetic solution to the social novel—the "refuge" of "sentences"—is, I think, the right one, or at least one of them, but his reasons for arriving at it are the wrong ones, such that they cast doubt on the certainty with which he believes in that solution. To begin with, the essay was so autobiographically infected that his argument too quickly sickened into subjectivity; predictably, it is just this autobiographical malady that has appealed to the media during the publication of *The Corrections*, so that the essay is increasingly read as if Franzen had merely complained about the feebleness of a particular genre of American novel and then decided, with *The Corrections*, to go ahead and invent a really strong one—above all, a novel that people really want. *Time* magazine, noting that one of Franzen's definitions of how seriously the culture takes fiction might be a *Time* cover about a novelist, delivered itself of a review whose explicit theme was: *The Corrections* must be an important novel if *Time* is running this review of it.

But Franzen partly has himself to blame for the idiocy of his coverage, for his essay repeatedly had recourse to the personal as a way of solving what should have been impersonal arguments. We read about his despair, his "depressing estrangement from the mainstream," his "hunger for a large audience," and his "isolation." At one point he said, in effect, that he was disillusioned with the novel because he had become so isolated; so he decided to go back into society, do a little journalism, go to some literary parties, write for *The New Yorker*, and so on—and then he began to feel much better about the novel! As a result of this kind of argumentative Twelve-Step, it is never entirely clear that Franzen is not declaring the social novel dead just because *his* social novels died . . .

But more important, although his solution may have been aesthetic, the reasons he offered for the difficulty of continuing with the social novel are themselves social reasons, not aesthetic ones. At no point did Franzen ask if topicality, relevance, a large audience, the mainstream, are things the novel should in fact be courting; he simply said that the novel had not successfully courted them. At no point did he consider the proposition that "social instruction," the bringing of "news," might have nothing much to do with art. Like Don DeLillo, whom he quoted in the essay, Franzen establishes a kind of competition between the novel and society, almost an equivalence. The novel must somehow match the culture, equal its potency. And since the novel obviously cannot do so, then the novel has somehow lost, and must fatten itself up. DeLillo, in an essay published in 1997 called "The Power of History," argued, rather shockingly to my mind, that "at its root level, fiction is a kind of religious fanaticism with elements of obsession, superstition and awe. Such qualities will sooner or later state their adversarial relationship to history." (Imagine what Tolstoy would have made of such incoherence.) Franzen has come to the much more acceptable conclusion that the novel should stop trying to act like the culture, and become properly aesthetic.

But despite his difference, Franzen's premises, like DeLillo's, actually flatter the culture the novel is supposed to resist. They do so because they assume that the culture has a power that must be socially attended to, rather than just aesthetically bypassed. Franzen laments "the failure of my culturally engaged novel to engage with the culture I'd intended to provoke." But doesn't Franzen mean by this "engagement with the culture" that really the culture should engage back with the novel? And doesn't the culture then become the judge of the success of that engagement, the controller of it, as precisely *Time* magazine decided? *Time* declared, after all and in effect: "Your culturally engaged novel has engaged us, and the proof is that we are here to tell you so, and to engage back with you." And Franzen's words can only really mean: "the failure of my culturally engaged novel to *provoke a response* from the culture I'd intended to provoke." Well, he has finally provoked his response.

The danger of this kind of argument lies in its utilitarianism. Reflect on what would count as evidence, for Franzen, that his novel had indeed engaged with the culture. Two hundred reviews and forty profiles? What would be the definition of a novel not published "in a vacuum"? Is it not true that even *The Corrections*, already a best seller and chosen by Oprah Winfrey as a book club selection, will also in the end be essentially published "in a vacuum"? The only success is aesthetic, and the "culture" will never validate aesthetic success, will never "engage" with that. And above all, *we* will not be the definitive judges of this final success: Dr. Johnson suggested that a hundred years' survival might be the test of a book's aesthetic power. Aesthetic success is measured in leagues of posterity. In this sense every great novel is published in a vacuum: it teaches the empty space around it. *Nausea* and *The Stranger*, for instance, are not great novels which successfully engaged with an existential culture, but great novels which taught a culture existentialism.

So when Franzen reaches for the autonomy of art—a new novel form that will appeal to the "refuge" of "sentences"—the gesture seems weak largely because he does not seem to believe in the autonomy of art. He seems to believe in the sociality of art. And what kind of "refuge" can be taken in an aesthetics that is drained of both the moral and the authoritative? For on the question of the moral, Franzen writes: "I can't stomach any kind of notion that serious fiction is *good for us*, because I don't believe that everything that's wrong with the world has a cure." (Reread that sentence, and it quickly becomes the very definition of a non sequitur.) And on the idea of aesthetic hierarchy: "I resist, finally, the notion of literature as a noble higher calling, because elitism doesn't sit well with my American nature, and because . . . my belief in manners would make it difficult for me to explain to my brother, who is a fan of Michael Crichton, that the work I'm doing is simply *better* than Crichton's." (Notice again the flight to the personal at the moment that logic threatens.)

An aesthetics without any faith in either morality or in the arguability of aesthetic distinction—without beauty or truth, in effect—is a starved one, starved down precisely only to the "refuge" of a few authentic "sentences." And it is hardly surprising, given this starved aesthetic, that most of Franzen's argumentation is either sociological or autobiographical. It would be impossible, on this aesthetics alone, to make a proper argument against the social novel and in favor of a different kind of American novel. Only gestures are possible within this kind of aesthetics; or, rather, what is only possible is what Franzen produced in his essay: a polemic that has a bit of everything—a bit of aesthetics, a bit of sociology, a bit of pragmatism, and a bit of autobiographical justification.

II

Franzen has so lengthily lamented the impossibility of producing the social novel that he seems, really, to be longing for its renewed possibility. He appears to be disillusioned only with the possibility of the social novel, not its desirability; he is still half in love with it. And just as his essay looks toward the social and toward the aesthetic at the same time, and combines all modes of argument, so his new novel is a kind of glass-bottomed boat through which one can glimpse most of the various currents of contemporary American fiction: there is domestic realism (a midwestern family); there is social and cultural analysis (a nasty Philadelphia biotech company straight out of DeLillo); there is campus farce; there is the broad Dickensianism which has decayed into crudeness in too much American fiction; there is "smart young man's irony" of the kind familiar to us in Rick Moody and David Foster Wallace (riffs on corporate gardens, on the politics of cuisine, on the Lithuanian black market); and there is, at times, an easy journalism of narrative style.

But to be fair to *The Corrections*, there is also considerable grace, power, comedy, and beauty; and these qualities appear most reliably when Franzen is cleaving to the human, when he is laying bare the clogged dynamics of his fictional family, the Lamberts. I do not mean by this the anti-intellectual faint praise that Franzen is at his most affecting when merely "telling a story," when eschewing the theoretical or ambitious. I mean that he is at his finest when being ambitious and even theoretical about the soul, when he is examining consciousness and finding, willy-nilly, that consciousness is the true Stendhalian mirror, reflecting helplessly the random angles of the age.

Franzen's *Harper's* essay proposed, in effect, a softened DeLilloism. What is retained from DeLillo is the tentacular ambition, the effort to pin down an entire writhing culture. The DeLilloian idea of the novelist as a kind of Frankfurt School entertainer, fighting the culture with dialectical devilry, has been woefully influential, and will take some time to die; nowadays, anyone in possession of a laptop is thought to be a brilliance on the move. Franzen has some of this portable theoretical "brilliance" or "smartness" and it can be wearying. But against this, he has politely implied that DeLillo's most ambitious novel of cultural critique, *Underworld*, is weakened by its total lack of characterological depth, and *The Corrections*, though nicely blurbed by DeLillo, imagines itself as a correction of DeLillo in favor of the human. This is welcome. More than welcome, it is an urgent task of contemporary American fiction, whose characteristic products are books of great self-consciousness with no selves in them; curiously arrested books which know a thousand different things—How to make the best Indonesian fish curry! The sonics of the trombone! The drug market in Detroit! The history of strip cartoons!—but do not know a single human being.

So *The Corrections* is a correction, and as such it succeeds marvelously. At its warm center—and it says much for Franzen's charm as a writer that his book should seem warm while it is in fact dark—are Enid and Alfred Lambert, retirees who live in a fictional Kansan city named St. Jude. They are the striving middle classes: Alfred, an old-fashioned authoritarian, worked for most of his life as an engineer at Midland Pacific, a big midwestern railroad company, and Enid, who stayed at home, has spent much of her life calibrating their slow social rise. Stubborn, repressed, self-denying, Alfred is the kind of adamantine patriarch who has always been a rocky obstacle to his children, either as example or as cautionary lesson; Enid is the kind of noisy, bursting mother who drowns her children in striving. She wants too much for them, but what she wants is not what they want. Franzen provides a nice example of one of her "florid biweekly letters" to her son Chip, begging him to abandon his Ph.D.: "I see your old science fair trophies . . . and I think of what an able young man like you could be giving back to society as a medical doctor, but then, you see, Dad and I always hoped we'd raised children who thought of others, not just themselves."

But their parental authority is dissolving: Alfred has Parkinson's disease, and is losing control of both his body and his memory, and Enid, forced to become his helper, is weakened by Al's weakness—her appeals to her three children have become increasingly shrill. Franzen intelligently explores the shadowed lives of those three adult children: Gary, a banker in Philadelphia, and the only one of the

three children to be married and have children himself; Chip, a former academic who has been wasting his time in Manhattan trying to
write a film script; and Denise, a successful chef who has opened a
trendy new restaurant in Philadelphia. The stately length of his book
enables Franzen to accumulate quiddity gradually and persistently,
so that we gather a sense of each Lambert. In particular, we see that
the Lambert children, despite their successful and free lives as adults,
are unfree, because they are still above all parented. All decisions,
consciously or not, are routed via the parental desk—and so the
Lambert children, like many of us, are really only honorary adults,
ex officio.

Family is the great determinism. One of the subtlest and most
moving aspects of Franzen's often distinguished book is the way he
develops the idea of "correction" as a doomed struggle against this
determinism. At its simplest, it is no more than the notion that children often believe themselves to be living lives that correct those of
their parents. Franzen writes of Gary that "his entire life was set up as
a correction of his father's life," and much the same might be said, in
different ways, of Denise and Chip. But parents may also imagine
their children as new corrections of themselves, and yearn to live
through them vicariously, as Enid so earnestly does. And yet again,
this yearning promises pain, because it is painful to be self-corrected:
sure enough, Enid is tormented by the sense that her children have
corrected her too sharply and too publicly. Why don't her children,
she thinks sorrowfully, want what the children of her neighbors want?
Why do her children live so far away, and why do they launch themselves into outlandish occupations like screenwriting and cooking?

This dream of correction is chimerical, of course, because family
determinism tends to turn correction into repetition. Denise repetitively inherits her mother's restlessness and her father's unhappiness;
Gary repetitively inherits his father's unhappiness. When Gary accuses his father of being depressed, Alfred says that on the contrary it
is his son who is the one who is depressed, at which Gary bursts out:

"My life is on a fundamentally different basis than yours." Family illusion of this magnitude and wrongheadedness is one of the great novelistic themes—vivid in *Buddenbrooks* and *Confessions of Zeno*, to take two modern instances—a source of both comedy and pathos, and it is this comic sensitivity which constitutes the best of Franzen's achievement.

The proof of the comparative weakness of the social novel is that although Franzen attempts to enlarge his theme of correction socially, the attempt stalls. He strives to link correction to the prosperity of the 1990s and the market "correction" that followed the nineties; and he labors to address America's dependence on antidepressants by figuring it as an enormous national attempt to "correct" the brain's chemistry. "Everyone's trying to correct their thoughts and improve their feelings and work on their relationships and parenting skills instead of just getting married and raising children like they need to," thinks one character—which may not be Franzen's sentiments at all, but certainly represents his attempt to thicken the idea of correction by seeing it as a larger American malaise. In various interviews, Franzen has suggested that his commentaries about American medicine and about the stock market are, as it were, leftovers from an earlier version of his novel, in which, struggling under the deluded ambition that he had to achieve a social realist masterpiece, he threw in a great deal of social information. Presumably, as he began to write the story of the Lamberts, that earlier ambition was still difficult to abandon. But the leftovers seems a little stale.

The novel's short coda, which is entitled "The Corrections," begins thus: "The correction, when it finally came, was not an overnight bursting of a bubble but a much more gentle letdown, a year-long leakage of value from key financial markets, a contraction too gradual to generate headlines and too predictable to seriously hurt anybody but fools and the working poor." This sentence is also broadly a description of the slow end and correction of the Lambert family: Alfred enters a nursing home and gently withers away, while Enid and her children regroup themselves without Alfred.

What grates is that there is no need to make enlargements of the theme in this way. What is larger, as a subject, than the eternal corrections of family? Since the Lamberts have not before been obviously linked to their times in this way, it seems somewhat desperate to be suddenly suggesting that their inner corrections are akin to the economy's, or to the society's. Far from enforcing such a link, Franzen's comparison seems only figurative, and once it begins to seem only figurative it becomes merely aesthetic, a metaphorical gesturing. So in a cruel self-punishment, the hard lunge toward the social dimension actually turns out to look like a soft lunge toward the aesthetic dimension.

And this, of course, is because the social already exists anyway, firmly embedded in the Lamberts and their doings. A blurb by Michael Cunningham swoons that *The Corrections* bears comparison to *Buddenbrooks*. But the lovely transparency of that novel lies in Mann's singleness of implicit purpose, whereby he never makes too explicit the larger sociology of his family fall. Franzen's wavering between the aesthetic and the social recalls the uncertainty of his *Harper's* essay, and is the more peculiar because he seems, at other moments, perfectly capable of trusting the bona fides of the implicit, perfectly capable of respecting the intrinsic and not chasing after the explicit. The theme of family corrections has a fine suggestiveness about it, and Franzen shows himself an intelligent manipulator of suggestive patterns.

Consider, for example, a moment early on in the novel when Alfred is having difficulty controlling his hands; his illness is already surging. In a delicate simile, Franzen likens the disobedient hands to children, and the implication rises that Alfred is a man being pitifully "corrected" by his own hands: "His affliction offended his sense of ownership. These shaking hands belonged to nobody but him, and yet they refused to obey him. They were like bad children. Unreasoning two-year-olds in a tantrum of selfish misery. The more sternly he gave orders, the less they listened and the more miserable and out of control they got. He'd always been vulnerable to a child's recalci-

trance and refusal to behave like an adult. Irresponsibility and undis-
cipline were the bane of his existence, and it was another instance of
the Devil's logic that his own untimely affliction should consist of
his body's refusal to obey him."

Such writing, clear, direct, humane, and sensitively intelligent, is
typical of this novel at its deepest. Alfred, a stern and proud man,
suffers awfully the indignity of his illness but rarely says more than
the stiff "I am increasingly bothered by my affliction," even as his
children, now returned home for a final family Christmas, are changing his underclothes and mopping up his urine. But finer still is the
unintrusive way that Franzen quietly expands this picture of Alfred's
hands as rebellious children. Later in the book, Chip, in a weak rage,
will deliberately burn one of his hands with his own cigarette; later
still, Gary, in a weak rage, will accidentally cut one of his hands with
an electric saw; and later still, Denise will show a group of strangers
her scarred and burned hands, the working hands of a chef. This patterning may be accidental, but is more likely planned. It is precisely
what the novel form exists for, how it justifies its difference as a
genre, earns its genre-salary. This is the language of the novel—the
language of the implicit, the suggestive, the formal, the figurative,
the musical. Alfred is indeed corrected by his hands; the novel shows
us how. And Alfred is also repeated by his hands.

Franzen errs when he leaves this path and noses along the trail of
his old love, the social novel. Whenever he does so, his tone begins
to crack, and Franzen the clever journalist, the pocket theorist, peers
through. The contemporary novel has such a desire to be clever
about so many elements of life that it sometimes resembles a man
who takes so many classes that he has no time to read: auditing abolishes composure. Of course, there are readers who will enjoy the fact
that Franzen fills us in on campus politics, Lithuanian gangsters,
biotech patents, the chemistry of depression, and so on. But such
people seem to me to be prisoners of circularity, whereby their definition of a novel that "engages with the culture" is one that tells the

culture things the culture already knows anyway. Franzen is surely intelligent enough to escape this circularity, and it is sometimes dismaying to see him falling into it.

For instance, he has an idea that medicalizing the language in which he describes his characters' various moods and motives carries an ironic charge, a way of acknowledging and thereby perhaps resisting the saturation of our mental language by chemistry. This, I suspect, is the notion; the result, as so often in mimesis, is simply the re-representing of that saturation for his readers in a way that looks a little close to complicity with it. So we learn that "the remorse neurofactor (Factor 26) flooded the sites in Gary's brain specially tailored by evolution to respond to it," and later we find "his glial cells purring with the first sweet lubrication of his drink." When Denise gets angry, Franzen writes that "the anger was an autonomous neurochemical event; no stopping it." In general, the prose loves nothing so much as a chance to show off a little technical know-how: Denise is irritated by "the bradykinetic languor" of her mother's old stove; when Denise is irritated by a new worker in her restaurant kitchen, we read: "Cooks were not supposed to be political. Cooks were the mitochondria of humanity; they had their own separate DNA, they floated in a cell and powered it but were not really *of* it." (Okay, we say to ourselves, Franzen has proved that he knows what mitochondria are!) And elsewhere: "Tonsils release an ammoniac mucus when serious tears gather behind them"; "bluish swirls of inhomogeneity in his milk." And of Chip's indebtedness to Denise, who has lent him a lot of money: "He'd lived with the affliction of this debt until it had assumed the character of a neuroblastoma so intricately implicated in his cerebral architecture that he doubted he could survive its removal."

At such moments, Franzen becomes the cultural ironist, always a twisted adjective ahead of his characters. The best example of this occurs at a moment when Gary, a stolid banking executive, is arguing with his sister in downtown Philadelphia. He is standing in a little corporate plaza, neatly planted with rows of corporate flowers. "Gary had always enjoyed corporate gardens as backdrops for the pageant of privilege, as metonymies of pamperment, but it was vital not to ask too much of them. It was vital not to come to them in need." This little passage might stand as a little metonymy of its own. It sounds like a hundred other smart American writers engaged in being clever: the prose fairly droops with smirking. The lit-crit coolness of that word "metonymy," the cute neologism of "pamperment," the ironic joke inherent in the idea of coming to a *corporate* garden "in need." It seems like good writing for about three seconds. And then one reflects that Gary would never think like this, would never formulate such language. So the thinking is Franzen's. But it is hollow. Who would ever "ask too much" of a corporate plaza? The unfortunate result is that the tone sounds as if Franzen is making fun of Gary, condescending to him a little, or perhaps to the reader—and this is surely not Franzen's aim.

The Corrections is a big book, and the prose, in its long course, is likely to cross a few plains and flats. But as soon as one compares this language of smart commentary with the language of truth which runs also throughout this book, one is struck by the superfluousness of the former. Alfred's awkward refusal to describe his illness as anything other than an inconvenient "affliction" is worth any number of clever paragraphs about neuroblastomas, glial cells, mitochondria, and neurofactors. Sometimes a single sentence lances the heart with its clear and sharp rightness. Franzen describes a familiar contrast in Denise's childhood, for instance: "She'd gone to school in a bright modernity and come home every day to an older, darker world." Yes, we think, we know this division. Or when Alfred, in a moving final scene, is dying, trapped on his bed, desperate to undo the belts that are tying him to the bed but unable to, Franzen finely writes: "He was like a person of two dimensions seeking freedom in a third." It might be Alfred's epitaph.

Likewise this novel, which swerves between various dimensions, some richer and freer than others. If it can be said that it unwittingly enacts a fine argument against the viability of a certain kind of social novel, it must also be said that it constitutes a fine case for the vivacity of another kind of book, the novel of character. This is—or should be—what Franzen means by the taking of refuge in "authentic" sentences. It is easy to imagine that the press of modernity makes authentic encounter uniquely difficult, that we are all belated exceptionalists. But this is postmodern provincialism, surely, and Franzen, in his heart, seems not to believe it either. We are not uniquely doomed by modern conditions; if we are doomed, then we are doomed in rather old-fashioned ways, as Cervantes and Sterne and Svevo knew. We are doomed because humans always flow over their targets; their souls are gratuitous and busy, clogged with aspiration and desire. This is the dark theme of Franzen's novel; this is its truest touch. All the rest is "social news," and may be turned off, as it deserves.

Tom Wolfe's Shallowness,
and the Trouble with Information

&❦&

Tom Wolfe's novels are placards of simplicity. His characters are capable of experiencing only one feeling at a time; they are advertisements for the self: Greed! Fear! Hate! Love! Misery! The people who phosphoresce thus are nothing like real people. They are instead big, vivid blots of typology: The Overweening Property Developer! His Divorced First Wife! His Sexy Young Trophy Wife! The Well-Dressed Black Lawyer Who Speaks Too White! The Oafish Football Player! They race through huge, twisted plots, their adventures hammered out in a banging and brassy prose.

What is so curious is that Wolfe thinks his fiction is realistic, and has used it as an example of how the American novel should develop. In 1989 he wrote a bouncy manifesto called "Stalking the Billion-Footed Beast," in which he championed "a highly-detailed realism based on reporting," like that of his own novel *The Bonfire of the Vanities*, which had appeared two years earlier. He complained that too few novelists were interested "in the metropolis or any other big, rich slices of contemporary life"; they had abandoned realism for what he called "literary games"—minimalism, or various sterile, white-coated avant-gardisms. Only by vigorously going out and reporting on American society could one bring it back and wrestle it into the novel. Zola had done this with French society when he went on his "documentation" trips, and Sinclair Lewis had done this with America in the 1920s and 1930s. It is reportorial detail that makes novels "engrossing" and "gripping" and "moving," said Wolfe—"the *petits faits vrais* that create verisimilitude and make a novel gripping or absorbing." This, he wrote, is the modern novel's gift to us, its sentimental education, which we can see in Dickens or in *Anna Karenina*. "No one was ever moved to tears by reading about the unhappy fates of heroes and heroines in Homer, Sophocles, Molière, Racine, Sydney [*sic*], Spenser, or Shakespeare," Wolfe catechizes in a remarkable sentence. But when Little Nell dies in *The Old Curiosity Shop*, everyone cries.

It is a strangely primitive mind that has never been strongly moved by a Greek tragedy, let alone a Shakespearean one; and it is an orphaned realism that not only excludes but actually sets itself against Shakespearean character. (Who is more Dickensian than Falstaff?) But Wolfe's essay is not really a response to American literature so much as a response to American film; and it is in turn not a literary response but a filmic one. For contemporary American fiction has not been at all negligent in its realist duties. Perhaps a little avant-garde starvation occurred in the 1960s, but since then we have had John Updike's suburban sediments, John Irving's infantile robustness, Richard Ford's New Jersey real estate, Robert Stone's racy, piratical worldliness. Philip Roth has become Newark's archivist. What was *Underworld* but an old-fashioned Dickensian novel about the bomb? There is far too much realism in American fiction; it has become an idle liberty.

Wolfe's essay reads as if he were not so much goaded by the failure of realism in American fiction as piqued by the success of realism in American cinema. One deduces this from his solution, which is entirely cinematic: Go out, fill up your notebook, and then uncomplicatedly stuff all this reality into the novel. (Shoot and then don't edit.) Like the commercial film director, Wolfe does not realize that his gaudy storytelling is mannered or sensational. He thinks that it is realistic, because life is gaudy; he is like a man with a very loud voice who thinks he speaks like everyone else. Thus although many writers have filled notebooks with "documentation," Wolfe prefers the cruder and more sensational examples of rewarded diligence, such as Zola and Sinclair Lewis, writers it is now hard to reread. Flaubert copiously documented the agricultural show that appears in *Madame Bovary*, and Thomas Mann, while planning *The Magic Mountain*, visited the sanatorium his wife was staying in. And Joyce . . . But Wolfe never mentions these more literary writers, because they demonstrate that what is done on the page with the *petits faits vrais* — their intellectual compression, the writerly theft that is meted out on them — is more important than their borrowed rawness. Wolfe is not in search of realism; he wants hot, brothy journalism.

And all this would be barely worth articulating were Wolfe not floating on a sea of smiles, with the press garlanding him as Dickens's heir. *The Washington Post* thinks *A Man in Full* is "tough, demanding, uncompromising stuff," that it "calls to mind the work of Dickens" and gets "to the innermost human soul." *Newsweek* says: "Right now, no writer — reporter or novelist — is getting it [America] on paper better than Tom Wolfe," while *Time* quivers that "no summary of *A Man in Full* can do justice to the novel's ethical nuances." *The New York Times* judges Wolfe to have written "passages as powerful and as beautiful as anything written not merely by contemporary American novelists but by any American novelist." So it seems worth explaining that the gap between *Anna Karenina* and *A Man in Full* is not merely one of talent but of genre: a fountain against an aerosol spray. Wolfe's novels are only crudely like Dickens's, since they are not literary. Despite their bulk and their immense twisted colons of plot, their ambition is the management of simplification.

By "realism," Wolfe means the recognizable. His characters are types: each is a special edition of generalities. The hero of the novel's title, for example, is a tediously obvious and uncomplex type: Charlie Croker is a southern, loutish, macho property developer who has fallen upon hard times. A former college football star, he is powerfully built and brutishly charismatic. Now sixty, he has divorced Martha, his long-serving wife, and married Serena, a lithe twenty-eight-year-old. He is one of the big men who have built Atlanta, where the novel is set. He dislikes his sensitive son Wally. He bullies his way through life, throwing off racist and homophobic remarks. When his financial empire begins to collapse, he reacts as you would expect him to, belligerently. Only toward the end of the novel do his anxieties about the money he owes force him into an apparent surrender which is actually a spiritual triumph. Until this moment of spiritual reversal—which seems an inadvertence on Wolfe's part, something absurdly rushed in an attempt to end the novel—Charlie Croker never says anything surprising or interesting or eccentric or meaningful or beautiful or even especially funny in the entire book. When you expect him to be angry, he is angry. When you expect him to be sad, he is sad. He is proud of exactly the useless baubles you would expect such a man to be proud of. He has no interesting or touching secrets, except his weakness, which is not interesting because it is exactly the kind of weakness such blustering men are commonly expected to have.

Atlanta in the 1990s is a forest of typologies, all of them swaying in Wolfe's gale-force prose. Around Charlie Croker sways the venomous Harry Zale, of PlannersBanc, who is determined to retrieve the money his firm has lent to Charlie. Elsewhere in the city, Fareek Fanon, a black football player for Georgia Tech, has been accused of raping Elizabeth Armholster, the daughter of one of Atlanta's richest and most powerful men, Inman Armholster. The shrewd black mayor, fearful that this story will tear the city apart, decides to try to get the famous Charlie Croker, who once played for Georgia Tech, to say a few public words on Fareek's behalf. The mayor uses as his courier Roger White, a suave black lawyer, who dresses fabulously but is afraid of seeming too white, as his college nickname, Roger Too White, reminds him. (All Wolfe's characters have one big anxiety or flaw, the kind that has been squeezed again and again by the media, and is therefore recognizable to readers. Martha is the Divorced Businessman's Wife; Roger White is the Successful Black Sellout; the mayor is the Unscrupulous Black Strategist; Fareek is the Black Athlete as Sexual Menace.) Meanwhile, in California, a young man called Conrad Hensley is working for Croker Global Foods. One day his path will cross with Charlie's, and he will change Charlie's life for the better . . .

But none of these people is an individual. They are all chosen from society's catalogue. Even the minor characters are typological. Wolfe cannot help registering this knowingness at the verbal level: "Buck McNutter was a prototypical Southern white boy." Or two policemen, "real country boys, the rawboned kind who liked to get drunk on Saturday night and go down to the railroad grade crossing and have a rock fight." A mean lawyer: "The man seemed to have only two expressions: Indignation and Contempt." (Well, that certainly makes his fictional representation easy!) One of Charlie's hands at his Georgia plantation: "Every time Charlie saw this big man and heard his deep Baker County voice, he just knew that he was the archetype of what the overseers had been back when overseers rode hard." Or Kenny, one of Charlie's employees in California: "He was one of those rawboned young California Okies, to use the local term for Redneck." Or Fareek Fanon: "You could see the dense muscles and cable-like tendons of the real ghetto boy." Or Inman Armholster. "He's a sort of fat white man who exists only in Georgia." Wolfe is, as it were, always writing that someone is "prototypical," or that he is "the kind of man who," or "the archetype of," or "the sort of."

Well, Wolfe has certainly been out to collect his *petits faits vrais*. And look—they are rows and rows of spangled typicalities:

> She had Black Deb written all over her. Her parents were no doubt the classic Black Professional couple of the 1990s, in Charlotte or Raleigh or Washington or Baltimore. Look at the gold bangles on her wrists; must have cost hundreds of dollars. Look at the soft waves in her relaxed hair, a 'do known as a Bout en Train . . . probably went to Howard or maybe Chapel Hill or the University of Virginia; belonged to Theta Psi.

"She had Black Deb written all over her." In fact, it is Wolfe who has "written all over her," so that she is covered with the advertisements of her type.

As if Wolfe is aware of these dangers, he tries to agitate his typology by making his characters physical gargoyles in a pseudo-Dickensian manner. He may also have studied Saul Bellow's tough-hided externals. Thus many of his men are outsize physical specimens, bursting out of their clothes. It is the principle that the quickest way to make somebody interesting is to make him physically eccentric. So his men are gargantuan. There is Buck McNutter, the Georgia Tech coach: "His neck, which seemed a foot wide, rose up out of a yellow polo shirt and a blue blazer as if it were unit-welded to his trapezius muscles and his shoulders. He was like a single solid slab of meat clear up to his hair, which was a head of hair and a half, a strange silvery blond color, coiffed with bouncy fullness and little flips that screamed $65 male hairdo." Five hundred pages later, this is almost exactly how Wolfe describes the massive Charlie Croker when Roger White meets him for the first time: "His neck, trapezius muscles, shoulders, and chest seemed to be a single unit-welded mass." (What is this thing about trapezius muscles? What *are* trapezius muscles?) Then there is the hugely fat Inman Armholster, and there is the mayor's chauffeur: "The man was a tank. His shirt-collar size must have been twenty at least." And a giant of a man who works for a tow truck company: "a regular giant, 250 pounds if he was an ounce. The sleeves of his shirt had been cut off at the shoulders, revealing his huge fleshy arms."

It is Wolfe's typology—his ideal of reportorial fidelity—that pushes him into melodramatic exaggeration. On the one hand, Wolfe gets the facts, harnesses America's sociological tides; and on the other hand, in reaction to the prosaic factuality of his information, his people are teased into grotesquerie, to make them more than merely typical. But then they are just grotesquely typical. What they fail to be is individual. They are skins only, pithless. Rushing to shiny extremes of characterization, Wolfe always neglects the subtly glamorous median. The *Los Angeles Times*, in a generally negative review, conceded that Wolfe's characters, "like Dickens's, are to a greater or lesser degree grotesques." But Wolfe's people are unlike Dickens's in every important literary respect. Dickens's grotesques are not recognizable but strange. Wolfe's prose always prefers the most ordinary, the most vulgar word. His descriptions have no capacity for simile or metaphor. But Dickens finds the unexpected detail, the vivid simile. Think of Joe Gargery in *Great Expectations*, "with eyes of such a very undecided blue that they seemed to have somehow got mixed with their own whites." Or, in *David Copperfield*, Dora's cousin "in the Life-Guards, with such long legs that he looked like the afternoon shadow of somebody else." Or Uriah Heep in the same novel, his mouth "open like a post-office." The delight of such wit has little to do, at times, with accuracy; a mouth never really looks like a post office (Dickens means a postbox, incidentally). The joy, the literary joy, is in the local fizz of each detail, and in the relation of each detail to the other, and then in the moral revelation that such similes provide. (Uriah Heep is like a post office, that is, he is everyone's willing courier.)

Literature is not always like life. Why should it be? Sometimes the real itself is not always realistic, because it is incredible. Dickens used to walk in a cemetery at Cooling where could be found a grave with thirteen little siblings, all of them from the same family, all of whom had died as children. When he stole this grave for the cemetery scene at the beginning of *Great Expectations*, he reduced the number of dead children to a less sensational five. What is good "documentation," good reporting, may be lousy literature. And there is another way, of course, in which the heavy documentation of detail is not necessarily realistic: it is not through documentation that most of us absorb or present or remember detail. We do not boil in a fever of *petits faits vrais*; we shiver in the cool temperature of particulars.

But Wolfe's characters are always presented to us as tumuli of data, and, oddly, they appraise one another like this. The description of the young woman who "had Black Deb written all over her" is actually seen through the eyes of Roger White, the smart black lawyer, who is watching her dancing in the street. Perhaps Roger White, who is conscious of status, might be just the man to flood the young woman in sociological detail; but he is more likely to have noticed something odd about her ears. When Levin, in *Anna Karenina*, nervously runs to the doctor to bring him to his wife, who has begun labor, he does not, as a Wolfean character would do, build an obtuse observational jigsaw for us—say, the fashionable street the doctor lives on, his trapezius muscles, his obviously cheap haircut, his eau de cologne from Paris (rue Diderot), his shirt from the well-known shirtmaker Pavel Suvorin in St. Petersburg. No, in his beautifully clumsy male anxiety, his first-time father's mistaken belief that his wife is about to give birth at any moment and that the doctor is being horribly slow, Levin fixates on the "thick cigarettes" that the doctor insists on smoking before leaving his house. The thick cigarettes make literature. In the whole of *A Man in Full*, there is nothing like those thick cigarettes. But then, such details are generally imagined, not doggedly "documented."

The kind of "realism" called for by Wolfe, and by writers like Wolfe, is always realism about society and never realism about human emotions, motives, and secrecies. To be realistic about feeling is to acknowledge that we may feel several things at once, that we massively waver. This is Shakespeare's realism—Shakespeare, who has never moved Tom Wolfe—that he sees how eloquently unfinished our inner lives are, how disappointed we are in the stories we tell, and how private and unknowable are our tragedies and comedies— or rather our tragicomedies, for a realism about emotion acknowledges that human stories are always junctions of difference, never merely one thing or the other.

But Wolfe's characters have only their simplicities. Charlie Croker is clearly modeled in part on Robert Maxwell, the entrepreneur and newspaper owner who died in mysterious circumstances, leaving his financial empire in tatters and some of his employees penniless. At one point in the book, Charlie recalls Robert Maxwell, and considers "disappearing" like Maxwell. But Charlie's cartoonish simplicity, his depthlessness as a fictional character, is only made more acute by reflection on a real tycoon like Maxwell. Like Croker, Maxwell seemed cartoonish. He was huge, and brutal, and coarse. But just because he was cartoonish, we know that Maxwell was much more complicated than a cartoon: Maxwell, who was Jewish, who was born in Czechoslovakia, who made himself into an unconvincing English gentleman, who was a tyrant but who was apparently loved by two loyal sons, who was a capitalist but who was known as a leftist and who published Ceauşescu's memoirs and fawning biographies of Mao. Maxwell had many interesting contradictions.

At least Wolfe's characters have vivid inner lives. About the only interesting aspect of his fiction is that Wolfe has a rather finely old-fashioned commitment to the stream of consciousness, the interior monologue. Wolfe devotes whole pages to the drifting internal anxieties of his characters, and sometimes, by dint of sheer perseverance, by sticking with a character's train of thought, he transmits a weak power. (The same applies to Wolfe's perseverance with speech, and with rendering slang and dialect phonetically. Sometimes the reportage is so good, the rendition so faithful, and the speech so strange, that a genuine power flickers on the page. A scene set in a California prison draws strength from Wolfe's painstaking and undaunted determination to capture the talk of the black inmates.)

Unfortunately, Wolfe's characters only feel one emotion at a time; their inner lives are like jingles for the self. As Picasso had his Blue Period, so Wolfe's characters have their Angry Period, or their Horny Period, or their Sad Period. But they never have them at the same time, and so the potential flexibility of the stream of consciousness, precisely its lifelike randomness, is nullified. The reader finds his eyes continually skipping to the end of each long patch of interior monologue, because he knows that its garish unity will be boring. And because these people think only one emotion, they feel their emotions very robustly, all the time. All the stream of consciousness in this book is excitable and melodramatic in the same way, regardless of who is thinking it, with screeching italics and arrow-showers of exclamation points, and ellipses like hysterical Morse code. Thus the great novelistic tool of individuality, the stream of consciousness, ends up demonstrating, in Wolfe's fiction, that everyone is the same. Everyone is scrawled with the same inner graffiti. On one of the earliest pages of the book, Charlie Croker blusters to himself about his wife's rudeness: "Why, the . . . the . . . the . . . the . . . impudence of it!" Yet two hundred pages later, his ex-wife, Martha, is sitting at a concert and thinking angrily about her ex-husband in exactly the same language:

> She had—had—had—had—well—created!—the Charlie Croker the world had come to know—and now after three decades, he had the audacity—the audacity!—to shuck her, to cast her off like any old piece of worn-out baggage, as if she had been merely lucky enough to come along for the great ride, as if he had introduced her to all the wonders of the Buckhead life rather than the other way around!

The delicacy of stream of consciousness is that it both discloses the movement of the mind and also gestures to what cannot be said, to what is unrepresentable; it is the soul's stutter. Wolfe may think that he is capturing some sort of mental stutter with his buffoonish "Why, the . . . the . . . the . . . the," but of course the very facility of this convention, and the fact that it is spread evenly among all the characters, suggests the opposite. It announces a complacency about how the writer captures the brokenness of thought. Wolfe says, in effect: "Here, this is how you do it, by repeating the definite or indefinite article four times, and tattooing some ellipses all over the page." In the process of apparently announcing the strenuousness of his realism, he in fact proclaims its easy conventionality.

Who, then, is playing what Wolfe called in his manifesto "literary games"? Borges, whom he disdains in "Stalking the Billion-Footed Beast," or Wolfe himself? Borges made literary games so beautifully that they are not games. Wolfe's unbeautiful, entirely ordinary "realism" is just a flat game that has forgotten it is a game. In life, no one actually thinks to himself, "Why, the . . . the . . . the . . . the . . . impudence of it!" Wolfe's realism, veering between the typologically drab and the monstrously melodramatic, is a set of unreal devices in which people breathe "stertorously" and think in conveniently spaced ellipses, and have two-page daydreams from which they are always jerked by the reality around them with a neat dash: "Oh, he felt—Just then a burst of static interrupted his thought . . ." The acceptance of this kind of writing as literature is dangerous not because anybody will confuse it with life, will think, "This is what life is like," but because readers may read it and think, "This is what literature is like." That this bumptious simplicity, this toy set of literary codes essentially indistinguishable from the narrative techniques of boys' comics, would call itself realism, and then be praised for its "unsparing" brutality, its capacity to reach the "innermost soul" of the human being, is an awful contemporary deformation, quite worthy of our appalled "documentation." But not by Tom Wolfe, please.

Salman Rushdie's Nobu Novel

❦

Fury, a novel that exhausts negative superlatives, that is likely to make even its most charitable readers furious, is a flailing apologia. It tells the story of an Indian professor, Malik Solanka, who has recently left his English wife of fifteen years and their three-year-old son and flown from London to Manhattan. Professor Solanka, who has made a lot of money by inventing and marketing a puppet, comes to America desperate to erase his past, to start over again, and to bury the guilt he feels not only about his separation but about a moment of "fury" in which he had held a knife over his wife's sleeping form and imagined stabbing her.

But in Manhattan—the boiling, zany, money-fattened Manhattan of the end of the millennium—Professor Solanka finds not peace but only a universal fury, and he obsessively wanders the streets, a tormented flâneur, angrily observing the madness of contemporary American life, inflamed by "the everywhereness of life, by its bloody-minded refusal to back off, by the sheer goddamn unbearable head-bursting volume of the third millennium." Solanka has an affair with a furious Serbian woman called Mila Milo (shortened from Milo-sevic—you see, even her name is furious!), and then with a beautiful Indian woman called Neela, "by some distance the most beautiful Indian woman—the most beautiful woman—he had ever seen." But Neela is furious in her way too—she is a political activist—and after some wild adventures Solanka loses her to that fury. The novel ends with Solanka returning to London and taking a suite at Claridge's, where he "lay wide-eyed and rigid in his comfortable bed, listening to the noises of distant fury." The next day he spies pitifully on his estranged wife and son as they walk on Hampstead Heath.

The novel appears to be an apologia in part because it is nimbused by a dirty cloud of reality. Many readers will know that Rushdie himself has suffered an actual separation from an English wife and child, and has embarked on a new life in America, and has a beautiful Indian girlfriend whom he met at the launch party of *Talk* magazine. Quite apart from these meshings of subject and theme, the novel seems to want us to read it as a species of feverish diary. *Fury* might as well be time-stamped, and it might itself be entitled *Talk*: most of it is relentlessly set in the New York of 2001, and records, as if offering the pages of a calendar, the city's large and small events.

Thus we read about the Puerto Rican Day Parade that ended in rapes, about Courtney Love. There are knowing references to Tom Ford of Gucci, Meg Ryan and Dennis Quaid, Monica Lewinsky, Naomi Campbell, Mark Wahlberg, Saul and Gayfryd Steinberg, Sophie Dahl, Lara Croft, Dave Eggers, Charlie Rose, Tommy Hilfiger, and so on. This is a novel that contains the sentence: "Thanks to Buffy on TV, vampires were hot." And this:

> The season's hit movie portrayed the decadence of Caesar Joaquin Phoenix's imperial Rome, in which honor and dignity, not to mention life-and-death actions and distractions, were to be found only in the computer-regenerated illusion of the great gladiatorial arena . . . In New York too, there were circuses as well as bread: a musical about lovable lions, a bike race on Fifth, Springsteen at the Garden with a song about the forty-one police gunshots that killed Amadou

Diallo, the police union's threat to boycott the Boss's concert, Hillary vs. Rudy, a cardinal's funeral, a movie about lovable dinosaurs, the motorcades of two largely interchangeable presidential candidates (Gush, Bore), Hillary vs. Rick . . . a cartoon about lovable British chickens, and even a literary festival . . .

Flourishing its glamorous congestion, *Fury* is immediately obsolete; its trivia tattoo has already faded. The decision to soften the task of fictional representation, to relax mimesis to this level of muscleless gossip, this bare recording of social facts, is obviously disastrous. For a start, it abolishes form: why should Rushdie's list ever end? There will always be a few more movies to include, and next weekend's parties. And when a writer is recording minor events only because they occurred, it is hard not to flatter them, hard not to be grateful to them for the small tenacity of their occurrence. Thus in the passage above, and throughout the novel, although Solanka (and, one imagines, Rushdie) seems to want to complain about all this ephemera and noise, and even to resist it, the actual tone of the citations is something closer to complacency, a clammy and hospitable irony.

Of course, all this weightless volume of reference is supposed to be part of "the fury"—the white noise to Solanka's black noise. We are often asked to picture Solanka lying on his bed with his hands around his ears, trying to banish the noise of Manhattan, "a city of half-truths and echoes that somehow dominates the earth." It is hard not to catch the tone of confession once again, the sound of a request for absolution: if a general fury surrounds Solanka, then perhaps his own sharp fury is less culpable, because he has merely been dipped, like the novel, in the madness of the times. And why should we blame Solanka for leaving his wife if he is inflamed, poor fellow, by nothing less than the instability of the fin de siècle?

It may seem unfair to make Rushdie merge with Solanka, but the novel's own corruptions force the identity. There is, throughout the book, a grievous uncertainty about whose voice is speaking. On the one hand, we are introduced to a supposedly fastidious European voyeur who appreciates "the old European subtleties": "Old-world, dandyish, cane-twirling little Solly Solanka in straw Panama hat and cream linen suit went by on his afternoon walk." Solanka is essentially an Indian version of Mr. Sammler; he even has the Jewish nickname Solly. As in Bellow, descriptions and criticisms are generally prefaced or followed by an almost programmatic "Professor Solanka thought." So we get: "America insulted the rest of the world, thought Malik Solanka in his old-fashioned way," or: "Solanka marveled, once again, at the human capacity for automor-phosis," and so on.

On the other hand, what does Solanka choose to see, and how does he represent it? What is Mr. Solanka's Planet? Here the novel disastrously wavers. It seems, in fact, that "old-world" Solanka is enormously interested in, and utterly *au fait* with, the celebrity houses in the Hamptons, the fancy new Manhattan restaurants Nobu and Pastis, Ellen DeGeneres, Tony Soprano, and Jennifer Lopez. At one moment Solanka recalls that his first wife is probably somewhere in Manhattan: "Sara Lear was probably right here in town, he suddenly thought. She would be in her late fifties now, a big shot with a booming portfolio, the secret booking numbers for Pastis and Nobu, and a weekend place south of the highway in, ah, Amagansett." Now, one sees why Sara Lear might know the secret numbers to Nobu and Pastis, but why would "old-world" Professor Solanka know about them? At another moment Solanka reflects that although he feels he may be going mad, he will be "avoiding head doctors. The gangster Tony Soprano might be going to a shrink, but fuck him, he was fictional. Professor Solanka had resolved to face the demon himself." At another moment he sees posters for *The Cell*:

> There were posters everywhere for *The Cell*, the new Jennifer Lopez movie. In it, Lopez was miniaturized and injected into the brain of a serial killer. It sounded like a remake of *Fantastic Voyage*, starring Raquel Welch, but so what? Nobody remembered the original.

Everything's a copy, an echo of the past, thought Professor Solanka. A song for Jennifer: We're living in a retro world and I'm a retrograde girl.

So Solanka, who seems to think that the corrective possession of deep historical memory will consist of familiarity with a Raquel Welch movie, also knows his Madonna.

And then there is the language in which Solanka makes his observations. For an Anglicized Indian professor, a former fellow of King's College, Cambridge (Rushdie's own former college), who has never before lived in America, Solanka's diction has gone peculiarly native. Solanka uses "gotten" and not "got," and thinks of one man as "his pal, his best buddy," and recalls getting "jiggy beside a big-assed Puerto Rican girl," and talks of "shrinks" and "head doctors," of "industry mavens," of "goddamn" noise and "the cheesiest daytime soap." When he complains to Neela about American power, he jitters explosively like someone trapped in a Philip Roth novel: "But, Solanka wanted to say, rising to the bait, what's wrong is wrong, and because of the immense goddamn power of America, the immense fucking seduction of America." One way of manufacturing a proper American "fury," clearly, is with the frequent oiling of the word "goddamn."

Is Solanka thinking or is Rushdie thinking? This is not a small complaint; not just a pedantic fussing about "point of view." For this instability of voice, this anarchy of borrowed languages, infiltrates and infects the fabric of the storytelling. A cartoonish and inauthentic voice produces a cartoonish and inauthentic reality. Consider the following fluorescences: "this glowing six-foot Cruella De Vil fashion plate of a mother"; "erect, wiry, with Albert Einstein white hair and Bugs Bunny front teeth"; "the owner-manager, a Raul Julia lookalike"; "she had become the Maya Angelou of the doll world"; "a petite Southern belle . . . who was a dead ringer for the cartoon sexpot Betty Boop"; "tall and skinny, with a sexy John Travolta

quiff"; "a Stockard Channing of the near-at-hand" (a particularly unfortunate echo of Augie March's self-characterization as a "Colum-
bus of those near-at-hand").

All these vulgarities, these hazy swipes at vivacity, are characters
(so called) in *Fury*, and all are seen in these terms by Professor
Solanka. Striving to be vivid, this writing produces only something
smaller than life, because it is distanced and mediated by anterior images: when a man is described as having Bugs Bunny teeth, you see
Bugs Bunny; you do not see the man. Or perhaps you do not even
see Bugs Bunny—who, frankly, would be a relief in place of the actual owner of the Einstein hair and the Bugs Bunny teeth, an octogenarian plumber named Joseph Schlink who arrives one day to
mend Professor Solanka's lavatory. Schlink speaks, writes Rushdie,
"with the unimproved accent of the transplanted German Jew," and
commits this monologue:

> My name amuses you? So laugh. The chentleman, Mr. Simon, calls
> me Kitchen Schlink, to his Mrs. Ada I'm also Bathroom Schlink, let
> zem call me Schlink the Bismarck, it von't bother me, it's a free
> country, but in my business I haff no use for humor. In Latin, hu-
> mor is a dampness from the eye. This is to quote Heinrich Böll, No-
> bel Prize nineteen hundred seventy-two. In his line of vork he alleges
> it's helpful, but in my job it leads to mistakes. No damp eyes on me,
> eh?, and no chokes in my tool bag. Chust I like to do the vork
> prompt, receive payment also prompt, you follow me here. Like the
> shvartzer says in the movie, show me the money. After a war spent
> plugging leaks on a Nazi U-boat, you think I can't fix up your little
> doofus here?

This cartoonishness, which has been Rushdie's weakness
throughout his career, and which has been lucky enough over
the years to be flattered by the term "magical realism," and which
really deserves the term "hysterical realism," only proves that he is
incapable of writing realistically—and thus oddly confirms the

prestige of realism, confirms its difficulty, its hard challenge, its true rigor.

It needs to be said again and again, since Rushdie's style of exuberance has been so influential, that such vividness is not vivacious, that in fact it encodes a fear of true vivacity, a kind of awkwardness or embarrassment in the face of the lifelike. There are certain kinds of critics who equate excess with nourishment, like someone who believes that only a fat baby is a healthy one. Such readers are doubtless likely to announce that Rushdie's new novel is "full of wonders, among them a learned riff on Raquel Welch and a plumber who looks like Einstein and chats easily about Heinrich Böll!" (This kind of critic always has a pen that whittles exclamation points!) But true vivacity—which is not necessarily the same as mere lifelikeness—has no need to shout. It goes by, in Yeats's words, with white footfall.

In general, Rushdie's observations pound a wilderness between incredibility and banality. Certainly the form of the novel is not suited to his screaming color range. Like a good number of contemporary novels, *Fury* makes use of the idea of an overloaded flâneur—a man goes out to record, with all the writer's fineness of observation on his side, what the writer would have seen were the writer able to speak autobiographically, like the "I" of a Romantic poem. The flâneur, of course, was born in Romantic poetry—the Wordsworth of *The Prelude* quite as much as Baudelaire—before being born again in modern prose in Benjamin, and in *The Notebooks of Malte Laurids Brigge*, and even in *Nausea* and *Mrs. Dalloway*. To this tradition, the contemporary novel adds the plausible idea that such a flâneur is not merely the writer's agent but in some ways a too-porous scout who has lost his way. The old maps have gone, and the new signs are unreadable; and so the modern flâneur is driven mad by the indecipherable abundance of contemporary signification. Bellow's Herzog stands on a sidewalk grate in Manhattan and feels the roughened surface "like Braille under his feet." The world pours in illegibly: it is Braille for those who cannot read it, the wrong answers to the wrong questions. Rushdie would like to add Professor Solanka, furiously reeling from fury, from "the everywhereness of life," to this literary inheritance.

Yet this is a difficult form to sustain, because it is managed and propelled largely by writerly tact and brilliance. In ordinary hands, where such brilliance is missing, the flâneur novel becomes merely a chance for the writer to have his say about some matters that occupy him; the novel becomes a series of ambulatory essays of variable interest and quality. *Fury* is a failure of this kind, because Rushdie lacks the literary fineness that is needed to keep descriptive analysis interesting. The prose is, without exception, flat and unoriginal, so that the details that Solanka observes lack any flame. And the analysis is itself often startlingly banal. Here is Solanka-Rushdie on TV ads:

> The commercials soothed America's pain, its head pain, its gas pain, its heartache, its loneliness, the pain of babyhood and old age, of being a parent and of being a child, the pain of manhood and women's pain, the pain of success and that of failure, the good pain of the athlete and the bad pain of the guilty, the anguish of loneliness and of ignorance, the needle-sharp torment of the cities and the dull, mad ache of the empty plains, the pain of wanting without knowing what was wanted, the agony of the howling void within each watching, semiconscious self. No wonder advertising was popular. It made things better. It showed you the road. It wasn't part of the problem. It solved things.

Apart from suffering the inconvenient disadvantage of being completely untrue, this passage is just a piece of "writing."

Worse, the flâneur novel, if weakened to pointlessness by limited literary talents, is entirely nullified by the magical realist or cartoonish impulse. If the flâneur is not an empiricist or an idealist but only a candy-colored animator, he might as well not go out onto the streets at all. Rushdie might reply that, far from failing at realism, he does not even attempt it, because he does not believe in it—hence the "magic" of his rollicking, unrealistic exuberance. To which the proper retort is that representation is both a realism and a magic. Fiction is itself chimerical, the manufacturing of inventions; and the effect of adding magic to chimera is not a kind of doubling of the chimerical, not a mere raising of the fictional temperature, but merely a miragelike false heat, resulting in total disappearance. For this reason, Schlink the plumber, the octogenarian European Jew, literally disappears into his "vividness" before our eyes. His complexity, his social history, his secret wants and sadnesses, his actual comedy: all this is abolished by excess, as great noise becomes finally inaudible.

The danger of this kind of "lively" writing becomes more apparent the nearer it aspires to conventional realism. For the nearer it reaches the real, the greater the surface of the real that it desecrates. Solanka sees a "middle-aged African-American woman sitting on the next bench" eating her way through "a long egg salad hero, advertising her enjoyment of every mouthful with loud mms and uh-huhs." The unwitting condescension of this vignette, the garishness of its minstrelsy—these blacks, the passage seems to scream, for them even a sandwich merits a gospel chorus!—is optimistically balanced by the wised-up correctness of the terminology: the lady may carry on like a crazy mama, but she is still an "African-American woman." Of course.

Perhaps Rushdie, in comparing his characters to film actors and the like, is making a point about the society of spectacle, about the ineradicably mediated nature of the contemporary American world? Look, even Professor Solanka cannot escape this corruption: he sees Jennifer Lopez and immediately thinks of Madonna! But to poison a whole book is a very lengthy way of making a point about a single modern germ. Besides, Solanka supposedly dislikes all this "fury"; it is he who condemns this "retro age," "this age of simulacra and counterfeits."

Alas, the contradictions of Rushdie's book (we are told also that the terrifically knowing Solanka apparently felt "alienated" by "the anonymous faces in magazines, faces that all Americans somehow recognized at once"), the unlikely vulgarities of Professor Solanka, taken alongside his equally incredible American argot, are so distorting that they abolish him as a character, and leave him only as a figment of Rushdie's painful confessional urge. *Fury* does not seem to present Mr. Solanka's Planet so much as Mr. Rushdie's Planet, which is all secret numbers for Nobu and fancy houses in the Hamptons. One sees now why Solanka-Rushdie reverently calls New York "a city of half-truths and echoes that somehow dominates the earth." It is because Solanka's idea of Manhattan is no deeper than the idea of the man who is "a Raul Julia lookalike." Indeed, the Manhattan of *Fury* is a city of half-truths precisely because Solanka-Rushdie peoples it with cartoons: Schlink is one of those walking half-truths.

And not just Manhattan. America, too, is seen cartoonishly in this book. Solanka, you recall, has come to America "to be devoured . . . He had come to America as so many before him, to receive the benison of being Ellis Islanded, of starting over. Give me a name, America, make of me a Buzz or Chip or Spike. Bathe me in amnesia and clothe me in your powerful unknowing. Enlist me in your J. Crew and hand me my mouse ears!" And thirty pages later Solanka returns to this theme:

> He had flown to the land of self-creation . . . the country whose paradigmatic modern fiction was the story of a man who remade himself, his past, his present, his shirts, even his name for love . . . [H]is old self must somehow be canceled, put away for good. And if he failed, then he failed, but one did not contemplate what lay beyond failure while one was still trying to succeed. After all, Jay Gatsby, the highest bouncer of them all, failed too in the end, but lived out, before he crashed, that brilliant, brittle, gold-hatted, exemplary life.

There is unwitting condescension in this prayerfulness. Perhaps Rushdie is unaware of the disdain that menaces his apparently lauda- tory words. The idea of America as a place of "amnesia" and "unknowing" represents a perfect coincidence of old-fashioned Eu- ropean dismissal and new-fashioned postmodern naïveté: in the older vision, America is always disapprovingly seen as the country with no real history; in the postmodern vision, America is always ap- provingly seen as the country with no real history, as one enormous inauthentic Disneyland, handing out Mickey Mouse ears to its grin- ning immigrants.

"Give me a name, America, make of me a Buzz or Chip or Spike": Rushdie seems not to realize that this might be a land of real names rather than a playground of floating signifiers, that some ac- tual Chips and Spikes live in America, that amazingly enough they have histories, even American histories, and do not stride forgetfully through clouds of "unknowing." Why, they might even know enough to not know what Nobu is! And Rushdie, solemnly deciding that America's founding modern myth is Gatsby's self-creation, seems unaware that there was the slightest tincture of irony or moral censure in Fitzgerald's novel. It is as if Solanka were saying to him- self: "Gatsby did it, so I do it, too." But the force of Fitzgerald's story was that Gatsby's life, however "brilliant," was a failure not because it crashed (Rushdie's apparently consequentialist standpoint), but be- cause Gatsby's ambition itself was corrupt.

Given these moral tremors, which speak brokenly throughout the novel, it seems preposterous and surprising when Solanka- Rushdie begins to plume himself up as a moralist toward the end of the book, excoriating America's corruption by materialism. Sud- denly Solanka has forsaken fascination with fashion, and is deciding the world, and ringing the metaphysical emergency bell: "All around him, the American self was reconceiving itself in mechanical terms, but was everywhere running out of control . . . For the real problem was damage not to the machine but to the desirous heart, and the language of the heart was being lost." Dazzled by the lovely and ardent Neela, Solanka appears to discover a conscience. He reflects that "behind the facade of this age of gold, this time of plenty, the contradictions and impoverishment of the Western human individual, or let's say the human self in America, were deepening and widening." All of a sudden Manhattan becomes "this Metropolis . . . [W]ealth was mistaken for riches and the joy of possession for happiness, where people lived such polished lives that the great rough truths of raw existence had been rubbed and buffed away":

> O Dream-America, was civilization's quest to end in obesity and trivia, at Roy Rogers and Planet Hollywood, in *USA Today* and on E! . . . or even at the unattainable tables of Jean-Georges Vongerichten and Alain Ducasse? Yes, it had seduced him, America; yes, its brilliance aroused him, and its vast potency too, and he was compromised by this seduction. What he opposed in it he must also attack in himself. It made him want what it promised and eternally withheld.

But it is too late to be coming on like Dreiser in *Sister Carrie*, flaying the corruptions of "The Walled City." This is supposedly a moral castigation, and perhaps a form of confession, but is it not really cousin to the earlier condescension? For Rushdie's view of corrupted America is as vulgar as his vision of uncorrupted America. Solanka's uncorrupted "devourer," the savior and eraser of the self, was Mickey Mouse; the corrupted civilization against which he supposedly pits himself is Roy Rogers, and possibly Alain Ducasse. Take your pick. But *Fury* speaks the language of corruption anyway, and so it has no rock, no Dreiserian sidewalk or Bellovian altitude, from which to launch this ethical armada. It has apparently been corrupted by the very corruption that it decries. It is Rushdie-Solanka, after all, who seems to have his head filled with Tony Soprano and J. Lo and Alain Ducasse. Perhaps the corruption here lies in knowing enough about such tiny figures to accuse them of being corrupters in the first place? Who will corrupt the corrupters? And so Rushdie manages the remarkable feat of being simultaneously Euro-condescending and American-debased.

It is one thing to write an allegory or an apologia about how America has compromised one's soul, but it is quite another to publish a novel that so emphatically reenacts that compromise.

Monica Ali's Novelties

❦

In the last twenty years, British and American fiction has been renewed by what might be called the immigration of content. In America, this useful novelty has tended to result from the inevitable hyphenation of the once apparently stable monad of Americanness (Cuban-American fiction, Puerto Rican–American, Asian-American, and so on). In Britain, the vast centrifuge of empire has more often resulted in fiction set outside Britain, or, when set in Britain, fiction explicitly about immigration (*The Satanic Verses*, *The Enigma of Arrival*). Hyphenation has been, for immigrants, a trickier train to catch in Britain than in the more hospitable United States.

Plenty of readers, critics, and academics have been grateful for the augmentation of material, the opening of "colorful" worlds, not to mention the at times radical literary techniques, that this new life has brought to fiction. At such times the etymology of the word "novel" is always mentioned, and Ezra Pound's definition of literature as "news that STAYS news" is reliably invoked. What is not so often said is that this new material has another and perhaps more momentous service to perform, which is to return fiction to its nineteenth-century gravity. This it does by reimporting into the

Western novel traditional societies, with their ties of marriage, burdens of religion, obligations of civic duty, and pressures of propriety—and thereby restoring to the novel form some of the old oppressions that it was created to comprehend and to resist and in some measure to escape. This was the case with Vikram Seth's massive panorama *A Suitable Boy*, and it is the case with Monica Ali's first novel, *Brick Lane*.

Ali's novel brings with it the undeniable fascination of novelty. Nazneen, a poorly educated eighteen-year-old Muslim girl from a traditional village in Bangladesh, is plucked by arranged marriage from the only place she has known to a grim housing estate in the East End of London, where she must live with her much more literate, patchily Anglicized forty-year-old husband. The miserable shock of immigration to Britain has been touched on by other writers— Naipaul, Rushdie, the Sri Lankan novelist Romesh Gunesekera— but no writer I know of has taken as her entire stretched subject the loneliness and the shabby poverty of these English near-ghettos. This is the world of sweatshops, and grim women doing piecework on sewing machines, and residents looking down on gray concrete courts from the tenth floor of council housing, and busy gangs of Bangladeshi youths, some radicalized by Islam, some stunned by drug addiction. Zadie Smith's multicultural North London was a fictional universe that readers wanted to visit, in part because it was new to them and in part because it was so essentially cheerful; but Ali's fictional world is shockingly monocultural—it contains only Bangladeshis who by choice and by necessity keep to themselves— and it is far from cheerful, even if her book is frequently comic.

This expansion of vision is the traditional benefit of new fictional material, and there is plenty of it here. (One of the characters, for instance, receives "salaat alerts" on his cell phone, regular reminders of prayer times from a commercial Islamic calling service.) But the novelty of Ali's world is also a restoration, for it allows her, quite naturally, to inhabit a fictional realm in which prayer, free will, and adultery all have their antique weight. Take adultery, for instance: once the great motor of the novel, it is now an idle cylinder, only formulaically or nominally used to give plot a bit of a lift. Adultery has withered as a fictional theme because it drags such little consequence behind it nowadays. In nineteenth-century fiction, by contrast, adultery was literally used by plot: it had weight by virtue of its place in a system of shame, punishment, desire, escape, and imprisonment, and to set it ticking was to set that system ticking, too.

So it is intensely gripping and involving when young Nazneen, who disliked her husband in the early years of their marriage and has only begun to tolerate his presence, finds herself distracted by desire for a young Bangladeshi Londoner, and begins an affair with him. For quite apart from the absolute censure of the community, Nazneen, who is a faithful Muslim, herself is certain that she will burn in eternal hell for her sin. Likewise, Ali's treatment of free will and determinism draws power from the fact that the novel's protagonist devoutly believes in fate. When Razia, her best friend in London, asks why her husband complains so much about Britain if his life there is better than it would be in Bangladesh, Nazneen has no answer: "She was in this country because that was what had happened to her. Anyone else, therefore, was here for the same reason." Again, some of the plottiness of nineteenth-century fiction was owed not merely to literary convention but also to the fact that many novelists believed in determinism, which was both obeyed and resisted by many heroes and heroines (especially the latter). Fictionally speaking, it takes a good deal of enactment, a good deal of story, for determinism to enact itself—for readers to feel that plot is being, as it were, rubbed into the very souls of the characters.

Ali's most daring decision may be her bestowal of what amounts to semiliteracy upon her heroine. Nazneen is not semiliterate, of course; but her abrupt arrival in London—a girl who had never seen much more than her village—and her inability at first to speak any English render her so in Britain. Ali keeps her narrative very close to

Nazneen's; we are never given independent access to any other character in the book; our sense of everything is passed through this
heroine's impressions. Thus all the new information that we learn
about this world, and indeed about the London world, is Nazneen's
information, approached as she approaches it. We have become so
used to the idea that new information is a chance for the writer to
show off a bit, to tell us how much he knows (goodness, he really
does know so much about real estate in North Dakota!), so used to
the idea of information as a part of writerly style, a ripple of style's
muscles, that it comes as a refreshing shock to encounter new information through what is a kind of antistyle.

But it is not, in fact, an antistyle; it is the suppression of obvious
authorial style in the interest of a character's style. (And so it is the
greatest style.) The result is a lovely simplicity, as we are led to inhabit the wide-eyed ignorance of a village girl from Bangladesh, and
to watch it develop itself. Early in the book, Nazneen sees a few minutes of ice-skating on television without understanding what she is
watching. Ali refrains from telling her or us what it is; we are to undergo the almost hermeneutic process of finding out:

> A man in a very tight suit (so tight that it made his private parts
> stand out on display) and a woman in a skirt that did not even cover
> her bottom gripped each other as an invisible force hurtled them
> across an oval arena. The people in the audience clapped their hands
> together and then stopped. By some magic they all stopped at ex-
> actly the same time. The couple broke apart. They fled from each
> other and no sooner had they fled than they sought each other out.
> Every move they made was urgent, intense, a declaration. The
> woman raised one leg and rested her boot (Nazneen saw the thin
> blade for the first time) on the other thigh . . .

This passage may not look like anything much, until one realizes
the care with which Ali makes Nazneen notice everything except
what would have been most obvious to a Western watcher: that this

is ice-skating. Nazneen sees instead the immodest private parts, the people clapping and suddenly not clapping at the same time (a brilliant touch—the staged decorum of such audiences must indeed seem a strange thing to one who has never witnessed it before), the free and erotic intensity between man and woman (Nazneen, by contrast, has recently overheard her husband Chanu telling a friend on the phone that his wife is "an unspoilt village girl" whose eyes are rather too close together, and "a good worker"), and finally, only then, the "thin blade" on the boot.

Seeing everything through Nazneen's eyes returns the gift of "estrangement" (as the Russian formalists used to call it) to fiction. Everything must be made new, in a halting journey of discovery. This becomes Ali's systematic procedure in the novel—refreshing and often wonderful in itself, and also of course succeeding in bringing us closer to Nazneen's travails and triumphs. A walk in the streets—the novel gets its title from the famous street in Tower Hamlets—is an oceanic voyage for Nazneen, at least in her early months in Britain. She sees many people dressed like her, in saris or in Punjabi pajamas and skullcaps, but then her eyes alight on a differently dressed pair, "in short dark skirts with matching jackets. Their shoulders were padded up and out. They could balance a bucket on each side and not spill a drop of water." Thus she discovers shoulder pads. (It is 1985.)

One day Nazneen strays from her familiar rounds and wanders toward the financial district of London. She sees a pair of schoolchildren, "pale as rice and loud as peacocks," and comes to a stop at the foot of a vast glass tower.

> The entrance was like a glass fan, rotating slowly, sucking people in, wafting others out . . . Every person who brushed past her on the pavement, every back she saw, was on a private, urgent mission to execute a precise and demanding plan: to get a promotion today, to be exactly on time for an appointment, to buy a newspaper with the right coins so that the exchange was swift and seamless, to walk

without wasting a second and to reach the roadside just as the lights turned red.

As a writerly description of a bustling London crowd, this may at first seem flat—where are the theoretical riffs on crowds, the slicing metaphors, the brilliant details? Until, again, one realizes that what has been beautifully captured, without any authorial commentary, is Nazneen's massive naïveté. There is the image of the revolving door seen as a massive fan—why should she have ever seen one of these doors before?—and then there is the almost childish certainty that because everyone is moving urgently on the street, each person is executing "a precise and demanding plan." And great subtlety is used in the fleshing out of Nazneen's very unworldly idea of what constitutes such a plan: "to be exactly on time for an appointment" or "to reach the roadside just as the lights turned red." This loose employment of what is called free indirect style works marvelously here.

But Nazneen is not simply a vessel for estrangement, vivifying as this effect is. The power of Ali's book is the way in which it charts its heroine's slow accumulation of English, her gathering confidence as a mother and a wife, and the undulations of her marriage to a man whom she eventually learns to respect and perhaps even to love. Again, this arc is traced in the subtlest ways. When Nazneen's first child dies in the hospital, the name of his illness is never given; we are told merely about "the rash" that brought him to the emergency room, "those little red seeds." This is in perfect accord with Nazneen's own linguistic and medical competence; she has barely learned the word "hospital," after all. So it comes as a pleasant shock, a measured gratification, when, a hundred or so pages and eight years later, Ali refers casually to one of Nazneen's daughters having been in the hospital with "tonsillitis." The daughters have taught their mother English, and her confidence, linguistic and medical, has grown.

Yet even when Nazneen has learned something, Ali takes care to

show how her knowledge is framed in ignorance. Halfway through
the book, when Nazneen has already experienced all kinds of instruction in life, she wanders down Brick Lane and notices the dif-
ferences between the cheap restaurants and the expensive ones (not
that she has ever set foot in either kind): "The tables were set far
apart and there was an absence of decoration that Nazneen knew to
be a style." "Knew to be a style": that is all. Nothing more. Because
that is all that Nazneen does know. She could not expatiate on what
we call minimalism; she has merely been long enough in London to
recognize a style. (An absence of decoration that is yet a style might
also be an apt characterization of Ali's prose.) Think how often fancy
restaurants are described in metropolitan fiction, and in such knowing waves of sarcasm! By contrast, such simplicity on Ali's part, such
authorial reticence coupled with such authorial sympathy, is a strenuous achievement.

Nazneen's marriage is at the heart of this book, and Chanu, her
husband, is its other leading character. He is a Biswas figure—
earnest, probably more self-educated than formally schooled (he has
a degree, or so he says, from Dhaka University), restless, yearning,
and vulnerable, desperate to escape his little world. Almost as soon
as he is married, he longs to return to Bangladesh, to remove his
family before they can be "spoiled" by British ways, and his constant
invocation—"By then we could be in Dhaka"—has a canonical, not
to say Russian, mournfulness. He is of course a stranger to Nazneen
when they marry: a plump, not very attractive middle-aged man who
works for the local council and dreams of a promotion that we know
will never come his way. About the marriage, Ali is devastating: "In
all her eighteen years, she could scarcely remember a moment that
she had spent alone. Until she married." Nazneen is wary of Chanu
at first, and loathes the physical impositions of their union—she has
to cut his corns and his hair; and it is not until their son dies and
Chanu becomes a real companion that she realizes that although she
does not love her husband, he is a good man, worthy of respect. A

hundred pages elapse before we witness physical tenderness or even shared laughter.

Since the fine comic-pathetic lineage of Biswas sits so obviously behind Chanu, he can at times seem only a recognizable type, even a somewhat literary one; and Ali does not really deepen him as the novel progresses. Just as Mr. Biswas corresponded with something called the Ideal School of Journalism, so Chanu keeps framed certificates on his wall, including one from Morley College, where he attended evening classes on nineteenth-century thought—though, as he explains to Nazneen, the college did not actually give him a diploma: "It's just directions to the school, but that's all they gave out. No certificates." She subtly captures his vulnerability and his bombast in comic scene after scene. Chanu invites Dr. Azad, the local physician and the most "respectable" Bangladeshi he knows, to supper, and at one point remarks, painfully, that "we intellectuals must stick together." But when Dr. Azad's fierce wife interrogates poor Chanu, he retreats into incoherence. Chanu has claimed, in his usual pontifical way, that "to be an immigrant is to live out a tragedy." But Dr. Azad's wife will have none of it:

"What are you talking about?"
"The clash of cultures."
"I beg your pardon?"
"And of generations," added Chanu.
"What is the tragedy?"
"It's not only immigrants. Shakespeare wrote about it."

Chanu is a defeated man, despite his rhetoric, or because of it; and one of the funniest and saddest scenes occurs when he returns home one day with a computer. He gathers Nazneen and his two daughters around him and proceeds to write something: "He examined the keyboard closely before each stroke, putting his face right down by the letters as though something valuable had slipped between the cracks. Minutes later he had completed a sentence . . . 'Dear Sir, I am writing to inform you.' 'It all comes back so quickly,' said Chanu, in English. His cheeks were red with pleasure."

There is much satisfaction to be had from the comic gentleness and the tact with which Ali animates this boisterous and anxious man: "Only his eyes were unhappy. What are we doing here, they said, what are we doing on this round, jolly face?" As Nazneen's affection for him develops, so does ours: "He came next to her and leaned on the radiator. If there was a solid surface in sight, Chanu would rest against it. Mental toil, he said. That is the real exercise. No harder work than mental toil." Ali subtly catches Chanu out without semaphoring her satire. Thus Chanu repeatedly refers to the Open University (where he began but did not complete a course) solecistically as "Open University," without the usual definite article. Even as the book ends, Chanu says to his wife, "The English have a saying: you can't step into the same river twice." His ignorance is gently undisturbed by the author.

Into this precarious marriage comes the violent disruption of Karim, a young activist prominent in the local Islamic group the Bengal Tigers. Nazneen, given a sewing machine by Chanu, has started doing piecework, and Karim is the middleman whose task is to collect and to deliver her work. Karim is the opposite of Chanu: he is young, good-looking, apparently invulnerable. He saunters around Nazneen's flat chatting on his cell phone (it is he who receives the "salaat alerts"), putting his feet up on the coffee table, and marking the space with his erotic spoor. Nazneen cannot keep her eyes off him: "When Chanu fidgeted he showed his unease. When Karim could not be still, he showed his energy." Despite her dread of the sin of adultery, Nazneen starts an affair with Karim, a relationship that precisely substitutes for the lack in her marriage: it is strongly physical, and Nazneen is indeed in love. A measure of her loneliness, in this deeply traditional society, is provided when she tries to tell her friend Razia about it. Razia's son has been discovered to be a drug addict, and thinking that one misfortune might be traded for another, Nazneen haltingly unburdens her secret. But Razia cuts her short. "You don't have to tell me," say Razia. "Just because I am in trouble, you don't have to make trouble for yourself as well." In this world, the economy of moral survival renders the lavish expenditure of "confession" mute. (The same economy rules the impoverished peasant world of Verga's Sicily.) Razia is an unconventional Muslim woman—later she will listen to the full story of the affair—but Ali captures the sense that merely to hear such news is to be tainted with it.

Interestingly, Nazneen's religiousness in some way enables, rather than arrests, her sinful relationship. For once she has decided that she will burn in hell for eternity, there seems nothing to do except submit to fate and continue sinning: she is utterly lost anyway. Calvinism provides the Christian version of this kind of predestination, and James Hogg's *Confessions of a Justified Sinner* is the famous fictional commentary. Nazneen's Islamic serfdom to fate is a good deal calmer than the Calvinist enslavement, and besides, it has a strong personal dimension: Nazneen has always believed in such submission, partly because, as her grandmother liked to tell her, when Nazneen was born she almost died, and her mother, ignoring pleas to take the baby to the hospital, left her to survive or die, with the words: "We must not stand in the way of Fate. Whatever happens, I accept it. And my child must not waste any energy fighting against Fate. That way, she will be stronger."

The family story of How Nazneen Was Left to Her Fate has been endlessly repeated. (And it provides a rather too neat frame for the narrative theme.) Nazneen grew up believing that "what could not be changed must be borne. And since nothing could be changed, everything had to be borne." Her sister Hasina had fought fate by running off with a lover when she was a teenager. Her subsequent tribulations, which include prostitution, have not inclined Nazneen to think highly of the liberation from fate. (Hasina's letters to Nazneen punctuate the novel.)

The burden of the novel concerns Nazneen's capacity to struggle with her own fatedness, and this struggle will gather around the question of whether she should leave her husband (now not only determined to leave for Dhaka but with a date in mind and tickets in hand) and marry Karim. Chanu, it is quietly suggested, knows about the affair or strongly suspects, and characteristically he shows both his strength and his weakness in his response. He does nothing, except to become markedly sweeter to his wife and children. In one of the finest scenes, Chanu decides that the family deserves a holiday, an outing. They get on the bus to see the sights—the reader registers with a shock that in more than ten years of married life in London, Nazneen has never seen Buckingham Palace or the houses of Parliament, has never been to central London. As the family sits on the grass at St. James's, eating the picnic provided by Nazneen, Chanu says unexpectedly, "You know, when I married your mother, it was a stroke of luck." *Brick Lane* is full of unobtrusive patterning, and Chanu's chivalrous admission comes as a surprise not only because it is one of the few compliments Chanu has uttered to his wife but also because it inverts, for the first time, his usual mantra, which is to remind Nazneen again and again of how lucky she is to have married "an educated man." Nazneen, meanwhile, is thinking about Karim, and trying to sort out in her head how much Chanu knows.

Brick Lane is a great achievement of the subtlest storytelling—the kind that proceeds illuminatingly, in units of characters rather than in wattage of "style." There is, of course, a great deal of literary style in this book, and Ali is quite capable of fine similes and metaphors. She has a sharp satirical sentence on how the radical boys at the Bengal Tigers meetings are dressed: "The boys wore jeans, or tracksuits with big ticks [i.e., check marks] on them as if their clothing had been marked by a teacher who valued, above all else, conformity." Or this, on the arrival of politicians to the housing estate after a race riot: "Politicians came and walked around the estate with their hands behind their backs to show that they were not responsible, leaning

forward slightly to indicate that they were looking to the future."
Though Nazneen is watching the Nike-daubed boys and the politicians, this is clearly not her language; Ali allows herself the freedom
to disengage every so often from Nazneen's perceptions. But the
bulk of the book is occupied by Nazneen; she is Ali's quarry, and the
great prize of the prose is the way it subdues itself to her fears, her
ignorance, her triumphs, and finally her comprehension. The novel's
ending is wisely ambiguous. Nazneen does not escape her fate, or
even necessarily resist it, but she understands it. Life has been her
Morley College.

Coetzee's Disgrace: *A Few Skeptical Thoughts*

※

J. M. Coetzee's distinguished novels feed on exclusion; they are intelligently starved. One always feels with this writer a zeal of omission. What his novels keep out may well be as important as what they keep in. And Coetzee's vision is impressively consistent: his books eschew loosened abundance for impacted allegory. *Waiting for the Barbarians*, his finest allegory, set in a nameless empire with resemblances to turn-of-the-century South Africa, has an Orwellian power. Even when his novels are set in a recognizable and local South African world, as is the case with Coetzee's new novel, the dry seed of parable can always be felt underfoot, beneath the familiar surfaces of contemporary life.

But this can be a harsh exchange. Coetzee's novels eschew society, and the examination of domestic filaments, for the study of political societies; they eschew the scrutiny of moral life for a more desperate search for ethical survival; they eschew the description of human consciousness in its fullness and waywardness for the description of the consciousness of pain in its monotonous density. They avoid the warm flavors of the comic-ironic for the bitter concentrates of the allegorical-ironic. (And is one not always a little suspicious of a writer without any comic impulse at all?) There is fantastic compulsion to Coetzee's lean, thrilling tales—they are always difficult to put down—but his novels are strangers to the patience of accumulation. His prose is precise, but not rare.

There are few writers in English who equal this South African writer's hard intelligence. Few are as philosophical, or as familiar with the languages and the modes of poststructural and postcolonial theory: Coetzee taught literature for many years at the University of Cape Town, and is a formidable theorist of the novel and of the novel's destiny in his native country. And few writers are as bleak, as painfully, repetitively honest. Coetzee returns to the same pain as if a joint were being broken again and again in the same place.

Still, what his books exclude almost constitutes life itself, and certainly constitutes much of the novel's traditionally victorious tourism of life. This seems a hard confinement, and it is something that Coetzee seemed to acknowledge, with characteristic probity, in his Jerusalem Prize speech in 1987. He claimed, perhaps too fatalistically, that South African literature was "a less than fully human literature, unnaturally preoccupied with power and the torsions of power, unable to move from elementary relations of contestation, domination, and subjugation . . . [I]t is exactly the kind of literature one would expect people to write from a prison."

But people like novels that, however intelligently, tell them what to think, that table ideas and issues—novels that are discussable. Above all, people like allegory, and Coetzee's books always incline toward this mode. Coetzee is very subtle and refined, so that much of the time he does not really seem to be telling us what to think; better still, his novels self-consciously display an involvement in their own modes of presentation, so that Coetzee will often seem to be telling us what to think about being told what to think (which is still a species of telling people what to think, of course). *Disgrace*, which is a kind of South African version of Turgenev's *Fathers and Sons*—an issue novel about the generation wars—is a novel with which it is almost impossible to find fault.

These somewhat unfair thoughts are stirred by *Disgrace*, which is a very good novel, almost too good a novel. It knows its limits, and lives within a wary self-governance. It sometimes reads as if it were the winner of an exam whose challenge was to create the perfect specimen of a very good contemporary novel. It is truthful, spare, compelling, often moving, and thematically legible: that is to say, it does not overflow interpretation. It does not quite rise to greatness, in part because of a certain formal, cognitive, and linguistic neatness—almost a somber tidiness, if such a thing can be imagined—that is obscured, and almost successfully subjugated, by what is most powerful about the book, its loose wail of pain, its vigorous honesty.

David Lurie, through whom all of the novel's action is seen, is a professor at Cape Town Technical University. He feels himself to be something of an irrelevance, a traditional humanist with a love of the Romantic poets in a world of student illiteracy and snarling theory. He has been bumped from teaching literature to teaching "communications," which he despises. He is old-fashioned in another way, too: he likes to sleep with his female students. He begins a brief affair with one of them, a young woman named Melanie, and is more deeply drawn to her than he expected to be. The relationship is consensual, except that Lurie never really feels that Melanie's heart is in it.

Lurie is honest enough to sense an atmosphere of exploitation. In one of their sexual encounters, he has the uncomfortable sensation that he has forced himself upon his student: "She does not resist. All she does is avert herself; avert her lips, avert her eyes. She lets him lay her out on the bed and undress her: she even helps him, raising her arms and then her hips. Little shivers of cold run through her; as soon as she is bare, she slips under the quilted counterpane like a mole burrowing, and turns her back on him." Lurie feels that this experience has been "not rape, not quite that, but undesired nevertheless, undesired to the core."

A complaint is made (probably not by Melanie but by her thuggish older boyfriend) and Lurie is told by an academic committee that he must apologize, and undergo counseling or some form of "sensitivity training." He admits his formal guilt, but he refuses counseling for something that seems natural to him, and even fine. Wearily stubborn, he loses his job rather than mimic a penitence that he does not feel, leaves the university in disgrace, and travels to the Eastern Cape to stay with his daughter Lucy, who lives alone on a smallholding.

Disgrace is written in a language that, even by Coetzee's standards, is savagely reduced. It never spills a drop. The reticent lyricism that sometimes overcame his earlier novels, like that fine book *Life & Times of Michael K*, is here abandoned. Scenes and characters are flicked with a word or two, and then dropped. The narrative is always restlessly propulsive. This, for instance, is how Lurie appraises Melanie's threatening boyfriend, and is the fullest visual description we are offered: "He is tall and wiry; he has a thin goatee and an earring; he wears a black leather jacket and black leather trousers. He looks older than most students; he looks like trouble." And this is how Petrus, a black neighbor of Lucy's, is seen: "Petrus wipes his boots. They shake hands. A lined, weathered face; shrewd eyes. Forty? Forty-five?"

Coetzee is always praised for his dignified bleakness, for the "tautness" or carefulness or grim efficiency of his prose, which is certainly good enough to embarrass the superfluous acreage of many supposedly richer stylists. But there is a point beyond which pressurized shorthand is no longer an enrichment but an impoverishment, and an unnatural containment. It is the point at which ellipsis becomes a formalism, a kind of aestheticism, in which fiction is no longer presenting complexity but is in fact converting complexity into its own too-certain language. Hemingway at his worst represents one extreme, as when the narrator of *A Farewell to Arms* sees his dead friend and tells the reader, bathetically: "He looked very dead. It was raining. I had liked him as well as anyone I ever knew."

The effect of such writing, when passed through the jaded or cynical eyes of the protagonist, is a nullification of what is described. The language simply refuses to extend the consequences of its findings. Among contemporary writers, Robert Stone and Joan Didion straiten themselves in this way; and Coetzee does so, I think, in this novel. Thus at the simplest level, no one is ever adequately described as simply "tall and wiry . . . a thin goatee and an ear-ring . . . black leather jacket." This is only the beginning of description, and a prose that treats it as finale is merely servicing its own requirements, rather as, when we find ourselves in a country whose language we barely know, we limit ourselves to what we know we can say, for self-protection.

At such moments, fiction is not open to reality. Instead, it is efficiently reproducing its own fictive conventions. One of those conventions is precisely that characters, and characters' bodies, are swiftly describable. Another is that a character can quickly range over the memory of many years and produce an instant summation. David Lurie is very much this kind of character; all his reflections and memories and thoughts are tightly marshaled in a spare line or two. When Lurie meets his ex-wife Rosalind, and they talk about his dismissal from the university, he recalls the early moments of their relationship:

> His best memories are still of their first months together: steamy summer nights in Durban, sheets damp with perspiration, Rosalind's long, pale body thrashing this way and that in the throes of a pleasure that was hard to tell from pain. Two sensualists: that was what held them together, while it lasted.

This passage would not be out of place in a mass-market thriller. It is the sheerest conventionality ("steamy summer nights . . . body thrashing . . . pleasure . . . from pain"). No one thinks of an entire marriage in such neatly summary terms except in novels, where men are strangely fond of this kind of thought, which exists in such novels as a code whose sole task is to announce, circularly enough: a man is now thinking about his failed marriage. (Particularly frustrating is that phrase "two sensualists," with its fraudulent confidence and its calm speaking on behalf of both parties.) If such writing seems "efficient," the compliment should only be backhanded, since its efficiency is to save the novelist time, and the reader effort. It is cheap writing, literally cost-saving. It is like the moment at the beginning of *Waiting for the Barbarians* when soldiers are seen slumbering, "dreaming of mothers and sweethearts." The point is to tell us: soldiers asleep. In the conventions of fiction, soldiers always dream about mothers and sweethearts.

It must be admitted, in fairness, that Coetzee is so agile and so intelligent that for every sentence that seems formulaic in his work, another springs out with life. And *Disgrace* is involved, as a theme, with its own verbal flatness. When Lurie and his daughter discover that they cannot communicate with each other, Lurie reflects that in South Africa language has become "tired, friable, eaten from the inside as if by termites. Only the monosyllables can still be relied on, and not even all of them. What is to be done? Nothing that he, the one-time teacher of communications, can see. Nothing short of starting all over again with the ABC." So some of the novel's linguistic scantiness can be laid at the door of David Lurie, who is disillusioned and cynical about language.

Yet a disillusioned and cynical consciousness is still a busy consciousness; it is one that is merely thriving on disillusionment and cynicism. The novelist's task is then to present in its fullness this sour mental prosperity. Coetzee fails, or refuses to do so, and he lets David Lurie's reduced language define David Lurie's inner life, which is to say that Lurie does not quite exist as an examined consciousness in this novel. He is an efficient flatness. Lurie—as the

novel shows us—becomes an active conscience; but as a consciousness he is little more than a conduit for Coetzee's taut language,
which makes Lurie too often merely the voyeur of his own weary
clarities.

The effect is limiting in ways that Coetzee did not perhaps intend, in ways that go beyond Lurie's own limitations. The novel always feels tightly poised, but never quite alive. Mental reflection is
shunted into swift sidings; and characters speak in those one-line
fouettés that are only ever used by people in movies or in Oscar
Wilde:

> He makes love to her one more time . . . It is good, as good as the
> first time; he is beginning to learn the way her body moves. She is
> quick, and greedy for experience . . . Who knows, he thinks: there
> might, despite all, be a future.
> "Do you do this kind of thing often?" she asks afterwards.
> "Do what?"
> "Sleep with your students. Have you slept with Amanda? . . .
> Why did you get divorced?" she asks.
> "I've been divorced twice. Married twice, divorced twice."
> "What happened to your first wife?"
> "It's a long story. I'll tell you some other time."
> "Do you have pictures?"
> "I don't collect pictures. I don't collect women."
> "Aren't you collecting me?"
> "No, of course not."

Lurie and his daughter have never had a very easy relationship, despite his fierce love for her. He is conservative, solitary; she is lesbian,
lefty, and also solitary, living alone on a small farm in a dangerous
area among blacks and armed Afrikaners. Her best friend, Bev Shaw,
runs an animal clinic, about which Lurie is initially dismissive. Father and daughter are brought together and further separated by
a horrendous event: three men burgle Lucy's home, set fire to
Lurie and lock him in a lavatory, and gang-rape Lucy. Coetzee

describes this moment superbly. In particular, one admires the boldness with which he presents David Lurie's racist fear and sense of powerlessness (the assailants are black): "He speaks Italian, he speaks French, but French and Italian will not save him here in darkest Africa. He is helpless, an Aunt Sally, a figure from a cartoon, a missionary in cassock and topi waiting with clasped hands and upcast eyes while the savages jaw away in their own lingo preparatory to plunging him into their boiling cauldron. Mission work: what is left behind, that huge enterprise of upliftment? Nothing that he can see."

Thus begins the novel's second half, a gripping and complicated examination of the two different responses that two different generations fashion to this dreadful eruption. As in *Fathers and Sons*, the younger representative is more politically radical than the older; but the power of the novel lies in the way in which Lucy begins to change her father's vision, for Lurie ends the novel very much more thoughtful and penitent than he began it, shaken by his solitude, and shaken by Lucy's arguments. Though Lucy and her father do not quite agree by the novel's close, and in some sense they are as separated as they have ever been, both have been changed by the effort of reconciliation.

Lucy's response to the rape, which her father finds bewildering, is to seek refuge in a damaged silence, and then in fatalism. She does not want to press charges, and refuses to move away from the area, in part because that will seem like a defeat, and in part because she begins to see the rape as the necessary price for her continued occupation of the land. The attack is a kind of historical reparation. "What if that is the price one has to pay for staying on? Perhaps that is how they look at it; perhaps that is how I should look at it too. They see me as owing something. They see themselves as debt collectors, tax collectors. Why should I be allowed to live here without paying? Perhaps that is what they are telling themselves." To which Lucy's father responds: "I am sure they tell themselves many things.

It is in their interest to make up stories that justify them." Yet only a few minutes earlier in the conversation, David himself had raised the notion that the attack was not personal but historical: "It was history speaking through them . . . A history of wrong. Think of it that way, if it helps. It may have seemed personal, but it wasn't. It came down from the ancestors."

But Lucy seems to share the self-justifications of her attackers, and when she discovers that she has been made pregnant by the attack she refuses to have an abortion. On the contrary, she expects to have the child, to raise it, and even to love it in time. Her father finds this grotesque, and accuses her of trying to "humble herself before history." He complains to Lucy's friend that "I don't know what the question is anymore. Between Lucy's generation and mine a curtain seems to have fallen. I didn't even notice when it fell."

The novel is interestingly divided on this rather shocking idea of rape as historical reparation, which, on the surface, is insulting both to its victims, who are seen to deserve it historically, and to its agents, who are no more than historically determined, and perhaps even racially determined ("It came down from the ancestors"), to keep on exacting it. The possibility that the novel discusses and then finally proposes this vision has earned Coetzee a certain amount of covert condemnation.

But the book is more complicated than that. First of all, a society such as South Africa is riven by just this kind of liberal white fatalism, in which black violence is seen as a baleful inevitability, as nothing more than just deserts. It is honest of Coetzee to let his characters give expression to it, and the novel is alert both to the imprisonment that this thought represents and to its subtle white racism, in which blacks are credited with no possible response other than the vengeful. In this sense, the novel discovers and dramatizes what unites David's and Lucy's different politics: both of them have depressingly low expectations for the future of South Africa, and both of them flatter themselves that whites will somehow have to act more "nobly" than blacks. Both espouse a kind of cynical "realism" that is in fact a variety of racist guilt. David thinks the historically determined criminals should be locked up with their own kind, and Lucy thinks that she should live penitentially among the historically determined criminals.

If both of them, at various moments, make black crime and white punishment appear inevitable, Coetzee seems to say, this only shows the imbrication of so-called conservative and liberal positions in South Africa. We should not be surprised that Coetzee's book develops this idea: in his novels and in his essays, from a staunchly liberal position himself, Coetzee has hammered on the way in which racism and conservatism have contaminated all political positions in South Africa, even their liberal inversions.

Still, David and Lucy do not simply "agree." Though David sometimes shares the idea of inevitability with his daughter, he does so to comfort her, having discovered what extremity of thought Lucy now finds consoling ("Think of it that way, if it helps"). David's occasional agreement is perhaps part his own fumbling, part his own inarticulacy in the face of the indescribable. Clearly David is fundamentally opposed to his daughter's masochistic politics, and is only occasionally dragged toward his daughter's position by the awful victorious logic of her interpretation. It is Lucy who refuses to move, and David, who anyway has fewer "convictions" than his daughter, must mold himself around her, however awkwardly. Equally clearly, David's narrative function is dialogical: Coetzee has him in place to oppose and to qualify Lucy's dark temptations of thought, so that the novel is finally incapable of doing anything as monologic as "propose" a single politics.

It is the form of *Disgrace*, not its content, that makes the reader uneasy. For the novel's shape—its very story, the allegory of its tale— *does* seem to insist on the necessity of Lucy's "punishment." It is a matter of symmetry. David has erred, committing a virtual rape against Melanie, and the novel's function is to wear down his complacent cynicism so that, in a late scene, he visits Melanie's parents and atones for his earlier involvement with their daughter. "In my own terms," he tells Melanie's father, "I am being punished for what happened between myself and your daughter . . . trying to accept disgrace as my state of being." This is David's "disgrace" and penitence. Lucy's "disgrace," of course, is not one that she earned or deserved; but in pairing the two forms of penitence, the novel comes unpleasantly close to suggesting a formal parallel of disgrace, in which both characters enact "necessary" falls. The idea of disgrace and penitence is forced to take too much weight; Lucy's rape is overdetermined—not merely by South African politics but by the novel itself.

This is a significant weakness, and it returns us to Coetzee's limitations, which are the limitations of allegory. *Disgrace* is so firmly plotted and shaped, so clearly blocked out, that it seems to request a kind of clarity of reading which is ultimately simplifying and harmful to the novel, in which "issues" are shared out between the generations, and split into willing binarisms: young and old, liberal and conservative, man and woman, straight and gay. Around this, the novel's architecture attempts to fuse these binarisms, to annul them, by arguing for a kind of parallelism. It is as if the form of the book tells us that despite the oppositions of Lucy and her father, both characters share more than they divide, for here are two people undergoing their different-but-similar forms of disgrace. And then, as a capstone, the novel's title powerfully extracts the essence of these two experiences, and unites them in one clipped word, and one strong theme: disgrace.

That these suspicions should arise has to do with Coetzee's fondness for intellectual and formal tidiness. Some will find this tension between the neatly allegorical and the complicatedly novelistic fruitful, and masterfully governed by Coetzee; but it is also possible to see it as a barely managed contradiction, in which the allegorical, alas, has pride of place in Coetzee's large quiver of talents. If the novel is finally more complicated than this, and more beneficially self-confounding, this is a tribute not only to Coetzee's difficult powers but also to the very nature of novelistic narrative, which inherently tends toward the dramatic corrugation, rather than the thematic flattening, of ideas.

Saul Bellow's Comic Style

❦

I

Everyone is called a "beautiful writer" at some point or other, just as all flowers are eventually called pretty. "Stylists" are crowned every day, of steadily littler kingdoms. But of course, there are very few really fine writers of prose. This is not surprising, since a prose is a vision, a totality. Great stylists should be as rare as great writers. Saul Bellow is probably the greatest writer of American prose of the twentieth century—where greatest means most abundant, various, precise, rich, lyrical. (Far more consistently fine than Faulkner, say.) This seems a relatively uncontroversial claim. The august raciness, the Melvillean enormities and cascades ("the limp silk fresh lilac drowning water"), the Joycean wit and metaphoricity, the lancing similes with their sharp American nibs ("He was meteor-bearded like John Brown"), the happy rolling freedom of the daring, uninsured sentences, the prose absolutely ripe with inheritance, bursting with the memories of Shakespeare and Lawrence yet prepared for modern emergencies, the Argus eye for detail, and, controlling all this, the firm metaphysical intelligence—all this is now thought of as Bellow's, as "Bellovian."

Reading Bellow is a special way of being alive; his prose is germinal. There is an image in *Ravelstein* in which the narrator describes how his neurologist, Dr. Bax, coaxed his very ill patient back from death to life: "Dr. Bax, like a shrewd Indian scout of the last century, pressed his ear to the rail and heard the locomotive coming. Life would soon be back, and I would occupy my seat in the life-train. Death would shrink to its former place at the margin of the land-scape." This lovely metaphor, celebrating life, also enacts it; the prose is in fact the life-train. Again and again, Bellow's writing reaches for life, for the human gust. Joyce is his only obvious twentieth-century rival. Indeed, sometimes they are eerily close. In *A Portrait of the Artist as a Young Man*, Joyce alights for a moment on Mr. Casey, whose fingers could not be straightened out: "And Mr. Casey told him that he had got those three cramped fingers making a birthday present for Queen Victoria." In *Humboldt's Gift* we come across the Russian Bath in Chicago: "On the second floor there had always lived aged workingstiffs, lone Ukrainian grandfathers, retired car-line employees, a pastry cook famous for his icings who had to quit because his hands became arthritic." It is a curious historical reversal —like Bruckner sounding Mahlerian—that Joyce can sometimes sound like Bellow, or that nothing sounds more like Bellow than Lawrence's description of the Rhine, from his short story "The Bor-der Line": "old Father Rhine, flowing in greenish volume."

This life-sown prose moves fast, logging impressions with bro-ken speed. Rereading *Herzog*, one encounters too many marvels to record: there is Herzog's mistress, Renata, sparkily described as "certainly not one of those little noli me tangerines." And there is a brief memory of Strawforth, a fat schoolboy, with his "fat curling thumbs," and a rabbi, "short-bearded, his nose violently pitted with black." And Nachman, who played the harmonica in the lavatory stalls: "You heard the saliva in the cells of the tin instrument as he sucked and blew." And the lightbulb that Herzog remembers at home, "which had a spike at the end like a German helmet. The large loose twist of tungsten filament blazed." Herzog recalls his asthmatic brother, Willie, in the grip of a breathing fit: "Trying to breathe he gripped the table and rose on his toes like a cock about to crow."

Of course, there is Valentine Gersbach and his wooden leg, "bending and straightening gracefully like a gondolier." There is the hospital Herzog remembers being in as a child, where the icicles hung from the hospital roof "like the teeth of fish, clear drops burning at their tips," and the Christian lady who comes to the young Herzog to read from the Bible, her hatpin sticking out from the back of her head "like a trolley rod." Passing a fish shop, Herzog pauses to look at the catch: "The fish were packed together, backs arched as if they were swimming in the crushed, smoking ice, bloody bronze, slimy black-green, gray-gold—the lobsters were crowded to the glass, feelers bent." In New York, Herzog passes a demolition crew, and this passage flows out, one of the great examples of urban realism, at once lyrical and robustly particular:

> At the corner he paused to watch the work of the wrecking crew. The great metal ball swung at the walls, passed easily through brick, and entered the rooms, the lazy weight browsing on kitchens and parlors. Everything it touched wavered and burst, spilled down. There rose a white tranquil cloud of plaster dust. The afternoon was ending, and in the widening area of demolition was a fire, fed by the wreckage. Moses heard the air, softly pulled toward the flames, felt the heat. The workmen, heaping the bonfire with wood, threw strips of molding like javelins. Paint and varnish smoked like incense. The old flooring burned gratefully—the funeral of exhausted objects. Scaffolds walled with pink, white, green doors quivered as the six-wheeled trucks carried off fallen brick. The sun, now leaving for New Jersey and the west, was surrounded by a dazzling broth of atmospheric gases.

Given so much, it might be easy for a reader to become blasé. Good writers tend to raise one up like canal locks, so that one swims at their level and forgets the medium that supports one. After a while, the reader might take for granted Bellow's exuberance of detail, might not notice that the squares of the harmonica are called "cells," that the tungsten filament in the bulb is seen not only as large but wonderfully as "loose," that the icicles have clear drops "burning at their tips" (the paradox of heat at the end of something cold, yet superbly right as a description of ice melting into water; and compare, incidentally, Lawrence, seeing oranges in a grove in Italy, "hanging like hot coals in the twilight"), or that the demolition ball, hard at work, is yet seen as "lazy" and "browsing"—and browsing *on* kitchens and parlors (Bellow adds strange prepositions to his verbs, as Lawrence does when he has a woman walking behind her lover "gloating on him from behind," or: "Banford turtled up like a fighting cock").

One realizes, with a shock, that Bellow has taught one how to see and hear, has opened the senses. Until this moment one had not really thought of the looseness of a lightbulb filament, one had not heard the saliva bubbling in the harmonica, one had not seen well enough the nose pitted with black pores, and the demolition ball's slow, heavy selection of its victims. A dozen very good writers—the Updikes, the DeLillos—can render you the window of a fish shop, and do it very well, but it is Bellow's genius to see the lobsters "crowded to the glass" and their "feelers bent" by that glass—to see the riot of life in the dead peace of things. Flaubert told Maupassant that "talent is a slow patience," and that "there is a part of everything which is unexplored, because we are accustomed to using our eyes only in association with the memory of what people before us have thought of the thing we are looking at. Even the smallest thing has something in it which is unknown. We must find it." Bellow is Flaubertian in this sense: either, by force of metaphorical wit, he makes us seize new connections and linkages—"the toes of his bare feet were pressed together like Smyrna figs"; cats with "grenadier tails"; a man's "dry-cereal mustache"—or he notices what is unexplored: "Her throat was ever so slightly ringed or rippled by some enriching feminine deposit."

II

There are three main areas of comedy in Bellow: the comedy of ideas, the comedy of spiritual or religious yearning, and the comedy of the body. Bellow has been so often discussed—mistakenly, I think—in the context of his many "ideas" that it is easy to forget that many of his heroes are failures or clowns in thought; the comedy of the novels has much to do with the prospect of the inefficacy of ideas, the piles of intellectual slack which truss these schlemiels like babies. "Oh so much human thread being wound on the most trivial spools," the narrator laments in *More Die of Heartbreak*. And Herzog wonders if thought can wake him from the dream of his mad existence, in which he runs chaotically from wife to mistress. "Not if it [thought] becomes a second realm of confusion, another more complicated dream, the dream of intellect, the delusion of total *explanations*." Out of this disjunction, between the rage to explain and the rage to experience, Bellow creates a distinctive modern irony—witty, heated, cerebral. He universalizes and simultaneously mocks the universalizing impulse: "Cops have their own way of ringing a doorbell. They ring like brutes. Of course, we are entering an entirely new stage in the history of consciousness," thinks Charlie Citrine, in his characteristic jumble, in *Humboldt's Gift*.

Moses Herzog is an adult child, flooded with memories of his close, stifling family life. He recalls his immigrant father, with his stern, furious face. Herzog hangs his head before great ideas, as a child might before his father. His intellectual patrimony is both parent and tyrant, and Herzog's wild and frequently funny letters to the great dead—"Dear Doktor Professor Heidegger, I should like to know what you mean by the expression 'the fall into the quotidian.' When did it happen?"—are like a son's wartime letters to his family, written at the battlefront. Nietzsche and Kierkegaard are, in effect, our parents, and we moderns are like spoiled children, bloated with a wealth we do not know how to spend wisely. Tommy Wilhelm, in

Seize the Day, complains that "the fathers were no fathers and the sons no sons."

This comedy is not only an intellectual or academic comedy; we are not merely laughing at the delusions of intellectuals but experiencing the pathos of their aspirations. And sometimes these comic creatures are not formal intellectuals at all, as Tommy Wilhelm is not, in *Seize the Day*, yet they wrestle comically with ideas. Perhaps nothing is more movingly comic in the whole of Bellow than the scene in *The Adventures of Augie March* in which Einhorn, a Chicago autodidact, writes an obituary of his father for the local newspaper. Stiff, clumsy, noble, the obituary is foolishly, ambitiously "intellectual," and the reader is able to see, in a paragraph, the quavering pretensions of a generation of intelligent American Jews:

> Einhorn kept me with him that evening; he didn't want to be alone. While I sat by he wrote his father's obituary in the form of an editorial for the neighborhood paper. "The return of the hearse from the newly covered grave leaves a man to pass through the last changes of nature who found Chicago a swamp and left it a great city. He came after the Great Fire, said to be caused by Mrs. O'Leary's cow, in flight from the conscription of the Hapsburg tyrant, and in his life as a builder proved that great places do not have to be founded on the bones of slaves, like the pyramids of Pharaohs or the capital of Peter the Great on the banks of the Neva, where thousands were trampled in the Russian marches. The lesson of an American life like my father's, in contrast to that of the murderer of the Strelitzes and of his own son, is that achievements are compatible with decency. My father was not familiar with the observation of Plato that philosophy is the study of death, but he died nevertheless like a philosopher, saying to the ancient man who watched by his bedside in the last moments . . ." This was the vein of it, and he composed it energetically in half an hour, printing on sheets of paper at his desk, the tip of his tongue forward, scrunched up in his bathrobe and wearing his stocking cap.

I doubt that this could be bettered by Dickens or Joyce. We begin the obituary in laughter and end it in tears, in a sublime dapple of emotions. Everything is here, beautifully ventriloquized: the clumsy, ungrammatical pompousness of the unpracticed writer ("leaves a man to pass through the last changes of nature who found Chicago a swamp" . . . "saying to the ancient man who watched by his bedside"), the rambling, feebly channeled anarchy ("He came after the Great Fire, said to be caused by Mrs. O'Leary's cow"), the intellectual exhibitionism which is in fact the purest non sequitur ("My father was not familiar with the observation of Plato that philosophy is the study of death, but he died nevertheless like a philosopher"), the autodidact's historical allusions hanging off the sentences ("in flight from the conscription of the Hapsburg tyrant"), and finally Einhorn's affecting, foolhardy American optimism, whereby this new land apparently proves that "great places do not have to be founded on the bones of slaves." No bones of slaves in America, indeed! — a marvelous idiocy of optimism. Note that Bellow does not have Einhorn write "Plato's observation that," which is the formulation a real intellectual would use, but the more upholstered and uneasy "the observation of Plato," a phrase whose awkwardness enshrines a certain distance from Plato; and what a marvelously, unwittingly comic word "observation" is — as if Plato were someone who threw out *mots* like Wilde.

III

Bellow's bodies are funny; he is a great portraitist of the human form, Dickens's equal at the swift creation of instant gargoyles. There is not only Valentine Gersbach in *Herzog* but Victor Wulpy, the great art critic and theorist, in "What Kind of Day Did You Have?" who is disheveled and "wore his pants negligently"; and Cousin Riva in "Cousins": "I remembered Riva as a full-figured, dark-haired, plump, straight-legged woman. Now all the geometry of her figure had changed. She had come down in the knees like the jack of a car, to a diamond posture"; and Pierre Thaxter in *Humboldt's Gift*, whose penis lengthens and contracts like a trombone; and Professor Kippenberg, in "Him with His Foot in His Mouth," a great scholar with bushy eyebrows "like caterpillars from the Tree of Knowledge."

What function do these exuberant physical sketches have? First, there is a simple joy to be had from reading the sentences. The description of Professor Kippenberg's bushy eyebrows as resembling caterpillars from the Tree of Knowledge is not just a fine joke; when we laugh, it is with appreciation for a species of wit that is properly called metaphysical. We delight in the curling process of invention whereby seemingly incompatible elements—eyebrows and caterpillars and Eden; or women's knees and car jacks—are combined. Thus, although we feel after reading Bellow that most novelists do not really bother to attend closely enough to people's physical shapes and dents, his portraiture does not exist merely as realism. We are encouraged not just to see the lifelikeness of Bellow's characters but to partake in a creative joy, the creator's joy in *making* them look like this. This is not just how people look; they are also sculptures, pressed into by the artist's quizzical and ludic force. In "Mosby's Memoirs," for instance, a few lines describe a Czech pianist performing Schoenberg. "This man, with muscular baldness, worked very hard upon the keys." Certainly we quickly have a vision of this "muscular baldness"; we know what this looks like. (Richter, in a word.) But then Bellow adds: "the muscles of his forehead rising in protest against *tabula rasa*—the bare skull," and suddenly we have entered the surreal, the realm of play: how strange and comic, the idea that the muscles of the man's head are somehow rebelling against the bareness, the blankness, the *tabula rasa*, of his bald head.

Bellow's way of seeing his characters also tells us something about his metaphysics. In his fictional world, people do not stream with motives; as novelists go, he is no depth psychologist. Instead, his characters are embodied souls. Their bodies are their confessions, their moral camouflage faulty and peeling: they have the bodies they deserve. Victor Wulpy, a tyrant in thought, has a large, tyrannical head; Valentine Gersbach, the adulterer with the roving eye, is hobbled by his lameness; Max Zetland, a reproving, withholding father, has an unshavable cleft or pucker in his chin, and when he smokes, "he held in the smoke of his cigarettes." It is perhaps for this reason that Bellow is rarely found describing young people; even his middle-aged characters seem old. For in a sense he turns all his characters into old people, since the old helplessly wear their essences on their bodies, like hides; they are seniors in moral struggle.

Like Dickens, and to some extent like Tolstoy and Proust, Bellow sees humans as the embodiments of a single dominating essence or law of being, and makes repeated reference to his characters' essences, in a method of leitmotif. As, in *Anna Karenina*, Stiva Oblonsky always has a smile, and Anna a light step, and Levin a heavy tread, each attribute the accompaniment of a particular temperament, so Max Zetland has his reproving pucker, and Sorella, in *The Bellarosa Connection*, her forceful obesity, and so on. In *Seize the Day*, probably the finest of Bellow's earlier works, Tommy Wilhelm sees the great crowds walking in New York and seems to see "in every face the refinement of one particular motive or essence—*I labor, I spend, I strive, I design, I love, I cling, I uphold, I give way, I envy, I long, I scorn, I die, I hide, I want.*"

IV

As for the comedy of religious or spiritual yearning: Bellow's characters are repeatedly tempted by visions of escape—sometimes mystical, sometimes religious, and often Platonic (Platonic in the sense that the real world is felt to be not the real world but only a place where the soul is in exile, a place of mere appearances). Charlie Citrine, in *Humboldt's Gift*, with his anthroposophical leanings, is the most celebrated example. Tommy Wilhelm, in *Seize the Day*, imagines a different world, one suffused with love, and Woody Selbst, in "A Silver Dish," is full of the "secret certainty that the goal set for this earth was that it should be filled with good, saturated with it," and sits and listens, religiously, to all the Chicago bells ringing on Sunday. Yet the story he recalls is a tale of shameful theft and trickery, an utterly secular story. The narrator of "Cousins" admits that he has "never given up the habit of referring all truly important observations to that original self or soul" (referring here to the Platonic idea that man has an original soul from which he has been exiled, and back to which he must again find a path). But again, the spur of his revelations is completely secular—a shameful court case involving a crooked cousin.

Bellow's characters all yearn to make something of their lives in the religious sense; and yet this yearning is not written up religiously, or solemnly. It is written up comically: our metaphysical cloudiness, and our fierce, clumsy attempts to make these clouds yield rain, are full of hilarious pathos in his work. In this regard, Bellow is perhaps most tenderly suggestive in his lovely late story "Something to Remember Me By" (surely a gentle homage to Isaac Babel's story "My First Fee"). The narrator, now old, recalls a single day from his adolescence, in Depression-blighted Chicago. He was, he recalls, a child dreamy with religious and mystical ideas, of a distinctly Platonic nature: "Where, then, is the world from which the human form comes?" he asks rhetorically. On his jobs delivering flowers in the city, he always used to take one of his philosophical or mystical texts with him. On the day under remembrance, he becomes the victim of a cruel prank. A woman lures him into her bedroom, encourages him to remove his clothes, throws them out the window, and then flees. The clothes disappear, and it is his task then to get home, an hour away across freezing Chicago, to the house where his mother is dying and his stern father waits for him, with "blind Old Testament rage."

The boy is clothed by the local barman and earns his fare home by agreeing to take one of the bar's regulars, a drunk called McKern, to McKern's apartment. Once there, the boy lays out the drunk and then cooks supper for McKern's two motherless young daughters — he cooks pork cutlets, the fat splattering his hands and filling the little apartment with pork smoke. "All that my upbringing held in horror geysered up, my throat filling with it, my guts griping," he tells us. But he does it. Eventually, the boy finds his own way home, where his father, as expected, beats him. Along with his clothes, he has lost his treasured book, which was also thrown out the window. But, he reflects, he will buy the book again, with money stolen from his mother. "I knew where my mother secretly hid her savings. Because I looked into all books, I had found the money in her *mahzor*, the prayer book for the High Holidays, the days of awe."

There are coiled ironies here. Forced by the horridly secular confusions of his day to steal, the boy will take this money to buy more mystical and unsecular books, books which will no doubt religiously or philosophically instruct him that *this* life, the life he is leading, is not the real life. And why does the boy even know about his mother's hiding place? Because he looks "in all books." His bookishness, his unworldliness, are the reasons that he knows how to perform the worldly business of stealing. And where does he steal this money from? From a sacred text. So then, the reader thinks, who is to say that *this* life, the life our narrator has been so vividly telling us about, with all its embarrassments and Chicago vulgarities, is not real? Not only real but also religious in its way — for the day he has just painfully lived has also been a kind of day of awe, in which he has learned much, a secular High Holiday, complete with the sacrificial burning of goyish pork.

This lovely tale, both wistful and comic, throws out at us, in burning centrifuge, the secular-religious questions: What are our days of awe? And how shall we know them?

V

Saul Bellow was nearly born in Russia. His father, Abraham Belo,
came to Lachine, Quebec, in 1913, and Bellow was born in June 1915.
He lived in Quebec for eight years before his father moved the family to Chicago, in 1924. Abraham Bellow went to work at Dworkin's
Imperial Baking Company. Repeatedly, in novels and stories, Bellow
has his protagonist dream back to the days of Bellow's childhood on
Saint Dominique Street in Lachine, or to the later years just east of
Humboldt Park, in Chicago. Though *Dangling Man*, his first novel,
is more contained than any of his later work, the true Bellovian note
bursts through at one moment, when Joseph is polishing his shoes
and recalls doing the same as a child in Montreal:

> I have never found another street that resembled St. Dominique . . .
> Little since then has worked upon me with such force as, say, the
> sight of a driver trying to raise his fallen horse, of a funeral passing
> through the snow, or of a cripple who taunted his brother. And the
> pungency and staleness of its stores and cellars, the dogs, the boys,
> the French and immigrant women, the beggars with sores and de-
> formities whose like I was not to meet again until I was old enough
> to read of Villon's Paris . . . a cage with a rat in it thrown on a bon-
> fire, and two quarreling drunkards, one of whom walked away
> bleeding, drops falling from his head like the first slow drops of a
> heavy rain in summer, a crooked line of drops left on the pavement
> as he walked.

The reference to Villon, the blood dripping heavily "like the first
slow drops of a heavy rain in summer"—it is all here, in little form, in
Bellow's first novel, written in his late twenties. In *Herzog*, Saint Dominique Street becomes Napoleon Street, and Herzog recalls "my
ancient times. Remoter than Egypt":

> Up and down the street, the brick-recessed windows were dark,
> filled with darkness, and schoolgirls by twos in their black skirts

marched toward the convent. And wagons, sledges, drays, the horses shuddering, the air drowned in leaden green, the dung-stained ice, trails of ashes. Moses and his brothers put on the caps and prayed together, .

"*Ma tovu ohaleha Yaakov . . .*"
"How goodly are thy tents, O Israel."

Napoleon Street, rotten, toylike, crazy and filthy, riddled, flogged with harsh weather—the bootlegger's boys reciting ancient prayers. To this Moses's heart was attached with great power. Here was a wider range of human feeling than he had ever again been able to find. The children of the race, by a never-failing miracle, opened their eyes on one strange world after another, age after age, and uttered the same prayer in each, eagerly loving what they found. What was wrong with Napoleon Street? thought Herzog. All he ever wanted was there. His mother did the wash, and mourned . . . His sister Helen had long white gloves which she washed in thick suds. She wore them to her lessons at the conservatory, carrying a leather music roll . . . On a summer night she sat playing and the clear notes went through the window into the street. The square-shouldered piano had a velveteen runner, mossy green as though the lid of the piano were a slab of stone. From the runner hung a ball fringe, like hickory nuts. Moses stood behind Helen, staring at the swirling pages of Haydn and Mozart, wanting to whine like a dog. Oh, the music! thought Herzog.

One of the significances of Bellow's career is that in the age of Beckett he has retained the soul-pungency of the nineteenth-century novelists, and the metaphysical leanings of the great Russians. He is like an earlier generation of writers in his determination to deliver his characters from the inessential. He once wrote that when we read "the best nineteenth and twentieth century novelists, we soon realize that they are trying in a variety of ways to establish a definition of human nature." In most contemporary literature, however, "this power to understand the greatest human qualities appears to be dispersed, transformed, or altogether buried." In his Nobel lecture, he wrote that "there is another reality, the genuine one, which we lose sight of. This other reality is always sending us hints, which, without art, we can't receive. Proust calls these hints our 'true impressons.' "

At the risk of sounding apocalyptic, we might say that Bellow has extended the life of the novel. He has reprieved realism, held its neck back from the blade of the postmodern; and he has done this by re-vivifying realism with modernist techniques. His prose is densely "realistic," and yet it is hard to find in it any of the usual conventions of realism. People do not walk out of houses and onto streets; his characters do not have "dramatic" conversations; it is almost impos-sible to find sentences in Bellow along the lines of "He put down his drink and left the room." That is because most Bellovian detail ap-pears as memory in his novels, as scenes which are filtered through a remembering mind. So detail is modern in Bellow because it is al-ways the impression of a detail; yet his details have an unmodern solidity—they are indeed "true impressions."

> My ancient times. Remoter than Egypt. No dawn, the foggy win-ters. In darkness, the bulb was lit. The stove was cold. Papa shook the grates, and raised an ashen dust. The grates grumbled and squealed. The puny shovel clinked underneath. The Corporals gave papa a bad cough. The chimney in their helmets sucked in the wind. Then the milkman came in his sleigh. The snow was spoiled and rot-ten with manure and litter, dead rats, frogs. The milkman in his sheepskin gave the bell a twist . . . And then Ravitch, hung over, came from his room, in his heavy sweater . . .

Herzog is recalling this scene, hence that aspect, so strong in Bellow, of a kind of emotional cubism, whereby the mind returns repeatedly, but with variations, to the same details, and ponders and reponders. It is a relaxed stream of consciousness, disguised by its relaxation so that it almost seems as if it were conventional realism. Of course, Bellow learned from Joyce that the stream of consciousness gives re-alism new life because it absolves realism of having to persuade in the conventional way. A standard realist account might try to convince us that the scene in Herzog's kitchen was happening as we witness it, or as another character witnessed it. In such a convention, for us to "believe" in the milkman would necessitate the conjuring into life of that milkman—a plausible description of his existence. But the memory can select and assert, can pounce on one small detail—the bulb with its large loose twist of tungsten—precisely because these events have happened long ago, and there is no pressure to convince us; there is not the pressure of simultaneity in which realism often awkwardly finds itself ("She entered the door and gave a sharp cough"). Bellow is using detail not to persuade us of the existence of something but almost the opposite—to confirm its absence. Realism is elegiac, a branch of consciousness in Joyce and Bellow.

Curiously enough, the stream of consciousness, for all its reputation as the great accelerator of description, actually slows down realism, asks it to dawdle over tiny remembrances, to circle and return. The stream of consciousness is really an ally of the short story, of the anecdote, the fragment—and it is no surprise that the short story and the stream of consciousness appear in strength in literature at about the same time, toward the end of the nineteenth century: in Hamsun and Chekhov. In a short story writer like the Russian Isaac Babel, for instance (who was translated into English in 1929, and whom Bellow read in the 1930s), one encounters small, sharp details, broken off and removed from the large sustaining network of conventional realistic narration. Sometimes the sound is very close to Bellow: "Even Shoyl, my grand-uncle, went along. I loved that boastful old man, for he sold fish at the market. His fat hands were moist, covered with fish-scales, and smell of worlds chill and beautiful . . . Besides the salesmen, old Lieberman, who had taught me the Torah and ancient Hebrew honored us with his presence. In our circle he was known as Monsieur Lieberman. He drank more Bessarabian wine than he should have. The ends of the traditional silk tassels poked out from beneath his waistcoat, and in ancient Hebrew he proposed my health."

Bellow's prose, like Babel's, moves between different temporalities, between the immediate and the traditional, present time and memory time, the short-lived and the long-lived. The narrator of "Something to Remember Me By" writes that at home, inside the house, they lived by "an archaic rule; outside, the facts of life." Bellow's prose marvelously moves in similar ways, between the "archaic," or traditional, and the immediate, dynamic "facts of life." It may not be an ideal style, but then no such thing exists: of course there are registers which Bellow cannot fathom, or has not chosen to fathom. But it grandly exuberates with more diverse elements—lyricism, comedy, realism, vernacular—than any other contemporary English prose, and in America it deserves more praise than Bellow's now elderly canonicity perhaps encourages.

The Real Mr. Biswas

❧

In his essay on laughter, Henri Bergson argues that comedy is chastening, not charitable. Laughter is defined by a certain absence of sympathy, a distance and disinterestedness, the philosopher tells us. A world full only of pure intelligences would probably still include laughter; a world full only of pure emotionalists probably would not. Bergson appears to have been universalizing from the example of Molière, and in so doing produces a description of comedy that is rather mightily contradicted by the novel form. For the novel's greatest and most authentic category might be precisely one of sympathetic comedy, in particular that paradoxical shuffle of condescension and affiliation we are made to feel by Don Quixote, or Uncle Toby, or Zeno, or Pnin, or Bohumil Hrabal's foolishly inspired heroes. Such characters have busy souls. They are congested by aspiration, an aspiration that outstrips their insight. They claim to know themselves, but their selves are too dispersed to be known. It is we who know them, because we know about them at least something: that they are self-ignorant. They are thus rich cavities into which we pour a kindly offering: once it is only we who can provide the knowledge they lack about themselves, then we ourselves have become that lack, have become a part of them.

V. S. Naipaul's great comic character Mr. Biswas belongs to this company. Generous, combustible, nobly hysterical, facetious when he would like to be solemn, stoical in resolve but crumbling in practice, free in spirit but actually tied to the train of his destiny by the modesty of his ticket, he is a very affecting comic creation, one of the few enduring characters in postwar British fiction. We watch Biswas become a signwriter (his first work, for a neighbor, is IDLERS KEEP OUT BY ORDER), and then a journalist at the *Trinidad Sentinel*. A dreamer, he likes to read fictional descriptions of bad weather in foreign countries. Eager to write his own stories, he corresponds with the "Ideal School of Journalism, Edgware Road, London," which advises him to write about "the Romance of Place-Names (your vicar is likely to prove a mine of colourful information)." Biswas has a kind of anxious serenity; he is a neurotic stoic: "When he got home he mixed and drank some McLean's Brand Stomach Powder, undressed, got into bed, and began to read Epictetus." This delicate sentence is characteristic of Naipaul's early comic writing: there is the lovely synchromesh of registers, stomach powder ennobled by Epictetus (and how nicely the sentence docks at its final, rising word); there is the mock-heroic absurdity of it, and a gentleness which is balanced between rebellion and fatalism: the stomach powder, like Biswas's soul, will keep fizzing even as Epictetus calms. Above all, there is the sympathetic identification—what Hugh Kenner, speaking of Joyce, calls the "Uncle Charles Principle"—whereby Naipaul's description so assumes Biswas's way of thinking that it comically, pedantically offers the precise brand name of the stomach powder, just as Biswas would if he were narrating the story. Here Naipaul, as we have, has become Biswas. Comedy is not distance but proximity.

One of the reasons, doubtless, for Naipaul's penetration into Biswas's happy chaos is that the young author, at the novel's deepest moments, was describing the essence of his father, Seepersad Naipaul. *Letters Between a Father and Son* shows us that Naipaul's father was less naïve, much less unlettered, and more worldly than Mr.

Biswas; but the two men share an ungoverned delightfulness, and are, at the same time, stalked by an ungoverned anxiety. Both are overflowing spirits, breathing the germs of vicarious aspiration over their clever and dutiful sons. This is often a hope, however unwitting, that the son may not resemble the father: Seepersad Naipaul, who had privately published his stories, writes several times to Vidia that he believes that his son will become a great writer; for himself, all he hopes is that he might one day be reputably published by an English firm. The spirit is not unlike that described in *A House for Mr. Biswas*, when Biswas tells his son, Anand, "I don't want you to be like me." "Anand understood," writes Naipaul. "Father and son, each saw the other as weak and vulnerable, and each felt a responsibility for the other, a responsibility which, in times of particular pain, was disguised by exaggerated authority on the one side, exaggerated respect on the other."

Seepersad so dominates the collection of letters between father and son that the book rather resembles a double bed of which only one side has been slept in. Seepersad rises off these pages as powerfully as, perhaps more powerfully than, Mr. Biswas rises off his; the young Vidia Naipaul, who is a student during the exchange of letters that comprises the book, emerges more intermittently. The letters sent between father and son begin in 1950, when Vidiadhar Naipaul—called Vido by his family—leaves Trinidad for Oxford, and they end in October 1953, when Seepersad dies at the age of forty-seven, from a heart attack. Seepersad Naipaul, called "Pa" in these letters, was working as a reporter on the *Trinidad Guardian* when his seventeen-year-old son left for Oxford. It was a gravely exciting time for both of them. Seepersad was frustrated in his job, and desperate to find the time to write fiction. The job ground him down. As he explains to his son in a letter written in October 1950:

> This is the time I should be writing the things I so long to write. This is the time for me to be myself. When shall I get the chance? I

don't know. I come from work, dead tired. The *Guardian* is taking all out of me—writing tosh. What price salted fish and things of that sort. Actually that is my assignment for tomorrow! It hurts. Now keep your chin up, and far more important: keep yourself out of mischief.

Love from Ma and all, Pa.

So in his liberated and intelligent son, Seepersad grounds his own dreams. "I have no doubt whatever that you will be a great writer," he writes to him during his first term at Oxford; "but do not spoil yourself: beware of undue dissipation of any kind . . . You keep your centre." Later, he writes to Vidia: "I am often tired after work, and must be in a good mood to get back to work [i.e., to writing fiction] after work. It takes all the juice out of a fellow." He tells his son that he scribbles down stories at night, in bed. "The fact is I feel trapped."

It is the varieties of Seepersad's vicariousness that make him so full of comedy and pathos. Though Vidia's letters are often warm, they are rarely needy; there is never a doubt in our minds that it is this teenage son, the eldest son, who has the greater power—the power to excite, to impress, and to disappoint his father. In one sense, then, Vidia outgrew his father before he himself grew up; and if this is the case, then he had always outgrown his father, because his father's emotional need of him had always been more acute than his of his father. Seepersad's letters are fulsome where his son's are controlled, for which Pa apologizes: "Sometimes in my letter you'll find me spouting a lot of talk; if you should find them absurd, forget them as so many banalities." Commenting ruefully on Vidia's early successes as a student writer, Pa exclaims: "My God! At your age I could hardly manage to write a good letter."

This outgrowing of one's father naturally produces at times a stiff loneliness, as when Vidia writes to his sister, during his first term at Oxford, that his parents' devotion to him makes him feel both loved and sad: "One feels too weak to be caring about such a big responsibility—the responsibility of deserving affection." At other times, that loneliness—or perhaps singleness is the better word—erupts into a strange, slightly grotesque hypertrophy of authority, in which the teenager feels impelled to instruct his father: "By the way, let Pa know that I don't like his I'd's and we've's. Use the apostrophe as sparingly as possible," the eighteen-year-old writes to his mother. More often Vidia's letters contain both warm respect for his father and the beginning of a necessary objectification of Pa, a novelist's weaning, in which the young man begins to see his father as others might—as a character. He writes home: "What a delight to receive Pa's excellent letter from home. If I didn't know the man, I would have said: what a delightful father to have."

And indeed, despite Vidia's unnatural advantages in authority and education and experience, the tone of this exchange is overwhelmingly warm, because Pa's warmth is so large and universal that it burns off all family chills. It seems characteristic that when Vidia intimates that he has become close to an Englishwoman, his father, after warning against mixed marriages, concludes his letter: "The only thing that matters to me—and to all of us at home—is your happiness." Not for the first time in this collection, the reader reflects that in some respects Seepersad Naipaul must have been an ideal father, because on the one hand he existed to be outgrown, and knew it; and yet on the other, his support of his seven children was absolute, and could never be outgrown, or even rivaled. His love was greater than his authority: thus he was never paternally ex officio, but always instead a kind of civilian in fatherhood, an amateur at paternity.

Like most parents who give their children opportunities they themselves have never had, Pa lives through his son's experiences, urging him to write long, detailed letters about daily life at Oxford, and especially about his encounters with "big-shots" (Pa's characteristic word, a word equally characteristically eschewed by Vidia). What is delightful about the father who lives in these pages, how-

ever, is that unlike most ambitious parents, he does not squeeze his
son for guilt. Quite the opposite. He does not envy his son his experiences, or reproach him for them, but instead identifies with them
so strongly that he warmly shares them, takes them over. He is not
really ambitious for his son so much as ambitious for himself; his
son is an edition of his own rich fantasy life. It is Pa who is really in
Oxford, arranging meetings with prominent people. Thus, one of
the greatest comic elements in Pa's personality is that he lives vicariously through his son's experiences while giving plentiful advice
about the very experiences he has never had. "Don't be scared of being an artist. D. H. Lawrence was an artist through and through," he
cheers on his son. When Vidia tells him that he has not succeeded in
meeting Professor Radhakrishnan, the professor of Eastern religions
at Oxford, Pa replies with a bustle of recommendations:

> I do hope you did succeed in meeting Radhakrishnan again. To get
> the notice of such men a "rebuff" or two is a cheap price for the
> privilege of an interview. And it is always the best to be quite frank
> about your position with such people. You could have said, in order
> to make conversation: "My father has always looked upon you as
> one of the greatest minds of modern India. He has often said he
> never understood Hinduism so well as when he read your book, *The
> Heart of Hindustan*." And you would have broken the ice, as they
> say. Contacts, Vido, contacts all the time. Let me go on. Suppose
> you had a fairly good chat with this great scholar, you could have
> described the experience of the incident to me in a letter—in a long
> letter, if that was necessary. I'd have delighted in the reading of such
> a letter, and I'd have kept it with other letters of yours. Write me
> weekly of the men you meet; tell me what you talked; how they
> talked . . .

It is hard to imagine that Pa could seriously be advising his
proud, anxious, precocious son to "break the ice" in this absurdly
voluble manner. But Pa is serious, and that is his comedy, and his
poignancy. Pa's advice is hopelessly misguided; but he acts with the

busy authority of one who has already been in this situation himself. He burrows his way into that Oxford room, and sets himself up in place of his son. And there is nothing especially oppressive about this, because his identification with his son has such a fantastic quality. It is as if Pa, in dispensing advice so freely and confidently, has already lived, in a previous incarnation, the experiences he so longs to hear about; his son is his avatar. And, of course, Pa *has* really lived these experiences, because he has imagined them so many times. There is a nobility in this, a mental triumph. Pa is the victor of systems, because his fantasy is an army, running on a thousand legs.

So Pa may be "trapped," but he is also free, because he is most himself when traveling out of himself. His cry to Vidia—"This is the time for me to be myself"—is anguishing. Yet such a man could probably never *discover* himself, or merge with himself, or "find" himself, as if his singleness were a mislaid object. His self is a traffic of identifications and imaginings. He does not know himself because his intelligence is poured not into self-scrutiny but self-fantasy, not into self-gathering but self-dispersing. His identity is identification— identification with possibility. With great tenderness, Naipaul caught this aspect of his father in *A House for Mr. Biswas*, in which Biswas daydreams while reading the novels of Hall Caine and Marie Corelli, and tries to use the word "bower" because he found it in Wordsworth (by way of the *Royal Reader*). The sadness clouding that novel is that one is always oneself even when one does not know it; one cannot escape *that*, and freedom is always qualified. Freedom is a shout between two murmurs. This is literally evidenced by a habit of Pa's which Vidia fondly recalls in a letter to his "darling Ma." In it, her son reflects on his growing likeness to his father: "Perhaps you know Pa's habit of getting up at 5 or so in the morning, making a row to get everybody else up, and then going back to sleep. Well, I have no one to make a row with, but I get up sometimes at 5, and then go back to sleep too." It is a fitting vision, somehow, of freedom's poor chink, opened and shared with everyone else in the family, whether they want it or not. Pa reminds one here not only of Biswas but of another great fictional fantasist, optimist, and father, Sam Pollit in Christina Stead's *The Man Who Loved Children*, of whom Stead writes: "Sam was always anxious for morning."

Pa is a seething optimist, and he practices a kind of corrective vicariousness, in which he tells his somewhat depressive son to maintain postures and emotions that he himself has clearly never mastered. "Do not allow depression to have too much of a hold on you. If this mood visits you at times regard it as a passing phase and never give way to it," he writes to Vidia in September 1950. Pa himself was clearly prone to depression and anxiety, like his son. But for a father writing to a son, there are always two chins to keep up: he consoles Vidia in July 1952 when he learns that Vidia's novel has been rejected. "People like us are like corks thrown on water: we may go down momentarily; but we simply must pop up again." And he urges Vidia to do what he lacks time or discipline to do, which is to keep writing. Alluding to the author of numerous how-to-write books (one can imagine Vidia's youthful shudders), he implores: "Do you recollect what Cecil Hunte has said on the importance of note-taking?—of jotting down your impressions of people and things (and I'd add, of capturing a mood)? It would be a God-send to you if you adopted this as a habit."

The son who caught these balloons of aspiration and advice in Oxford seems at first unrelated to his emotionally ragged Pa. He tends to hoard himself where his father spreads himself. While his father is animally generous to all, Vidia can be royally haughty to others. "I met Ruth," he writes from New York, on his way to Oxford, in 1950. "She gave me a very unpleasant afternoon. I think she is a stupid, self-pitying shrew. A most detestable woman." While Pa is uncertain, burying his fragility in a muff of warm advice, Vidia seems adamantine, extraordinarily confident and penetrating for his years. While his father is lavish with banality, Vidia's letters are defined by the thrift of their omissions. One has a sense of a young man reserving the self for his work, and sharing only his dilutions with his family. (This is in fact the case: Naipaul wrote several novels while at Oxford.)

But Vidia does reveal himself in time, and the reader is able to discern an anxiety and pride that seem reminiscent of his father's. Above all, these letters allow us to trace a journey, from the rim of things to the uncomfortable center. Vidia set out from Trinidad in August 1950, by way of New York. "For the first time in my life people are calling me sir at every min.," he reports to his family. "It quite took my breath away. I was free and I was honoured." This young man already has an incipient aristocratic liberty of mind, while his father has labored all his life for his small supplement of liberty. The difference is partly because Vidia, unlike his father, is able to feel free on so little freedom. The passing respect of a black porter suffices, because although such gestures are essential to Vidia's sense of life, they are not essential to his sense of self. Pa's political metabolism is, by comparison, inefficient; his sense of freedom too clumsy and massive to be nourishing. There are too many wants to please. Vidia's wants are superbly narrow: he wants to be respectfully left alone, so that he can concentrate his self-originated freedom, and convert it into fiction.

In other words, Vidia is a much more efficient fantasist than his father, which is one definition of a novelist over a daydreamer. In July 1951, after he has been a year at Oxford, Vidia asks his father not to send money, because

the discipline, you know, of not having anyone but yourself to depend on is quite good, especially for a man like me. I discover in myself all types of aristocratic traits, without, you know too well, the means to keep them alive. Whenever I go into a new town, I go into the best hotel, just to feel comfortable, sit in the lounge, read all the newspapers . . . and drink coffee. I like comfort. And whereas in Trinidad, I was tremendously shy of going even into a Civil Service Office, now I go everywhere, firmly believing that I have as much right to be there as anybody else. That is the one good thing Oxford has done for me.

Vidia needed only a year at Oxford to set himself up.

Vidia's descriptions are always precise, concrete, often evocative. In December 1950 he sees his first snow and, writing home, says: "The closest thing I have seen to it in Trinidad is the stuff that gathers in a refrigerator." Naipaul is always relevant. T. S. Eliot refers to the necessity of "relevant intensity" in good style. Pa, of course, the delightfully inefficient fantasist, has the trick of irrelevant intensity down to a tee. Pa has a reverence for useless details, which hang off his letters like sloths. He thus has the mind of a writer—a willingness to take pains with detail—but the eye of a solipsist: he sees only what is relevant to himself. He is always itemizing costs, especially those involving the car ("Battery is giving way after 18 months' use and I need a tyre and tube," he writes to his son). He tells Vidia that he has recently lost his glasses "at Forest Reserve Oilfield, and replacing them has meant $34." When Vidia sends him a copy of *Isis* with one of his pieces in it, Pa praises him, but quickly gets absorbed in questions of subediting: "The by-line to the article 'Literary Schizophrenia' might have given the page a better appearance if it had been placed, say, midway into the middle column—and boxed."

Pa is helplessly theatrical, but Vidia learns to perform at Oxford, to act a part. Again, one has the impression of a true self, a writing self, kept in the wings. About a social occasion, Vidia writes, "I performed (that's the way I usually do things) no blunders." His letters are streaked with anxiety and pride, but one has to search for the stains of vulnerability. Early on, in his first few weeks, he writes: "The people here accept me." (Already, in a sign of how strange a writer Naipaul would become, this phrase of apparent humility before polished Oxonians sounds instead like the proud satisfaction of a conqueror among savages!) But the ghost of a rather harder assimilation appears four months later, in a letter to his sister, Kamla: "My

English pronunciation is improving by the humiliating process of error and snigger." When the dean of his college generalizes about "Indians," Naipaul tells his father: "I took all this in good humour." Vacations were often difficult for Naipaul. He was very poor ("literally penniless . . . [T]he man at the Ashmolean Museum at Oxford bought me regular teas"), and very lonely. One can only scrape the crust of desolation that is briefly hinted at in this sentence: "I spent Christmas Day at my boarding house. There was a little party given by the housekeeper. Terribly dull."

Both father and son, then, were keeping brave faces, but Vidia was under the greater pressure, because while Pa believed in his own optimism, Vidia, a pessimist, did not. Pa's brave face *was* a face; Vidia's was a mask, and a desperately important one. At times the young Naipaul can seem hard on his less educated family, but that is because he has been so hard on himself. When a cousin writes to him as "Mr Vido Naipaul, Oxford University, London, England," Naipaul sounds a tone that is now familiar to his later readers: "It is very flattering to be addressed Mr Naipaul, Oxford University, and have letters reach you. But think of the colossal ignorance." The arc of his development and escape from Trinidad, so fought for, will not become the casual doorway of some idle relative. If his father's watchword is the heuristic "Contacts, Vido, contacts," Vidia's is the militant "Vigilance, Vido, vigilance." His confidence, and what can seem like arrogance, are really no more than the units of his desperation, as a letter sent at the end of his first term artlessly reveals. Reviewing some of the essays he has written during the term, he tells his father that "they do read quite well." But then he adds: "I want to come top of my group. I have got to show these people that I can beat them at their own language."

Still, Naipaul's letters are by no means all carapace and control. His family, and especially his abundant father, provoke his warmth. When Pa develops a passion for growing orchids, Vidia smiles: "Well, it is mad, perhaps, but I like it," he writes home in September 1951. "I approve, if my approval helps at all, that is!" His family had been sending him food parcels, and had been hiding contraband cigarettes in tins of sugar: "What amateur and immature Customs-dodgers you are, my dear people . . . [T]here were these incriminating cigarette packets sitting so obviously, so loudly begging to be sent, that I am surprised that you have not been rounded up for questioning." And when Naipaul is lonely, he softens into homesickness: "I feel nostalgia for home. Do you know what I long for? I long for the nights that fall blackly, suddenly, without warning. I long for a violent shower of rain at night. I long to hear the tinny tattoo of heavy raindrops on a roof, or the drops of rain on the broad leaves of that wonderful plant, the wild tannia." At such moments, the son is quite the equal in charm of his father.

Over the Christmas vacation of 1951–52, Naipaul, again lonely and homesick, suffered some sort of nervous collapse. In response, family knots are tightened, and letters become warmer than ever. Pa worries about Vidia's depressions, and responds characteristically: "I'm sending you by sea mail the book *You and Your Nerves*. I think it will help you resolve a good many of your worries. Most of the things over which we worry are really no true cause of worry at all." But there were true family worries surfacing. Vidia had mentioned his English girlfriend, Pat, and was making it clear that he could not live in Trinidad. "I don't want to break your heart," he writes to his father in September 1952, "but I hope I never come back to Trinidad, not to live, that is, though I certainly want to see you and everybody else as often as I can. But Trinidad, as you know, has nothing to offer me."

Then, in February 1953, Pa collapsed from a heart attack. Vidia's elder sister, Kamla, writes to Vidia that the reason for the illness is that Pa has been worrying about her and Vidia: a vicarious heart attack. She adds that "Pa's greatest worry is that he cannot get his stories published . . . Now will you, in the name of Pa's life, see immediately to his short stories and write him a nice, cheering letter."

Naipaul's letter to his father is very moving, so exemplary is its tenderness and concern, and yet so poignant the sense it imparts of the son holding the damaged egg of his father's soul in his all-powerful hands: "You should not have thought I was uninterested in your writing," says Vidia to his father. "You ought to know that I am perhaps more keen on your work than anyone else is. And, furthermore, as I have often told you, you have the necessary talent . . . Please have courage and try to trust me."

Pa was severely weakened by his attack. He was let go from the newspaper at the end of July 1953. Much of his old buoyancy had absconded. This was no longer the man who had once included at the end of a letter to Vidia this jumble of passions: "Next week I might have the outside of the house painted. We never forget you for a day." Depleted though he was, however, Pa had not lost his talent for Pyrrhic persistence. In June 1953 he urged Vidia to sell his father's stories in London, and added: "If my own matter is not enough to make a normal-size book, what about adding your own stories? The by-line would thus be—By Seepersad and Vidia Naipaul. I don't know. It's up to you." Seepersad lived to hear Vidia read one of his father's stories on the radio in July. He died in October 1953, and his son sent this telegram home: HE WAS THE BEST MAN I KNEW STOP EVERYTHING I OWE TO HIM BE BRAVE MY LOVES TRUST ME—VIDO.

V. S. Pritchett and English Comedy

࿔

A friend once told me a true story, about a provincial dentist, a man called Miller, who kept a copy of *Who's Who* open on the waiting room table. The book was always agape at the letter *M*, indeed at the pages of notable Millers, as if the dentist wanted his patrons to notice something. But the dentist was not one of those Millers; he was nowhere to be found in *Who's Who*. He kept the book open at the place where he *would* be, if he *were* in it.

This little tale seems comic, universally and in a local English application. It might be Russian, or French, or even German (one might recall the dentist in *Buddenbrooks*, that surprisingly comic novel, who keeps a parrot in his office pretentiously named Josephus). The universal element is the comedy of desire, our sense of the provincial dentist as the possessor of an energetic soul, full of misplaced aspiration. He is a man in some ways free in spirit, free to expand and enlarge himself on private gusts of want. But he is also a figure of comic pathos because we sense his actual lack of freedom; he won't, as it were, ever get to Moscow. Surely we both laugh at and feel sympathy for the dentist. We feel a paradoxical estrangement and identification, a combination of affiliation and distance, because the dentist is himself so paradoxical: he is defying society in one sense, but also yearning to belong to it in another. He is absurd, not wrong. He lives in two societies, ours and his own; he is a solipsistic universalist.

The particular English inflection has to do with the nature of the dentist's aspiration, the snobbery of his desires, their pettiness. Smollett, Sterne, or Dickens might easily have invented such a man; Austen's Sir Walter Elliot is a dislikable, upper-class version. Schopenhauer, in *The World as Will and Representation*, argues that comedy frequently arises from the incongruity between our concepts and objective reality, which seems a fair definition of the dentist's plight. Schopenhauer mentions a drawing by Tischbein, of a room entirely empty and illuminated by a blazing fire in a grate. In front of the fire stands a man whose shadow starts from his feet and stretches across the whole room. Tischbein has this comment beneath his drawing: "This is a man who did not want to succeed in anything in the world, and made nothing of life; now he is glad that he can cast such a large shadow."

Schopenhauer asserts that the seriousness expressed by this drawing and this kind of humor is of the kind encapsulated in the advice "Get beyond the world, for it is naught"—which Schopenhauer the pessimist would say. But the seriousness of Tischbein's drawing surely also resides in the serious and forlorn prospect of a man consoling himself with the fantasy that even if he cannot be a success in the world, he can be a success in his own home and right now with his own shadow! In other words, we are brought back again to the dentist and the comic pathos involved in modest aspirations that do not know their own modesty.

This universal comedy of aspiration, and of the incongruity between the real and the perceived, is richly found in the comic world of V. S. Pritchett, a writer both very English and in revolt against Englishness. Pritchett has disappeared into a vague posterity; indeed, even while alive he became somewhat cloudily venerable. He may not be very much read now, and even to his admirers may seem only a fine minor writer. But he may also be exemplary, because his gentle literary struggle—that of broadening, Russianizing, internationalizing English comedy—is still significant even as his stories fade a little from the canon.

Pritchett was born in 1900, in Ipswich, into a lower-middle-class family, and died in 1998, in London. His mother was illiterate but a natural storyteller; his father, a Micawber-like figure who became a Christian Scientist, saw himself as the hero of a story, his own. Pritchett once said that his father "must have been very shy, for in public he had somehow to make himself into a person visible to all. In restaurants he was a mixture of the obsequious and the bumptious; he would speak to the manager in a very pretentious way." In his autobiography, he beautifully fixes his father in a moment of small desire: "I loved seeing the sad voluptuous pout of his lips as he carved a joint and the modest look on his face when, at my house, he passed his plate up and said, as his own mother had before, 'Just a little more.' It should have been his epitaph."

Pritchett's world, like Larkin's or Orwell's, is distinct, in a modern-antique way: velvet-lined pubs, cocky salesmen with poor teeth, tired municipal grasses, inflamed women, and sherry-fed courage. He sees the managed restlessness of ordinary life in such communities, he sees that such societies organize themselves like morbid conspiracies, and that the surest way of escaping such a world may be internal—by living out some kind of theatrical expansion of the self, by turning life into performance and spectacle. He got much of this from Dickens, and indeed Dickens has been the decisive influence on postwar English comedy: in Muriel Spark, in early Naipaul, overwhelmingly and detrimentally in Angus Wilson, also in Salman Rushdie (again detrimentally), in Angela Carter and Martin Amis, one finds Dickens's impress, in particular the interest in the self as a public performer, an interest in grotesque portraiture and loud names, and in character as caricature, a vivid dab of essence.

Pritchett was perhaps the most subtle Dickensian of these post-war writers: he represents, if it were possible, an attempt to blend Dickens and Chekhov. He wrote very well about Dickens, and the way his characters "take on the dramatic role of solitary pronouncers. All Dickens's characters, comic or not, issue personal pronouncements that magnify their inner life . . . [W]hat we find in this comedy is people's projection of their self-esteem . . . [A]ll are actors . . . They live by some private idea or fiction . . . Our comedy, Dickens seems to say, is not in our relations with each other but in our relations with ourselves." They are people, he wrote, whose inner lives hang out of them on their tongues. Likewise, many of Pritchett's characters, in the stories he wrote between the late 1930s and the late 1980s, are internal expansionists. The theatrical, expansive tendency is the closest we get to a definition of human nature in Pritchett's work.

Often, as in the true story about the dentist, these little billowings of pride and greed are social, and have to do with stolen calibrations of prestige. In his story "Sense of Humour," published in 1938, a young couple are having to drive a corpse, in a hearse, to the mother of the deceased. The circumstances are both grim and banal. They have the use of the hearse because the father of the driver is an undertaker. As they proceed through small English towns, so bystanders take off their hats, and others salute. The man driving the car thinks that it is like being at a wedding; the woman by his side laughs that "it's like being the King and Queen." A characteristic principle of English comic inversion is taking place here: what should be sad is actually funny, and it is hard not to think that Pritchett had in mind Mrs. Gargery's funeral in *Great Expectations*, which is comic when it should be solemn, and grotesquely ritualized when it should be spontaneous; the reader perhaps drifts from Pritchett's scene back to Dickens and on to "The Whitsun Weddings," and how Larkin describes the women at those weddings as sharing the secret "like a happy funeral."

There is an English dialectic, in Pritchett's comedy, of shyness and public performance. The shyer his characters are, the more they are likely to perform and expand in public; but the more they expand and perform, the lonelier, more secretive they actually are. This is the case in one of his most celebrated stories, "The Fall." A group of accountants are having their annual dinner in a drab, large Midlands city that "smelled of coal." One of their number, the inappropriately named Mr. Peacock, is dressing for dinner. He is a shy fantasist, a man who has to gather his selves for public events, and then display them in a series of performances. His social origins, about which he is touchy, are humble: his parents had a fish-and-chips shop. At the dinner, we see him falling into comic routines which he has rehearsed, and doing different voices—American South, Scots, Cockney.

But Mr. Peacock has a secret pride as well as a secret vulnerability: his brother is a famous movie star, and he is quite pleased to let people know it. His brother has a well-known stage fall; a big man, he can collapse with impunity, and then get up. Peacock starts showing his colleagues how this is done. At first, they are admiring, but Peacock, who has had too much to drink, doesn't know when to stop: " 'My brother weighs two hundred and twenty pounds,' he said with condescension to the man opposite. 'The ordinary person falls and breaks an arm or a foot, because he doesn't know. It's an art.' His eyes conveyed that if the Peacocks had kept a fried-fish shop years ago, they had an art." He accosts strangers, and offers to show them the famous stage fall. Soon he is alone in the large dining room, falling and rising, falling and rising, the only audience of his performance. The story has an immense comic pathos, because of the power of its irony. We see things through Peacock's eyes, yet we can see what he cannot: that he has become a boring drunk who falls to the floor, heavily and without his brother's grace. The story, one of great delicacy, ends with Peacock standing in an empty lounge in the hotel, not unlike the man in Tischbein's drawing, before a portrait of Queen Victoria, preparing to fall to the ground.

What is especially English, apart from the settings, about Pritchett's comedy? After all, these winds of fantasy and dream are everywhere in comic literature. How is Peacock different, really, from Gogol's Akakay Akakievich, an internal expansionist who, once he gets his fine new coat, is described thus: "From that time onwards his whole life seemed to have become richer, as though he had married and another human being was by his side." As I have suggested, Pritchett's comedy, grounded in the quixotic battle between internal fantasy and objective reality, certainly has a universal dimension. But distinct English lineaments emerge, too. One of those is the class-saturation of the comedy. Another is the subtle way in which Pritchett implies that these characters' expansions are cheap domestic versions of their country's enlargements: as their country once expanded, so they now expand. Each is a pocket imperialist, in a colony of one. Pritchett liked the way Dickens's characters drew on their sense of themselves as what he called "walking legends," and he liked to quote this outburst by Pecksniff, in which Pecksniff historicizes his feelings by comparing them to the princes who were murdered in the Tower of London: "My feelings, Mrs Todgers, will not consent to be entirely smothered like the young children in the Tower. They are grown up and the more I press the bolster on them, the more they look round the corner of it."

In his own work, many of his characters link themselves, with clinging grandiosity, to British history and expansion. There is Peacock, anachronistically offering himself, as it were, to Queen Victoria; or the couple in "Sense of Humour," riding in the hearse and imagining themselves royalty. And there is a wonderful moment in a story called "The Wheelbarrow," in which a Welsh taxi driver, Evans, has offered to help a lady clear out her late aunt's house. Evans has been truculent and obscure, but suddenly bursts into evil foliage when he picks up a volume of verse from an old box in the house, glances at it, and then throws it down: " 'Everyone knows,' he said scornfully, 'that the Welsh are the founders of all the poetry in Europe.' "

Or consider "When My Girl Comes Home." In this long story, written shortly after the Second World War, a young woman, Hilda, returns from a Japanese prison camp to London—or so her family thinks, a tight-knit, mean little court of judges. Initially, all of them want to bathe in the reflected glory of Hilda's return. Mr. Fulmino, a relative by marriage, has been responsible for the logistics of this homecoming: "Mr Fulmino . . . expanded in his chair with the contentment of one who had personally operated a deeply British miracle. It was he who had got Hilda home." She arrives by train, and her mother announces with what Pritchett calls "acquisitive pride" that Hilda was "in the first class."

In fact, Hilda was not really in a prison camp. She had been living in India with an Indian husband, who died, and then married a Japanese man, who also died, and is now waiting for the arrival of a wealthy American, Mr. Gloster. Her family, at first dazzled by her celebrity and her expensive clothes, becomes jealous, decides that she is a whore, and closes ranks against her. (Surely Pinter read this story, and worked a variation on it in his play *The Homecoming*.) Mr. Fulmino is tremendously proud that he has brought Hilda home: " 'I wrote to Bombay,' said Mr Fulmino. 'He wrote to Singapore,' said Mrs Fulmino. Mr Fulmino drank some tea, wiped his lips, and became geography." Recall Pinter, who learned so much from Pritchett about comic speech: in *The Homecoming*, Lenny, as it were, colonizes Venice. For no apparent reason, and with splendid illogicality, he says: "Not dear old Venice? . . . You know, I've always had a feeling that if I'd been a soldier in the last war—say in the Italian campaign—I'd probably have found myself in Venice." Lenny speaks of Venice as if he were speaking of dear old London, or dear old Blighty.

There is an obvious paradox, however: Pritchett's characters colonize at a time when their country was withdrawing from empire. They are children of diminishment. One might call them fat ambassadors of their country in a lean age. In this sense, they are not really linked to English history, and are not the retroactive thief of history that Dickens presents in Pecksniff. They are trying to escape from history, they are traveling in the opposite direction of the little gray determinism of their times. But to no avail. Pritchett's stories overflow with failure. And one notices something very English, that unlike the comic fantasists in Proust or Gogol or Tolstoy, or even sometimes in Chekhov, comic expansion is simultaneously the measure of the characters' failures. Indeed, one notices that Pritchett's descriptions of the way his characters' bodies change when they are expanding themselves tend to convert those moments into areas of shame: "One Sunday Argo looked at his feet sticking out boastfully from the bottom of the bed." Or this marvelous phrase: "He had also the look of a man who had decided not to buy another suit in his life, to let cloth go on gleaming with its private malice." Or this: "By nature Dr Ray was a man of disguises, and a new one with every sentence. Two whiskies stabilised him. A heavy, guilty blush came down from the middle of his head, enlarged his ears, and went below his collar." Elsewhere, Pritchett writes of a woman who became "swollen with shame." There is a sense in which all of his characters blush to have aspirations at all; they blush to colonize.

So much for Pritchett's Englishness. As with his characters, what is interesting about Pritchett is both his deep Englishness and his deep flight from Englishness. He was a great traveler, was fluent in French and Spanish, and had read deeply the entire European canon of the novel. Like one of his characters, he was in disguise: he played the role of English mildness and softened ambition. But English comedy clearly frustrated him. Unfairly (and uncharacteristically unfairly), he lumped together Fielding, Scott, Jane Austen, Trollope, George Eliot, Kipling, Wells, Waugh, and Powell into a so-called masculine tradition, which he characterized, in his book *George Meredith and English Comedy*, as "sanguine, sociable, positive, morally tough, believes in good sense . . . suspects sensibility." His own comic tendency inclined toward what he called "the feminine, the affectable." "Suppose you value your privacy," he wrote, "value imagination and sensibility more than common sense. Suppose you live not by clock time, but by the uncertain hours of your feeling . . . Then you will be with Sterne in the disorderly, talkative, fantasticating tradition." This tradition, he wrote, included Peacock, Dickens, Meredith, Joyce, and Beckett.

Of course, Pritchett's chosen "feminine" tradition actually represents a good description of Jane Austen, a supposedly "masculine" writer: sensibility finally triumphing over sense, as it always does in her novels. But I think that Pritchett invented this unfair division because he was really defining himself against the dominant English comedy of his day—that of Waugh and the early Powell, in which characters are clicked like checkers across metropolitan boards; a comedy of apparent heartlessness, in which the novelist is always a knowing adjective ahead of his characters.

The kind of English comedy Pritchett opposed can be found throughout Waugh's early novels. The famous passage in *Decline and Fall*, for instance, about the Welsh brass band is still praised as a characteristic piece of English literary fun:

> Ten men of revolting appearance were approaching from the drive. They were low of brow, crafty of eye and crooked of limb. They advanced huddled together with the loping tread of wolves, peering about them furtively as they came, as though in constant terror of ambush; they slavered at their mouths, which hung loosely over their receding chins, while each clutched under his ape-like arm a burden of curious and unaccountable shape.

Pritchett never wrote about this passage, but seen from his eyes, it must only have seemed the crudest comedy. First that adjective, "revolting," is clumsy because it so brutally reveals the author's cards, and sets up the passage in such undergraduate terms. And then there is the way Waugh lumpily insists on the men's animality, telling us first that they were "wolves," and then reminding us that they "slavered" and were "ape-like." And then there is the foundation of the comedy itself—the idea that humor is skin-deep, for one thing; and that the Welsh are inherently funny, for another. One naturally thinks by contrast of Pritchett's Welshman, Evans, who is so subtly mocked and yet so subtly comprehended when he attempts to make his claim for the Welsh as the greatest poets of Europe.

Faithful to Dickens but eager to expand English comedy, Pritchett Russianized it, finding above all in Chekhov an inwardness and hospitality to fantasy which he could make use of. His phrase about not living by "clock time, but by the uncertain hours of your feeling" (as well as exemplary of the gently metaphorical style of Pritchett's criticism) is acute, for in Chekhov we feel that his characters' inner lives have a limitless quality, that they are laxly calendared. And like the Chekhovian Henry Green, Pritchett found a way of speaking from within his community—precisely what shocked Waugh when he read *Loving*. (Waugh wrote to Green that he found the book "obscene": "You are debasing the language vilely.") The English novelists, after all, are remarkably intrusive, always breaking in to speak over their characters and tell us what to think, mummifying them somewhat in strips of essayism: this is true of Fielding, Eliot, Forster, and on to Angus Wilson and A. S. Byatt. In Chekhov, however, the prose has the texture of its content: it doesn't seek to illuminate its perfection but lightens a path for its own developing cognition. When similes, metaphors, and images are used, they are poetic, but also the kinds of observations the characters themselves might have used.

Pritchett's detail has this quality. Sometimes by the use of free indirect speech, at other times by handing over his stories to narrators, he produces a strange, rich prose, full of traveling hesitancies, which might nevertheless have been alighted upon by his characters. In "Sense of Humour," the man who narrates the story is sitting in the hearse next to a woman who says, in Chekhovian manner, "I want to get away . . . I've had enough." And the narrator adds, superbly: "She had a way of getting angry with the air, like that." Or take the moment in "When My Girl Comes Home" when Hilda describes her mother's death. Hilda is in the kitchen, and hears a shout from the bedroom—"like a man selling papers." That really is as good as Chekhov. Or this from "The Necklace," in which a man who does not understand his wife—he is an uneducated window cleaner—watches her put on a necklace, and comments: "When women put on something new, they look high and mighty, as if you had got to get to know them all over again." Even when Pritchett uses what Roland Barthes called the reference code—in which authorial appeal is made to something we all know, a consensual or universal truism—it is from within, not without: "We were in the middle of one of those brassy fortnights of the London summer when English life, as we usually know it, is at a standstill, and everyone changes."

Pritchett said that it is very hard for an English writer to write like Chekhov, with the Russians's open-endedness, "since some sort of practical or responsible instinct works against it," but, along with Green, Pritchett brought, in moments like these, something new to English comic narrative—a curious mysterious delicacy, not unlike a softer and more ironic Lawrence, so that Pritchett stories creep up on the reader, not frontally but sideways or from behind, as a ship is boarded. Like Shakespeare and Dickens, he saw that the metaphorical is central to writing, and central to character; that characters expand via metaphor—they are, as the word suggests, carried over, changed into something else in the process of using metaphor—and that readers expand metaphorically when they encounter metaphor. It can and should be said of Pritchett that he secures the Englishness of metaphor while carrying it over into something forever un-English, forever changed.

Of the three modern English writers—Woolf, Green, and Pritchett—who were explicitly influenced by Chekhov's mastery of the apparently superfluous, his talent for making fiction a bashful drift, Pritchett was the least significant figure. Most readers would agree that he never wrote anything on the order of *To the Lighthouse* or

Loving. To reread a great number of his stories is to find, curiously enough, that his characters, for all their English expansions, do not expand strangely or deeply enough. Pritchett's stories, perhaps like his criticism, do not have the instability of greatness. He was a great minor writer, and perhaps knew this himself; to be a great novelist, he once wrote in an essay about George Eliot, "a wide and single purpose in the mind is the chief requirement outside of talent; a strong belief, a strong unbelief, even a strong egoism will produce works of the first order." Pritchett lacked that singleness; by comparison he was a shy English pointillist. But I hope he will last.

Henry Green's England

❦

English modernism must be measured in units of exhaustion or negation. There is so little of it, and its life was so softly fleeting, that it is difficult to seize it. And it is not only in size or historical passage that it seems evanescent; as art, it is itself frequently muted, pastoral, and elegiac. The absence of a true urban modernism is perhaps most striking. London makes appearances, of course, in English modernism, but there is no modernist Dickens—and no English Dos Passos, Céline, Joyce, Bely, or Döblin.

In music, there was William Walton and Ralph Vaughan Williams, in art Stanley Spencer, and in fiction Virginia Woolf and Henry Green. These artists took what they needed from the hard modernism of the Americans, the Irish, the Russians, and the continental Europeans and mixed it with the gentler seeds of native English life. Walton was influenced by Prokofiev, but softened the Russian by passing his steely interruptions through the smooth wooden enclosure of that most English of instruments, the viola, in his Viola Concerto. Henry Green made an English modernist fiction out of his hospitality to Chekhov, Proust, and Joyce.

Green is the least known of these figures, partly by his own design. He gladly disappeared into a public espionage of his own making. "Henry Green" was a nom de plume (he was born Henry Yorke). He resisted all forms of publicity or even biography, and he preferred to be photographed from behind, like a surrealist clerk, faceless in bondage. Though he was utterly unprecious about what he called "literature, that overblown trumpet"—he was a businessman for most of his life—he doubted that he could be popular, and for many years he chose not to be published in paperback. His novels, most of them given one-word gerundive titles, appeared between 1926 and 1952, and then stopped, though Green was barely forty-seven: he began very early, publishing his first novel, *Blindness*, in 1926, when he was twenty-one, and his next novel, *Living*, in 1929. Ten years passed before the cluster of books that are his real achievement: *Party Going* (1939), *Pack My Bag* (1940), and, above all, *Loving* (1945).

Yet the deeper reasons for Green's relative obscurity have to do with the gentle comic reticence of his art. A girlfriend of his once remarked that he was hardly there, that he lived off the fat of others. As far as is possible in fiction, he tried to live off the fat of his characters. Though his prose is intensely distinctive, it strives to so mold itself around the characters of his novels that it might be the plausible emanation of those characters themselves. His later books are written almost entirely in dialogue, and all the speech in all his novels proceeds, like Green's prose, through indirection and obliquity.

Like Woolf, he was influenced by the new translations of Chekhov that were appearing by Constance Garnett in the teens of the last century. He saw that Chekhov had discovered that people express themselves most tellingly in their irrelevances; that people seem real to us when they seem real to themselves, and that they often seem real to themselves when they are being most private, strange, and fantastic. He saw that people in life often refuse to present themselves, and swerve away from purpose. But fiction, alas, and drama too, often bullies characters into formal self-presentation, in a way that has more to do with the conventions of art than the anarchy of existence. This was what Chekhov surely meant when he complained that Ibsen was "no playwright. In life, it simply isn't like that at all."

Just as art often forces characters into unnatural presentation, so it forces itself into shapely presentations of one kind or another—and these artificialities, too, Green sought to annul, by creating an art of disheveled purpose. His books truly seem to drift, and at times he takes the reader to the limit of patience, as his scenes wind and tremble through half-thought and secret surmise. He is best known for the extraordinary delicacy with which he listened to speech, especially to English dialect. He began his second novel, *Living*, just after leaving Oxford, while he was working on the factory floor of his father's engineering firm. Here, one of the workers describes a fellow patient in the hospital:

> There was a feller opposite my bed that had lengths cut out of his belly and when they brought 'im in again, an' he come to after the operation, they told him 'e could eat anything that took 'is fancy. So he said a poached egg on toast would suit 'im for a start but when they took it to 'im he brought it up. Black it was. And everything they took him after he brought it up just the same till they were givin' 'im port, brandy and champagne at the end.

This is remarkably good for any twenty-three-year-old writer, but Green would become much more expert at letting his characters reveal themselves in scrambled increments.

Though he was fascinated by the way Chekhov used irrelevance, the major precursor was almost certainly Shakespeare (and Dickens after him). In *Loving*, characters are continually expressing the most important things about themselves in speeches of apparent indirection and irrelevance. And in all of Green, there is a distinctive spatial movement, between the local and the general, and the prosaic and the lyrical. In *Loving*, Mrs. Welch, an embittered and sometimes drunken housekeeper, denounces the butler, Raunce, and the maid with whom he is in love, Edith, to the lady of the house:

> That's just it mum. For this is what those two are, that Raunce and his Edith. I don't say nothin' about their being lain all day in each other's arms, and the best part of the night too very likely though I can't speak to the night time, I must take my rest on guard and watch as I am while it's light outside, lain right in each other's arms . . . [T]he almighty lovers they make out they are but no more than fornicators when all's said and done if you'll excuse the expression, where was I?

The moment of spatial shift in this passage occurs when Mrs. Welch, with wonderful absurdity, tells her mistress that she can't watch Raunce and Edith at night—"I can't speak to the night time, I must take my rest on guard and watch as I am while it's light outside." Suddenly we gain access to the daily habits of Mrs. Welch, and by means of her ridiculous pomposity she enlarges before us, so that she almost becomes the light itself ("as I am while it's light outside"). In this moment, the speech deepens, from merely a comic denunciation of envied and imagined erotic bliss into an appalling, unwitting confession, in which Mrs. Welch almost seems to be implying that she will keep watching Raunce and Edith as long as there is light to watch them by.

This quick shift or leap is one of the finest things in Green's prose. In *Living*, he writes of a woman who is falling for a fellow worker: "From joking with him and from the long day talking with him her laughing went out all at once into confidences." It is hard to say why that phrase "went out all at once" is so right, and—despite its careful vagueness—so precise. But we know the ways in which, suddenly, our intimacy with someone else goes out all at once into confidences, and deepens.

Green's prose "goes out all at once" in the same way; and suddenly goes in, too. In *Pack My Bag*, which is a memoir written just before the outbreak of the Second World War, Green described the large house and grounds in which he was born, and mentioned a gardener who had worked at the house for forty years. The gardener was called Poole: "The house washed over in pink, was built raised up above these lawns on a low embankment, and it troubled Poole to mow the sides, he had a bad leg." In this characteristic run-on sentence, that little tail—"he had a bad leg"—takes the reader from contemplation of the house to Poole, and then to Poole's leg, and it does so in the swift, homely way that Poole might have put it.

Green describes the ancestral family house, Forthampton, in Gloucestershire, near the Severn River: "We lived here in the early years, in soft lands and climate influenced by the Severn, until my grandfather died and we moved to the big house a mile nearer the river where it went along below the garden." Again, description quickly swells, goes out from the local and enlarges itself—"in soft lands and climate influenced by the Severn"—before contracting again into the domestic ("until my grandfather died"). One notices first the plural: not "land" but "lands," giving the sentence an air of cobwebbed national magic (as if Green were speaking of "the ancient lands of the Britons," something mythic and literary; and Green surely recalled how Milton wrote about the "rushy-fringèd bank" of the Severn in *Comus*). And how subtle is that verb "influenced," whereby Green activates the Latin root of the verb. We usually think of seas or lakes as "influencing" a climate, but not rivers. Isn't there a gentle Englishness of tone at play here, a modesty of assertion, in claiming that a *river* might influence a climate? And since a river will obviously have a smaller impact on weather than a larger body of water, then what better verb, as a way to capture this gentleness of impact, than "influenced," which suggests the lightest ancestral touch, the smallest historical nudge on the climate. A verb not only rhetorically perfect in its "Englishness" but alertly in accord with the social world Green is here describing, an upper-class realm of centuries-long social privilege and "influence." All this in a sentence!

But then *Pack My Bag* is full of such exquisite prose:

> Again, each Sunday afternoon we had a walk still dressed in our best and we could draw in the sweet country air, this island's attar of roses, coming from the sea overland to where we meandered, the woods all about us, rooks up in the sky, the cattle in the fields . . . [W]e had that view over all the county where it lay beneath in light haze like a king's pleasure preserved for idle hours.

In the same book, Green writes that prose is not to be read aloud "but to oneself alone at night, and it is not quick as poetry but rather a gathering web of insinuations . . . Prose should be a long intimacy between strangers with no direct appeal to what both may have known."

In the passage above, when Green moves between a Sunday walk and "this island's attar of roses" (encompassing the whole country in that phrase, as well as lodging his language within the English poetic tradition) and likens the rural view to "a king's pleasure," we see enacted what he means by a gathering web of insinuations and a long intimacy. As *Pack My Bag* is a kind of self-elegy, written in the prospect of certain war and possible death, so it is also an elegy for England in its long last summer of peace.

Henry Yorke was born in 1905, into one of the more prominent English aristocratic families. His mother, Maud Wyndham, was the daughter of the second Baron Leconfield, who lived in Petworth, one of England's finest houses, in Sussex. The Yorkes, unlike many of their English coevals, were neither philistine nor unintelligent. Henry's father, Vincent, had taken a double first in classics at Cambridge, and been a fellow at King's. As a young man, he had been an adventuring archaeologist, and had identified a Kurdish village as the birthplace of the Greek satirist Lucian. By the time Henry was born, he was living two lives, one as the managing director of Pontifex, the family firm that made brewing equipment and plumbing for bathrooms and lavatories, and another as a traditional English squire, running his estate, riding to hounds, and dominating his three very intelligent sons, of whom Henry was the youngest.

Green was precocious: at Eton, he wrote several stories for the school magazine, which have been published in a posthumous collection of miscellaneous writings called *Surviving*. As schoolboy fingerings they are astoundingly assured, and already portend the kind of writer that Green will become. One of them, "Emma Ainsley," begins with a conversation between two women, overheard on a train: "What a lot Nuneaton meant to Emma!" says the first. The other replies: "Mary, she deserved it." Green would listen very hard to conversations on buses and in pubs, though he never regarded writing dialogue as simply a reportorial or fiduciary matter. Dialogue, in Green, is not about the writer "getting it right," as creative writing workshops insist. It is both a fidelity to the actual and an unreal infidelity, as in Shakespeare and Dickens; both a report and a dance.

Green left Oxford before taking his degree, and embarked on a radical act: he went to work on the factory floor of Pontifex (which his friends called Pontifex Maximus) in Birmingham. In *Pack My Bag*, he writes that most of the workers assumed that he had been sent there by his father as a punishment. In the factory, he listened with love to the dialect-pitted speech of his fellow workers. His father had been interested in the way that the servants and staff at Forthampton spoke, and often consulted his dialect dictionary. Green had an interest in, and a sympathy for, the English working classes, and in particular for servants, which was certainly political, and it produces an interesting politics in the novels. But it is stranger than politics. Green was a curious mixture of the conventional and the radical. He was snobbish, shy, patrician; and yet he tended to see English society from the bottom up, as if lying on the ground. It was this that his friend and rival, Evelyn Waugh, disliked in his work, sensing class guilt.

But Green did not have the politics, nor the class guilt, of his fellow Old Etonian George Orwell. In *Pack My Bag*, he argues simply that working-class speech is more poetic than conventional middle-class or upper-class speech, and he gives examples of language overheard in the factory: "His eyes started out of his head like little dog's testicles." Or this, a laborer talking about his brown dog: "What he likes is I take him out into the fields week-ends and he rolls 'im white in the grass." When workers describe, he writes, "they are literally unsurpassed in the spoken word." This unsurpassed spoken poetry is the fabric of Green's second novel, *Living*, which is set in a Birmingham factory and takes place largely among the factory's employees.

But *Loving*, published in 1945, is a much more considered achievement, and it is rightly thought to be his best novel. It is set in a country house in Ireland during the Second World War, and depicts a kind of Shakespearean saturnalia, not unlike the world of *A Midsummer Night's Dream*, in which the servants effectively take over the house when the mistress, Mrs. Tennant, leaves to go to England for a few days. There is little in the way of dynamic plot, and yet the book's bashful, shaded drift brings to our sympathy several souls. There is Charley Raunce, who has recently become the head butler, and Edith, the housemaid with whom he is in love, and whom he intends to marry. There is Edith's friend Kate, also a maid, who loves the Irish stable hand. (The domestic staff, as well as the Tennant family, are English.) There is Mrs. Tennant and her daughter-in-law Mrs. Jack, whose husband is away on military duty. Mrs. Jack is having an affair with a neighbor, Captain Davenport.

The speech in this book is a constant joy, and a poetry so entwined with Green's lyricism that the dancer and the dance really cannot be separated. What delights are not only the many dialect pungencies—"Oh there's no call for you to fash yourself Mr Raunce," "Mortal damp these passages are" (Green might well have got this use of "mortal" from Joyce's "The Dead"), "for land's sake" (used as one might say "for God's sake"), "because I know how it is at their age always worriting"—but also the Shakespearean way in which new words are created to mime the effect of dialect. Talking about Mrs. Jack's children, Edith wonderfully says, "Well I've got to take those little draggers out this afternoon." The words "fash" and "draggers" are both in the *OED*. "Fash" is northern dialect, meaning "tire" or "tired." Green uses the slang conventionally. But "draggers" according to the *OED*, means only "one who drags." There is no entry in which it is applied to children. (Green's use is not quoted.) Perhaps it was northern dialect to use the word about children, who so frustrate adults when they drag their feet and fall behind. But one's suspicion is that Green is here creating poetry—taking a word and making it new by fusing it with a new context. In so doing, he endows his maid, Edith, with poetry while making it look like mere easy slang. In one stroke, Green furthers both his characterization and his prose; fills Edith with reality while creating something stylistically exciting on the page. The word is also charming and funny; few readers can resist a smile when they encounter it.

In a marvelous scene, Edith, who speaks especially colorfully, comes into Mrs. Jack's bedroom and finds her in bed with Captain Davenport. Mrs. Jack sits up in shock, realizes she is naked and is revealing her breasts, and retreats beneath the sheets. Edith is shocked, but once recovered she happily tells the other staff about it, and comically takes pride in her witnessing: " 'Well then isn't this a knock out?' she asked. 'An' it happened to me,' she added. 'After all these years.' " Later still, she again remembers Mrs. Jack, and the way "she sat up in bed with her fronts bobblin' . . . like a pair of geese." Green does the same with "fronts" as he does with "draggers."

It is easy to forget that, despite Shakespeare's great example, the English novel, a bourgeois form, tended not to bother itself with women like Edith and men like Mr. Raunce. George Eliot apologizes to her readers for having to dwell briefly on rural bumpkins, and Forster, in *The Longest Journey*, writes that Mr. Ansell, a draper, should be classed with the phenomena that are not really there. Hardy and Lawrence (in some of the early stories) were the great pioneers in the art that Green brought to such perfection. In the fictional worlds of Chekhov and Giovanni Verga (whom Lawrence translated in the late 1920s), we see a narrative style in which the author's commentary and the characters' thoughts are so at one that the similes and metaphors provided by the writer might easily have been invented by the characters. Thus Chekhov describes, in a peasant village, the music of "an expensive-sounding accordion," and both Chekhov and Verga describe a man's handwriting as looking like a mess of fishhooks. In such cases, the writers have disappeared into their characters' imaginations.

Green was obsessed with this kind of disappearance, and extended —perhaps further than any writer ever has—this principle of invisibility. In *Living*, he removed many of the definite articles, running words together so that even passages of description or authorial commentary read like speech or stream of consciousness. In *Loving*, he removes the *-ly* of the descriptive adverb after speech, in an attempt to mimic the dialect of his characters. Thus: " 'Come on,' she whispered, brisk," since Edith would probably contract the word. And so we have "Raunce eyed her very sharp," "Kate finished dogged," and so on, throughout the book.

The smallest passage shifts its registers like a canal moving through locks, as Green inhabits his characters, then briefly comes out, then reenters them. Take the scene where Edith has come upon Mrs. Jack and the captain in bed:

A movement over in the bed attracted her attention. She turned slow. She saw a quick stir beside the curls under which Mrs Jack's head lay asleep, she caught sight of someone else's hair as well, and it was retreating beneath silk sheets. A man. Her heart hammered fit to burst her veins. She gave a little gasp.

Then the dark head was altogether gone. But there were two humps of body, turf over graves under those pink bedclothes. And it was at this moment Mrs Jack jumped as if she had been pinched. Not properly awake she sat straight up. She was nude. Then no doubt remembering she said very quick, "Oh Edith it's you it's quite all right I'll ring." On which she must have recognized that she was naked. With a sort of cry and crossing her lovely arms over that great brilliant upper part of her on which, wayward, were two dark up-raised dry wounds shaking on her, she also slid entirely underneath.

It is a superbly vital and flowing piece of writing. We travel from Edith's perception, expressed in a language she might use ("Her heart hammered fit to burst her veins") to a metaphor which lies somewhere between the literary and the vernacular, somewhere be-tween Green himself and Edith—the sheets over the humps of body likened to "turf over graves"—to a register frankly literary and lyrical, in which Green, always beautifully attentive to female forms, notes Mrs. Jack's "lovely arms" and her "wayward" breasts, like "two dark upraised dry wounds shaking on her"—the same breasts which, forty pages later, Edith will convert into her speech, and call "her fronts bobblin' . . . like a pair of geese."

Green differs from Chekhov and Verga in the intensity of his lyri-cism: only he would dare to call Mrs. Jack's arms "lovely." He is, in this sense, a modernist stylist. But the peculiar effect of this rapid in-terchange between speaking-through-his-characters and speaking-as-himself is that his lyricism undeniably issues from the author but appears so briefly that it seems to be denied its moment of issue. Thus Green's lyricism, while always and only his, seems not quite to come from its maker, who slips away while his different styles mingle.

His prose, constructed of course with utmost care, has an air of carelessness. In this he resembles Lawrence, both of them attempt-ing to dive through prose to a submarine vitality. Lawrence uses rep-etition to startle words out of their accretions, and to show that words change color, as it were, as they are repeated. Green is un-afraid of repetition, but his stylistic principle is a Joycean run-on: "coming over the hill to the first sight of where one is to fish, where under the withies nodding low into moving water chubb lie in wait to pick up what falls to them from those sharp pointed leaves." This fast, largely unpunctuated welter intensifies each word even as it seems to throw out the words as they are speedily consumed. In its air of careless largesse, Green's writing retains a certain aristocratic elegance.

As a man, Green appears to have been evasive, passionate, and sad. He was tall, handsome, an extremely hospitable listener—that writer's ear, his greedy gatherer—with a quick and loud laugh. Though he could be a very funny anecdotalist, he was happiest, like Chekhov, when he found himself a little to one side of a social event. He was extremely attractive to women (again, like Chekhov) and had numerous affairs, each prefaced with the commandment that they should be limited, since he adored his wife and would never leave her. (He did so only by dying before her, in 1973.)

Eudora Welty told Green's excellent biographer, Jeremy Treg-lown, of a meeting that she had with Green in London in 1950. It gives us something of Green's engrossing flavor. Welty had been snobbishly received by most of the London literary crowd, and was introduced to Green at a party. She was thrilled, having read *Loving* on the boat from America. The two spoke animatedly, and Green in-vited Welty to his house. He was not physically attracted to the American writer (at this stage in his life he was drawn to debutantes and socialites in their early twenties), but the two had a passionate encounter of a kind, talking for hours in Green's study and, years later, exchanging letters which, Treglown says, on Green's side read almost like love letters. "He was a terribly attractive man, of course," Welty said, and he had a mixture of spontaneity, mischief, and hu-mor, "a hilarious streak that goes all through his work. And he had that wonderful sudden laugh, just explosive."

If Welty did not see a sadness in Green, it was because she did not become his lover. Other women apprehended a painful vulnera-bility. By the late 1940s Green was drinking very heavily, and was becoming convinced that he could not write. His last novel, *Doting*, appeared in 1952. For most of his adult life, he had gone to work in the Pontifex office in London, where he was the managing director, and had come home to write in the evenings. But the writing would not come, and the daily commute to the office had become calcified habit. He acted like a man much older than he was, and indeed he was going prematurely deaf. In an interview, he spoke, alongside his love of jazz, of "the aching shallows" of middle age.

Green developed a kind of agoraphobia, and stopped going out. "The whole thing is really not to go out," he said, "if one can afford it, the best thing is to stay in one place, which might be bed." He was eased out of the family firm in 1959, when the directors, at a board meeting, noticed that the glass of clear liquid that Green had at the table was not water but neat gin. Treglown writes that by the mid-1960s "his main interest was to watch sports on television."

If "a hilarious streak goes all through" Green's work, as Welty rightly says, then a melancholy one goes through it, too. One of the beautiful effects of Green's unstopping and tissueless sentences, winding on without delay of punctuation, is not only the intensification of language that they bring but also the intensification of sentiment, by making it seem careless, or even social. Waugh, like Green, gets much of his comic effect by speeding up his prose to the pace of speech, and clippingly excluding available sentiment; but in Green, who has a far deeper lyrical impulse (and is a far deeper novelist), the evasion of sentiment only excites, by its lack, the desire for sentiment.

In *Pack My Bag*, Green recalls that when he was at prep school, during the First World War, it was a rule that when a boy's mother came to take out her son for tea, the boy had to bring along a friend.

This rule was unbreakable and it so happened that when a friend's father lost his life and his mother came down to read out his last letters home I went out with them and after tea we sat in that park I have described and they both cried over his letters as we sat with our backs against a tree. You would have thought this rule could be re-laxed at such a time but there was no question of it. We always had boiled eggs when out for tea.

Again, the sudden contraction of the sentence, from grief against a tree to habitual boiled eggs. But more than that, the casual speed of the sentence—moving at the brisk, clipped pace of upper-class English speech—evacuates sentiment from its society, has no room for sentiment, which is then achingly provided by the reader. The same kind of principle is at work in *Loving*, whereby the servants ef-fectively push the Second World War out of their world, only ever referring to Hitler as "he": "But perhaps he will keep to London with his bombing."

In this latter case, the principle of exclusion seems joyful rather than clipped; and yet both passages express a reticent stoicism, which Green indeed found characteristic of both upper-class and working-class English manners. In his work, both types of the En-glish tend to speak past or round each other rather than at each other, in crescents of evasion. *Loving* might as well be called *Living*, since we love, Green shows us, in the same way that we live, by re-fusing to surrender our singleness and privacy.

If Green remains, in the end, a very fine minor novelist, it is per-haps because he is too generous toward drift and half-thought. The fine determination not to prosecute a purpose—he is the opposite of the didactic Lawrence in this regard—creates an exquisitely unpress-ing art, unlike any other. But it leaves us with characters who only have motives in relation to each other, and never burn singly, under the flare of an idea, an ideology, a demonic want. Chekhov, after all, has his intellectuals, however thwarted and foolish they are. Green has only his unfurious English, softly passionate and melodic. But how beautifully he served them.

A Long Day at the Chocolate Bar Factory:
David Bezmozgis's Compassionate Irony

❦

Chekhov may be divine, but he is responsible for much sinning on earth. The contemporary short story is essentially sub-Chekhovian. It is most obviously indebted to what Shklovksy called Chekhov's "negative endings"—the way his stories expire into ellipses, or seem to end in the middle of a thought: "It was starting to rain." This is so invisibly part of the grammar of contemporary short fiction that we no longer notice how peculiarly abrupt, how monotonously frag-mentary much of what we read has become. (And we ignore how full even the shortest Chekhov story seems.) Consistent with this abruptness is the contemporary idea that the short story present itself as a victim of its own confusion, a poised bewilderment, in which nothing can really be sorted out; the necessary vehicle for this bewil-derment is the first-person narrator, who must get along amidst modern confusions without the help of an all-knowing, third-person authorial patron. Chekhov's simpleness and lucidity—it is easier to see his transparency than to sense his complexity and lyricism—seems to cast its shadow over the quick, skinned, blank language of so much American short fiction; a prose whose thin roof often houses, unsurprisingly, characters who are themselves rather blank and affectless, as if stunned by the hammer blows of the age. And Chekhovian irony also finds its debased correspondence in contemporary writing; though where Chekhov's irony is often savage, modern irony is often merely all-nullifying.

It says much for David Bezmozgis's considerable talents, then, that his apparently skinny, crafty, ironic stories, narrated entirely in the first person in simple, unmetaphorical prose, and fond of abrupt closures, should seem to dip so obviously into the common pool and yet avoid, on the whole, the commonest failings. These tales, collected in a volume entitled *Natasha,* sometimes surrender to an easy irony or a convenient blankness of narration, but the best of them are passionately full of life; above all, they are true examples of storytelling. Here, Bezmozgis's great advantage, other than his literary skills—remarkable for a thirty-one-year-old writer whose book is his first—is his material: he writes, in this book, exclusively about recent Russian-Jewish immigrants to Canada, trailing with ardent curiosity his own world and the world of his parents and grandparents (Bezmozgis was born in Riga in 1973, and moved to Canada in 1980; the stories are chronologically loyal to that history and dedicated to his parents).

There is such a thing as the glamour of geography in fiction. Some of the pleasure we get from reading Conrad, say, lies in the way in which he strings an exotic sketch of a minor character along a rope of exile. Stein in *Lord Jim,* for instance, with his collections of butterflies and "catacombs of beetles," is said to have taken part in the revolutions of 1848, then fled to Trieste, and then to Tripoli, "with a stock of cheap watches to hawk about. . . ." David Bezmozgis is similarly alive to what immigration and exile can do for him as a writer. He enjoys seeding his paragraphs with little jolts of far-flung historical reference. In "Roman Berman, Massage Therapist," the story's narrator describes his father, who had worked in Latvia for the Ministry of Sport, and had judged weightlifting contests: "My father was dressed in his blue Hungarian suit—veteran of international weightlifting competitions from Tallinn to Sochi."

Bezmozgis knows that the Western reader will roll cities like Tallinn and Sochi on the tongue, as alien grapes, enjoying their strange flavors. In general, he is expert at prodding on his stories with unexpected exoticisms; or indeed, opening them thus, too. "An Animal to the Memory" begins: "On the railway platform in Vienna, my mother and aunt forbade my cousin and me from saying good-bye to our grandparents." And "The Second Strongest Man" starts: "In the winter of 1984, as my mother was recovering from a nervous breakdown and my father's business hovered precipitously between failure and near failure, the international weightlifting championships were held at the Toronto Convention Centre. One evening the phone rang and a man invited my father to serve on the panel of judges." It is hard to resist such wide and dashing beckonings.

Bezmozgis is not just a good opener, however, but a very good continuer. He has a way of making his sentences jump from one to the other, as if the ordinary connective tissue has broken down:

> Night after night for more than a year, my father tortured himself with medical texts and dictionaries. After a long day at the chocolate bar factory he would come home and turn on the lamp in the bedroom. He would eat his soup with us in the kitchen, but he'd take the main course into the bedroom, resting his plate on a rickety Soviet stool. The work was difficult. He was approaching fifty, and the English language was more an enemy than an instrument. In Latvia, after resigning from the Ministry of Sport, my father had made a living as a masseur in the sanatoriums along the Baltic coast. He'd needed no accreditation, only some minimal training and the strength of his connections. But in the new country, to get his certificate, he was forced to memorize complex medical terminology and to write an eight-hour exam in a foreign language.

This is the first paragraph of "Roman Berman, Massage Therapist." It may look like simple enough prose, but its jumpy vitality has to do with its subtle manner of starting and stopping, and of secreting in almost every sentence an eccentric fact. The first sentence tells us about Roman's "torture" by dictionary; the second that he works in a chocolate bar factory (an oddly childish, fairy-tale aura attends this fact); the third slips in the detail that he rests his plate on a "Soviet" stool (what, the reader thinks, would that look like?); the fifth that English was his "enemy"; the sixth that Roman worked as a masseur along "the Baltic coast." Bezmozgis has surely learned from the Russian short story writer Isaac Babel, even if his sentences lack the blazing oddity of the Odessa master. He has learned from Babel how to turn his sentences into provocations and near-exaggerations—"torture," "enemy," "Soviet stool"—so that the prose becomes a kind of battle of vivid propositions.

One of the characters in this book is said, indeed, to be "right out of the pages of Babel," and Bezmozgis's funny and vibrant portraits of Baltic Jews, Soviety weightlifters, whorish cousins, weeping aunts, and sourly fierce rabbinical teachers have a theatrical pungency strongly reminiscent of Babel, filtered perhaps through the early Philip Roth. This collection of linked stories is narrated by Mark Berman, a little boy in the first four tales, and a teenager in the final three. Over the course of the book we get to know Mark's parents, Bella and Roman, and various relatives and friends. In Latvia, Roman's life had been comfortable, professionally at least. After working for the Ministry of Sport, he became a head administrator at the Riga Dynamo gymnasium. In 1979, the Bermans left Latvia for Canada, making their home in a section of Toronto already populated by Russian-Jewish immigrants:

> My parents, Baltic aristocrats, took an apartment at 715 Finch fronting a ravine and across from an elementary school—one respectable block away from the Russian swarm. We lived on the fifth floor, my cousin, aunt, and uncle directly below us on the fourth. Except for the Nahumovskys, a couple in their fifties, there were no other Russians in the building. For this privilege, my parents paid twenty extra dollars a month in rent.

Roman Berman's early years in Canada are much more arduous and uncertain than anything he experienced in the Soviet Union. He and his wife speak almost no English, and their isolation turns them into children, reliant as immigrant parents often are on their more adaptable children, who become their doves, pushed out to test the height of the floodwaters. "I was nine, and there were many things I did not tell them, but there was nothing they would not openly discuss in front of me, often soliciting my opinion. They were strangers in the country, and they recognized that the place was less strange to me, even though I was only a boy."

In "The Second Strongest Man," a Soviet delegation of weightlifters arrives in Toronto for the International Weightlifting Competitions. Roman Berman is asked to be a judge. Mark is excited because he remembers how Sergei Federenko, the gold medalist, used to visit the Bermans in Riga, and how he used to lift Mark's entire bed, with the boy in it, high off the ground. Yet when Sergei competes in Toronto, he loses first place, and only gets silver. Mark's hero is suddenly only "the second strongest man" in the world. Later in the story, one of the members of the delegation says that Roman is lucky because he has such a good life in Canada, where even the beggars on the street are wearing Levi's jeans and Adidas running shoes. Roman replies that appearances are deceptive, that he often thinks of returning to Latvia, and that "every day is a struggle." His friend refuses to believe him: "I see your car. I see your apartment. I see how you struggle. Believe me, your worst day is better than my best." The story delicately holds together its different depictions of shifting hierarchies and the changed fortune that exile brings: the gold medalist is only a silver medalist in the West, and no longer the idol he once was; yet the struggling Russian immigrant, whose life seems to be day upon day of hard graft, is envied by the visiting Soviet.

Bezmozgis has a compassionate irony; the compassion irrigates his irony, which might get a little dry without it, and the irony crisps his occasional descent into Jewish burlesque. Of the latter, "An Animal to the Memory" is a good example. It concerns little Mark's troubled days at his Jewish school. Mark has been caught fighting

and has already been cautioned by the headmaster, Rabbi Gurvich.
On Holocaust Remembrance Day, the schoolboys bring in all kinds
of relevant objects, artworks, and memorabilia, in order to build appropriate installations and shrines. Bezmozgis is tartly satirical at the
school's expense: "We had crayon drawings done by children in
Theresienstadt. We had a big map of Europe with multicolored pins
and accurate statistics. Someone's grandfather donated his striped
Auschwitz pajamas . . ." (There is something very wicked about that
scandalously soft word, "pajamas.") On the day itself, the rabbi sings
to the memory of the six million, and Mark feels the voice reach into
"that place where my mother said I was supposed to have the thing
called my 'Jewish soul.'" But Mark ends up fighting again, and
breaks one of the memorial displays, and is soon in the rabbi's office.
A story that seems to be in danger of becoming a Jewish romp —
rebellious boy larks around with Holocaust memorabilia, is scolded
by hideous bearded rabbi — is saved by the nice irony of its final paragraph. The rabbi grips Mark very hard, and forces him to shout out
that he is a Jew and is unashamed to be one. The humiliation makes
the little boy cry, at which the rabbi bitterly remarks: "Now, Berman
. . . now maybe you understand what it is to be a Jew." Does this
mean Mark has a "Jewish soul" or not? The story breaks off. . . .

The best examples of Bezmozgis's ironic compassion are to be
found in "Roman Berman, Massage Therapist," and in the collection's best and final story, "Minyan." The former recounts, with
rueful comedy, Roman's attempts to set himself up in Toronto
as a massage therapist. An office is secured, and advertisements are
placed, and everyone waits for the phone to ring. The only people
phoning, of course, are family members: "Everybody called to see
whether anybody had called." Eventually a mysterious physician, Dr.
Kornblum, phones. He invites the Bermans over to dinner at his
large house. He and his wife have an interest in helping Russian-
Jewish immigrants, especially refuseniks. Mrs. Berman bakes an apple cake to take along. But the dinner is inconclusive, and obscurely

disappointing. Despite his promises, it is not clear if Dr. Kornblum will refer his patients to Roman's services. Bezmozgis uses the absurd apple cake as the story's ironically pathetic symbol. Mrs. Kornblum returns it, uneaten, to Mrs. Berman at the end of the evening, because the Kornblums keep kosher. So the Bermans leave the house exactly as they arrived. And "it was unclear whether nothing or everything had changed." The story ends here, in proper contemporary fashion, denying us the knowledge of Roman's eventual career and prosperity. But this is an example of a Chekhovian "negative ending" perfectly placed, for we leave the story sharing the Bermans' own uncertainty, like them arrested in potential on the Kornblums' front lawn.

"Minyan" seems different in kind and depth from anything else in the book; it is tempting to speculate that this young writer wrote these stories sequentially, and that this last fruit is just a little riper than its younger siblings. It leaves the world of the Bermans to concentrate on two old men, Herschel and Itzik. Herschel is a Holocaust survivor from Lithuania, and Itzik, the man described as walking straight out of the pages of Babel, was a taxi driver in Odessa. They are both widowers, living in a Toronto apartment block. When Herschel's wife died, he moved into the apartment of Itzik, who was already widowed. They have become dear companions.

Mark Berman gets to know Herschel and Itzik because his grandfather has recently moved into the same apartment complex of subsidized housing for elderly Jews (for which there is a long waiting list). Mark quickly learns that the residents are suspicious of Itzik and Herschel; they disapprove of the couple, and hint that they may be homosexual, and all but ignore them. Itzik had a son, but Herschel had no children, because his wife refused to. After the Holocaust, Herschel tells Mark, there were two types of people. "There were those who felt a responsibility to ensure the future of the Jewish people, and then there were those, like Herschel's wife, who had been convinced that the world was irrefutably evil."

Itzik dies, and in an extraordinary scene his son, long estranged, arrives at the funeral. Bezmozgis provides one of his unexpected lurches, in which the son suddenly turns on the memory of his hated dead father, a man the reader has known only as a shrunken, fond, enfeebled widower:

> He turned back toward Itzik's grave. He spent seven years in jail, my father, did you know that? I have brothers and sisters all over Russia. I don't even know how many. For him nothing was forbidden. That was my father, you understand? He raised his fist to his face. He was like this, Itzik's son said. He drove his fist into a snowbank. He looked at me to see if I understood. I nodded that I understood. Like this, he repeated, his fist in the snowbank.

After Itzik's death, other elderly Jews start agitating to claim his apartment. It is inconceivable, they say, that Herschel would be allowed to stay in a subsidized apartment just because he lived with Itzik; he is not a relative (and besides, he may be homosexual).

"Minyan" is poignantly about the savagery of survival—and of survivorship—and about what we leave after ourselves. Itzik, the tough bully from Odessa, was loved, it seems, only by Herschel. He was a man who ran his own business and "never asked anyone for anything." His only known survivor, his son, hates his memory. Herschel will leave nothing behind him because his late wife refused to bear children. Thus the two old exiles mournfully cancel each other out, leaving behind nothing worth having. Except their apartment, which is only rented anyway, and over which other tough survivors, the victims of pogroms and holocausts and inexhaustible exile, are fighting. It is a sad and affecting story, whose placement at the end of this often ebullient and warmly comic book bathes what has gone before in grave twilight.